THE FOUNDER OF
MODERN EGYPT

THE FOUNDER OF MODERN EGYPT

A STUDY OF
MUHAMMAD 'ALI

BY

HENRY DODWELL

*Professor of the History and Culture of
the British Dominions in Asia, in
the University of London*

———————

CAMBRIDGE

AT THE UNIVERSITY PRESS

1931

REPRINTED

1967

Published by the Syndics of the Cambridge University Press
Bentley House, 200 Euston Road, London, N.W. 1
American Branch: 32 East 57th Street, New York, N.Y. 10022

PUBLISHER'S NOTE

Cambridge University Press Library Editions are reissues of
out-of-print standard works from the Cambridge catalogue. The
texts are unrevised and, apart from minor corrections, reproduce
the latest published edition.

First published 1931
Reprinted 1967

First printed in Great Britain at the University Printing House, Cambridge
Reprinted in the United States of America
Library of Congress Catalogue Card Number: 31-22265

CONTENTS

CONTENTS

PREFACE

The following pages constitute an endeavour to escape from the traditional hero of French and villain of English writers, and to ascertain by a study of original materials what Muhammad 'Ali really did. In many respects this task has become much easier of late years than ever it was before. A large amount of most important matter has been published by the Société Royale de Géographie d'Égypte, under the wise patronage of His Majesty King Fouad. Its publications include French, English and Italian documents of great interest and value.

Besides these I have examined in detail the reports of our own agents preserved among the records of the Foreign Office and the India Office.

By the courtesy of M. Cattaui I have been enabled to make use of the yet unpublished reports of the Russian consuls-general, especially those of Count Medem, the Russian agent during the most critical period of Muhammad 'Ali's career.

Lastly, by the permission of His Majesty King Fouad, I have been enabled to examine valuable series of letters and orders issued by Muhammad 'Ali to his principal officials.

In this connection I must acknowledge the special assistance of M. Deny and M. Gelat Bey, who always found time to afford me help whenever I needed it in the course of my work at Cairo.

I owe special acknowledgments to M. Georges Douin and to Professor L. M. Penson—to the first for the extensive use I have made of the volumes which he has contributed to the series published by the Société Royale de Géographie d'Égypte, and to the second for reading my proofs and favouring me with valuable criticisms.

H. D.

School of Oriental Studies,
   Finsbury Circus, London.

Chapter I

THE RISE OF MUHAMMAD 'ALI

We are perhaps still disposed to undervalue the force
and originality of our eighteenth-century ancestors.
Their formal manners, their decorative dress, their
heroic couplets, their sentimental novels, their super-
ficial histories, easily suggest the sophisticated ending
of an old rather than the beginning of a new world. Yet
it is hard to over-estimate our modern debt to them.
They conceived and handed down to us not only
humanitarian ideas and evolutionary theory, but also
the application of steam to industry and a most complete revolution in the art of war—the great points on
which our modern history and ideas have turned. In
fact they revolutionised the sources of power. And in
so doing they begot the ruin of the great oriental
empires. Power was no longer bestowed by the descendants of those nomad tribesmen who had burst east,
west and south from the steppes of Central Asia, carrying in their train havoc and empire. It now belonged
to the western races, with their highly disciplined infantry able without fear to confront any horsemen, with
their siege guns able to blast a way through walls
however stout, with their fieldpieces that could scatter
any concentration of Asiatic cavalry. By the close of
the period the states of India had already experienced
the force of the new weapon and were bending before
it; and in the Nearer East the Turks, who had not so
long ago pierced the Carpathians and almost taken
Vienna itself, could no longer hold their own. Their
frontier guards were being driven in; province after
province was being wrested from them; their hold on

nople itself was relaxing. And the growing
military inferiority was carrying with it a
e of moral consequences. As self-confidence
d, mutual confidence weakened. The sar-'askar
commander of the host—mistrusted his lieutenants, and was mistrusted by his men. That Might of
Islam to which such noble mosques had been dedi-
cated in the past was visibly sinking to the ground. Even
the despised Christian subjects, who for centuries had
tilled the fields and paid the infidel poll tax as un-
murmuringly as the Hindu subjects of Delhi, were
beginning to raise their heads and whisper of independence, and the pashas of the Sultan, like the nawabs and
nazims of the Moghul Emperor, now executed those
orders only that were beneficial to themselves. The
pashaliqs of Baghdad, of Damascus, and of Cairo were
hardly more than nominal dependencies.

The province of Egypt had indeed long been suffering
from a more than Turkish misrule. Its relations with
the empire, even in the early days following Salim's
conquest, had always been of the loosest. It had been
entrusted to the tyranny of such of the Mamelukes as
had survived massacre and had proved their unworthi-
ness by deserting their own master. Over them indeed was set a pasha appointed from Constantinople,
often changed, but seldom more than a governor in
name. The beys, as the Mameluke chiefs were called,
sought nothing but personal and private ends. Their
followers, recruited as slaves from Circassia and Georgia,
were sedulously trained as irregular horse and formed
perhaps the most gallant, certainly the most magnificent body of irregular cavalry in the world. But they
cherished few but personal objects. All the revenues
that could be wrung from the country went to cover
them splendidly in armour, to fill their stables with the
noblest Arab stock, to adorn their palaces with the

finest carpets of the East, to crowd their harims with beautiful slaves and to guard them with negro eunuchs. Under the rule of these picturesque but stupid warriors the resources of Egypt rapidly decayed. The canals on which cultivation depended choked themselves by neglect. The desert encroached, while the cities shrank. Alexandria from a great and flourishing port dwindled to a town of 5000 inhabitants. Wandering Bedouins perpetually raided the settled areas. Caravans from Suez or Kossir to Cairo could pass in safety only under a strong military escort. In fact what Sind was under the Mirs, Egypt was under the Mamelukes.

The advent of the Ottoman Turks had led to the abandonment of the ancient trade routes by Baghdad and the Persian Gulf and by Alexandria and the Red Sea, which for ages had borne the bulk of the traffic between the East and West. But in the middle of the eighteenth century events in India called for swifter communications with Europe than could be provided by way of the Cape. The schemes of Dupleix, the achievements of Clive, the struggles of Warren Hastings, the whole absorbing question whether India and the Indian trade was to be controlled from Paris or London, demanded prompt decisions and early reinforcements. Conditions in Egypt, Syria and 'Iraq became therefore matters of considerable interest to the rival western powers. From early times the English East India Company, whenever it had had urgent news to send eastwards, had despatched couriers overland, usually by way of Aleppo and Baghdad, to take ship at the head of the Persian Gulf. But this route had presented many disadvantages. The growing disorder of the pashaliq of Baghdad, and the frequent depredations of the Arab tribes had rendered it very insecure. The Company's packets contained nothing to excite Arab greed; but even if the tribesmen did not fancy the messenger to be well supplied with money, they might always be carried away by the sporting pleasure of slaying the infidel. Though many packets reached their destination, there was always a good chance that the bearer might be murdered or at least be obliged to destroy his papers.[1]

There was however an alternative route by way of Egypt and the Red Sea. This had the advantage of offering a shorter passage through nomadic areas—merely from Cairo to Suez; and, providing an agreement could be reached with the beys, it promised much greater regularity and security. When in 1768 the traveller James Bruce visited Egypt, he found Ali Bey, the virtual ruler of the country, in open revolt against the Turks and not at all unwilling to make friends with the infidel as an insurance against Turkish hostility. He was moreover enlightened enough to perceive that by encouraging trade he might enlarge his revenue. Bruce's suggestions, backed by Italian merchants settled at Alexandria, were reinforced by the direct proposals of British sea captains, who found the Red Sea trade decaying and fancied that they might find a good market for their Bengal goods in the bazaars of Cairo. Ali Bey was sufficiently interested to address a letter to the English authorities in Bengal, suggesting that they should open a direct trade to Suez, in defiance of the Sultan's orders that no Christian vessels should be admitted to any ports north of Jidda.[2] When Warren Hastings became governor of Fort William in 1772, he perceived at once the advantages that might accrue to Bengal from these proposals. Under his auspices more than one expedition was despatched, and a provisional treaty was actually signed by which Ali Bey's successors guaranteed the safe passage of goods from Suez to

[1] See for instance the adventures of Captain James Barton (Madras Public Consultations, August 10, 1758).
[2] Cf. Charles-Roux, *Autour d'une Route*, pp. 29 *sqq.*

Cairo.[1] But these arrangements pleased neither the East India Company nor the Sultan, who had just recovered something of his precarious power over Egypt. The Sublime Porte feared that the Hijaz revenues would suffer if the Indian trade were diverted from Jidda to Suez; while the Company feared that the trade development of the Egyptian route would lead to a breach of its monopoly by the export of prohibited goods from India to Europe by way of the Mediterranean. So in 1777 the Company forbade the despatch of vessels with trading cargoes to any port north of Jidda, but at the same time obtained from the Porte a verbal promise of free passage through Egypt for its despatches and couriers. This of course had little effect. Neither Company nor Porte could fully enforce these orders. Packets were made a pretext for surreptitious cargoes; and in 1779 and again in 1780 bearers of English packets were seized and imprisoned.[2]

Meanwhile the French had shown themselves keenly alive to the possibilities of the Egyptian route. To them it promised an incalculable advantage—a way of minimising the English superiority at sea which had exerted such a distressing influence on the course of the Seven Years' War. If the main stream of the Indian trade could be turned into the Mediterranean, not only would the opportunities and advantages of French merchants be greatly enhanced, but also the duties of the French navy would be greatly reduced. Such ideas too seemed the more timely in view of the evident decay of the Turkish empire. When it actually should collapse, that event would of course immediately benefit neighbours such as Austria and Russia; but, as a French

[1] Brit. Mus. Add. MSS, 29210, ff. 422 *sqq.* A copy of the treaty occurs in the India Office Factory Records, Red Sea, vol. 5 A.

[2] Charles-Roux, *op. cit.* pp. 124, 148. James Wooley, one of those concerned, had been commandant of the Nawab of Arcot's artillery (Madras Public Sundry, No. 4).

memoir of 1783 observed, their advantages might be easily and appropriately counterbalanced by a French occupation of Egypt.[1] An alternative plan, which had the merit of being immediately practicable, was that of entering into an alliance with the beys. This was done. Early in 1785 a French agent signed agreements with the leading bey, with the chief customer, with one of the Bedouin chiefs, for the safe transit of French goods on favourable terms.[2] This arrangement however, like Warren Hastings' provisional treaty, only served to emphasise the uncertainty of the Egyptian situation. Not only did the Porte refuse to confirm the French treaty, but once more reasserted its fluctuating authority at Cairo.[3] For the moment, therefore, this danger to the English position in India vanished; but none the less it remained true that at any time the French might establish themselves in Egypt either by force or by negotiation.[4]

We therefore followed the French example. George Baldwin, who had played a prominent part in our earlier projects, was named consul-general, with instructions to get from the beys as good a treaty as had been obtained by the French. The revival of Turkish influence rendered that harder than had been expected. Year passed after year, and, as far as the Foreign Office could see, Baldwin was drawing £1400 a year for doing nothing; Grenville resolved in 1793 to abolish his post, since if he was worth keeping in Egypt at all his pay should be found by the East India Company.[5] This decision was promptly followed by news that at last Baldwin had got his treaty. But with the

[1] Charles-Roux, *op. cit.* p. 167.
[2] *Idem*, pp. 168 *sqq.*
[3] Hailes to Carmarthen, October 12, 1786 (India Office, French in India, vol. 13).
[4] Eton, *Survey of the Turkish Empire*, p. 495.
[5] Dropmore MSS, II, 263, 273.

exception of Dundas the government of the day had lost all interest in Egypt in view of the much more immediate danger arising from the revolution in France.

The French themselves, however, soon dispelled our indifference. In the winter of 1797–8 a number of converging influences led them to plan a great expedition eastwards. In the spring Grenville learnt that the state libraries had been ransacked for the works of travellers in Egypt, Persia and India; that the services of Arabic, Turkish and Persian scholars had been requisitioned; and that the expedition was said to be designed to occupy Egypt and cut through the isthmus of Suez.[1] It was not known how much of this could be taken seriously. But Dundas thought the project "a great and masterly stroke";[2] and the Governor-General at Calcutta resolved to break or bridle Tipu Sultan before Bonaparte's "desperate and enterprising spirit" could find the means of joining him with a body of French troops.[3] In England it was resolved that, whatever might be the purpose of the armament assembled at Toulon, every English ship that could be spared should be sent to disperse or destroy it. "Never", wrote Mornington with great truth, "was a public measure taken with more wisdom or spirit."[4]

Meanwhile Napoleon had sailed from Toulon with some 38,000 men on May 19. On June 12 Malta surrendered to him. At the end of the month he landed on the Egyptian coast near Alexandria, promptly occupied that city, and then marched southwards. On July 18 he crushed the Mamelukes opposite Cairo at the battle of the Pyramids, and entered the city on the 24th. Eight days later Nelson found the French squadron, which he had been hunting for weeks, and destroyed it in Abukir Bay. Then the throttling effects of superior sea power

[1] Dropmore MSS, IV, 192–3. [2] *Wellesley Despatches*, I, 348.
[3] *Idem*, I, 322. [4] Dropmore MSS, IV, 385.

began to display themselves. Cut off from supplies, from reinforcements, and even from news on which he could rely, Napoleon might employ his matchless powers of organisation, creating a government, conciliating the religious leaders of Cairo, suppressing tumults, framing magniloquent proclamations, but, from a French point of view, he was merely ploughing unwatered sand. He sought to break out by way of Syria, but again the ships of his enemies carried to Acre supplies and men and a leader who frustrated the French efforts to take the place. He might announce to the citizens of Cairo that he had beaten down the walls of Acre and bombarded the city till there remained not one stone upon another,[1] but he was defeated. In sullen recognition of the fact he deserted his army in Egypt, and sailed for France on August 23, 1799. Kléber, who was left in command, with good reason disliked and distrusted his position. When a Turkish army advanced against him, he entered into negotiations with Sir Sidney Smith, the defender of Acre. By the convention of Al-Arish, signed on January 24, 1800, it was agreed that the French should evacuate Egypt in vessels to be collected and supplied by the Turks. But, while the Turks were assembling ships in their usual leisurely manner, the English cabinet had time to decide, on a false estimate of the French position, that the convention should not be carried into effect. This costly blunder involved us in a special expedition to turn the French out of the country. At the close of the year Sir Ralph Abercromby was sent with 15,000 men for this purpose, while a force from India co-operated on the side of the Red Sea. Abercromby landed at Abukir Bay on March 8, 1801. By this time Kléber had been murdered, and the command of the French had devolved upon Menou, an incapable

[1] Jabarti, *Merveilles Biographiques et Historiques*, VI, 132.

soldier who had espoused Islam and an Egyptian wife.
A battle was fought outside Alexandria. Abercromby
perished, but the issue was that one body of the French
shut itself up in Alexandria while the remainder, 12,000
men, manned the walls of Cairo. This unenterprising
behaviour promised no obstinate resistance. First Cairo
and then Alexandria surrendered, and the French
occupation of Egypt came to an inglorious end. But it
had been far indeed from fruitless. It had shaken
Mameluke power; it had fully awakened English
minds to the strategic importance of a country placed
midway between East and West; it had illustrated
Turkish incompetence; and incidentally it had brought
to Egypt an Albanian adventurer, Muhammad 'Ali.

Muhammad 'Ali had been born in 1769 at the tiny
walled seaport of Kavala, in a little house in one of the
old winding streets. Of the origins of his family nothing
is positively known. Turkish and even Persian ancestry
is claimed for him; the first seems corroborated by the
sturdiness of his physique and the fortitude of his
character, the second seems to accord better with his
subtle, flexible intelligence. In any case his family was
undistinguished. His father, Ibrahim Aga, commanded
a small body of local irregulars in the governor's service; but, dying while his son was still young, left him
to the care of the governor. The boy's education must
have been severely practical. He was fed and clothed,
he learnt his prayers, he was taught to ride, he was
practised in the use of arms. As soon as he was old
enough he must have accompanied parties sent out to
capture bandits or get in the revenue, and so learnt the
rudiments of war, the art of surprise, the manner of
command. He is said himself to have conducted some
of these parties with remarkable success, but here we
are at the mercy of the anecdotist, who loves few things
so well as to explain mature eminence by early traits of

genius and to contrast present greatness with past humiliations. When the boy was eighteen, he was married to one of the governor's relatives, who became the mother of five of his ninety-five children. He then embarked on the tobacco trade—the finest Turkish tobacco grew in the district lying inland of Kavala— but on what scale we do not know. Some have fancied him trading largely with a fortune derived from a wealthy wife;[1] others repeat stories of his having been helped out of a difficulty by a trifling loan of a couple of *rubiehs*.[2] But all we really know is that he himself looked back upon this early life with affectionate regret, towards the end of his days revisiting his birthplace and endowing a school there which still survives.[3]

When under British pressure the Porte assembled forces in the vain hope of expelling the French, the governor—Shorbashi was his Turkish title—of Kavala was called upon to furnish a contingent of 300 men. This party was sent under the command of the governor's son, 'Ali Aga, with Muhammad 'Ali as his lieutenant. But the passage to Abukir was stormy, and the Turkish force on landing had to bear many privations before it was unceremoniously bustled back into the sea by the French. The story runs that in this hurried re-embarkation Muhammad 'Ali himself was nearly drowned, and was rescued by a British man-of-war's boat. Be that as it may, the commander of the Kavala contingent was disgusted by the sea-sickness, hunger, and thirst that he encountered, and speedily returned home, leaving Muhammad 'Ali in command. The latter's spirit and resource attracted the attention

---

[1] Sabry, *L'Empire égyptien*, p. 24.
[2] Politis, *L'Hellénisme et l'Égypte moderne*, p. 179.
[3] Letter to the Governor of Kavala, 9 Shawal, 1246 (Abdine Palace Records); and Stoddart, No. 7, August 29, 1846 (F.O. 78–661 B).

of the Turkish commanders, while his forethought and attention secured the confidence of his men; thus he became by 1801 one of the two chief officers in command of the Albanian troops who formed the main strength of the Turkish force in Egypt.

This body had co-operated with the English expedition to the extent of plundering the open country and occupying the places not held by French troops. Hutchinson, Abercromby's successor in the command, soon formed the poorest opinion of its value, and gravely doubted its ability to maintain itself in Egypt,[1] and this view was confirmed by the request made by the Porte itself that a British force should remain in the country after the expulsion of the French, as a precaution against any renewal of their attempts.[2] The occupation of strategic points such as Alexandria and Suez, at all events till the end of the war, was suggested by the Russian ambassador[3] and advocated by the Governor-General of British India.[4] Pamphlets were written in the same sense,[5] and Dundas, who had always held strong views on the importance of Egypt, favoured the idea. Hawkesbury's ministry inclined to the same plan and was especially anxious to secure such a settlement of the relations between the Sultan and the beys as would prevent the recurrence of that misgovernment which had assisted the French occupation. With this object it was proposed that the rights and duties of the Mamelukes should be defined, that the collection of the revenues should be regulated, and that a fixed amount should be assigned to the maintenance of a military force under the command of British

[1] Cf. Charles-Roux, *L'Angleterre et l'Expédition française en Égypte*, II, 262. Douin and Fawtier-Jones, *La Politique Mameluke*, p. 5.
[2] Charles-Roux, *op. cit.* II, 268.   [3] Dropmore MSS, VII, 15–16.
[4] *Wellesley Despatches*, II, 588.
[5] *E.g.* Baldwin, *Political Recollections relative to Egypt.*

officers.[1] Unfortunately, Elgin, our ambassador at the Porte, was not the man to persuade Turks that a disagreeable or honest measure could be to their advantage. Instead of making terms, they promptly gave a striking demonstration of their proverbial bad faith. The Capitan Pasha—as the Turkish admiral was called —lured a body of Mamelukes on board two barges, where they were suddenly fired upon, and those who were not killed were made prisoners. This significant episode nearly led to blows between the Turk and English forces, and the Turks were only induced to release their captives by threats.[2] The beys then retired to Upper Egypt, out of Turkish reach.

While these commotions and disputes had been going forward, the Treaty of Amiens had been signed, declaring that Egypt was to be restored to the Sultan. This gave the French the right to demand its prompt evacuation by the English forces. After a few faint-hearted attempts to settle the question of the beys, the English commander was satisfied by the issue of orders that the beys were to be pardoned and granted the province of Assouan. The troops were then embarked; one of the Mameluke leaders, Elfi Bey, accompanied them on a visit to London; and Major Missett was appointed English agent to watch over the behaviour of both Turk and Mameluke, and do everything in his power to keep the French out of the country. The English occupation thus ended in March, 1803.

Missett's appointment as English agent was no doubt meant to counteract the intrigues of the consuls whom the French reappointed after the Treaty of Amiens. Similar agents were sent by the other Mediterranean

[1] A good summary is given in Ghorbal, *Beginnings of the Egyptian Question*, p. 166. The document is printed *app.* Douin and Fawtier-Jones, *op. cit.* p. 50.

[2] Douin and Fawtier-Jones, *op. cit.* pp. 160 *sqq.*

powers, and later on by Sweden, Prussia and Russia. These European agents were sharply divided into two classes according as they devoted most of their time to trade or to political functions, and naturally this division tended to follow the relative importance of the powers whom they represented. In the early years of the nineteenth century political functions amounted to little. Early consuls-general like Salt or Drovetti spent as much time collecting antiquities as in representing their national interests. But from 1830 onwards their political duties developed a new importance, and they became in fact, though not of course in form, diplomatic agents stationed with the pasha and seeking to guide his action in accordance with national policy. Some became close and intimate friends of Muhammad 'Ali, and the personal influence of Colonel Campbell weighed much with him in determining his administrative, if not his external, policy.

The English departure cleared the stage for as pretty a piece of skilful intrigue, plot and counter-plot, as ever was brought to a triumphant conclusion. In appearance only two parties were seeking the possession of Egypt—the Turks and the Mamelukes. But in reality matters were less simple. The Turks themselves were divided. On the one side were the troops who would obey the orders of Khusrau Pasha, appointed by the Sultan to govern Egypt; and on the other were the Albanians indisposed to obey anyone except their own chief leaders, Tahir Pasha and Muhammad 'Ali. The Mamelukes too had their own Bardissi and Elfi factions, each much more disposed to destroy the other than to make common cause against a common danger. The possible combinations were thus considerable, and the only rational forecast that could have been made at the moment was that none of them would be likely to endure long.

The first to disappear was Khusrau Pasha. When at a later time he had become Grand Vazir of the empire, western diplomatists regarded him as "a shrewd, bold, illiterate barbarian".[1] But in 1803 his character hardly seems to have yet risen to these heights. He is described at this time as possessing no knowledge of war, politics or administration beyond the cutting off of heads.[2] He lay, of course, at a considerable disadvantage in Egypt. The Turks were there regarded with even more hatred than the French. Their ignorance and mispronuncia-tion of the sacred language, their pride, their claims to rule the country, helped to rob them of all local sup-port. "God destroy them all", sighs the pious chronicler of the period.[3] Meanwhile at the head of the Albanian troops was Tahir Pasha, who had originally commanded a band of professed brigands in his native country with sufficient success and ferocity to merit admission to military rank in the Sultan's army. In Egypt he had displayed much courage and resource, but had been disappointed of his promised reward.[4] His followers too were dissatisfied with their lack of pay. Accordingly in May, 1803, they mutinied at Cairo. This was of course a mere everyday incident in a Turkish army. But when Tahir offered his mediation, Khusrau refused it. The next day Tahir at the head of his Albanians attacked and occupied the citadel. Khusrau fled to Damietta, and Tahir assumed the government of the city. As he had not been joined in this movement by the Osmanli troops, he called in the Mamelukes to his aid; but before they could arrive, he was murdered. His death, however, made no difference to the immediate situation. His place was taken by Muhammad 'Ali;

---

[1] Bulwer, *Life of Palmerston*, II, 252.
[2] Douin, *L'Égypte de 1802 à 1804*, p. 18.
[3] Jabarti, *op. cit.* VII, 241.
[4] Leake, *Observations upon Greece* (F.O. 78–57).

and the Mamelukes with the Albanians defeated Khusrau before Damietta, and finally conducted him a prisoner to the citadel of Cairo. Here then was the first combination: Albanians and Mamelukes against the Turks.

When all this was known at Constantinople, another governor, 'Ali Pasha, was hurriedly despatched with 1500 men to replace the deposed Khusrau.[1] He reached and occupied Alexandria, but promptly embroiled himself with the consuls of the European powers established there. He publicly declared that no capitulations held good where he was governor. He exercised no control over his troops, who amused themselves by firing at the Swedish arms over the consulate. He even sought to interfere with a decision of the local court which had inexplicably gone in favour of the Frank.[2] Early in 1804, expecting the assistance of the Albanians under Muhammad 'Ali, he moved southward against Cairo.[3] But the Albanians did not move. The pasha was captured and put to death by Bardissi Bey.[4]

He was succeeded by a third pasha, Kurshid. By this time the alliance of the Mamelukes and Albanians was wearing thin. The latter were exigent over their pay. The beys were reduced to forced loans and other violent expedients. It grieved them to the heart, to rob for other men's benefit. Moreover they inclined to support Kurshid as pasha, by reason of his pacific and moderate character.[5] A new grouping was therefore indicated, and developed with all the certainty of predestination. Elfi Bey returned from England in February, 1804. Instantly the Bardissi faction, with the support of the Albanians and perhaps with the encouragement of Muhammad 'Ali, attacked Elfi's

[1] Douin, *L'Égypte de 1802 à 1804*, pp. 55–6.
[2] *Idem*, p. 113.   [3] *Idem*, p. 143.
[4] *Idem*, pp. 156, 170.   [5] *Idem*, p. 155.

followers, whose houses in Cairo were plundered. Muhammad 'Ali was delighted at this division of the beys,[1] and promptly sought another ally, the new pasha who still lingered at Alexandria. He told the French agent at Cairo that as soon as the Albanians could get some pay, eight months in arrears, from the Mamelukes, there would be such an explosion as would restore the former to the Sultan's favour. "What can we, their natural enemies, expect", said he, "from men so ready to betray their own brethren?"[2]

The explosion followed in due course. On March 11 the Albanians at Cairo attacked the houses of the leading beys. The citadel surrendered; and Muhammad 'Ali proclaimed the farmans appointing Kurshid Pasha Wali of Egypt.[3] The pasha naturally proceeded to join his ally, and there followed some months of fighting around Cairo, between the beys on the one side and the pasha and Muhammad 'Ali on the other. But whereas in the previous year Albanians and Mamelukes had had to unite to expel Khusrau, now Turkish power had fallen so far that Kurshid was dependent on Muhammad 'Ali, who was visibly waxing in authority. The pasha, Lesseps reports truly enough, was nothing but an instrument which the Albanians could use at will.[4] In the autumn of the year this fact was exhibited in a most striking manner. The Albanians were weary of Egypt, and many desired to return home with the plunder they had obtained. But Kurshid felt that he could not maintain his position without the cool, resolute and dexterous aid of Muhammad 'Ali, and induced the latter, we must suppose without much difficulty, to remain.[5] The misery of Cairo at this period was extreme. Muhammad 'Ali's troops had to be satisfied, and

[1] Douin, *L'Égypte de* 1802 *à* 1804, p. 173.
[2] *Idem*, p. 180.   [3] *Idem*, p. 190.
[4] *Idem*, pp. 207, 211.   [5] *Idem*, p. 242.

Kurshid had to renew for their benefit the exactions formerly enforced by the Mamelukes for the same altruistic purpose. The leading Copts, for instance, were led up into the citadel and requested to provide 2000 purses.[1] The Mamelukes ranging round Cairo cut off supplies of grain so that famine raged in the city. Good Muslims began to regret the infidel government of the French.[2]

The foreign agents in Egypt contemplated these events with the normal human inability to forecast the future. A couple of generations later, with a view to stimulating Khedivial generosity, a story was put about that Lesseps, the French agent, had early recognised the genius of Muhammad 'Ali and contributed to his rise by his countenance and advice. In striking contrast with this romantic tale is his actual language to Talleyrand: *Je ne crois pas qu'il ait le génie de concevoir un plan vaste et les moyens pour l'exécuter.*[3] Accordingly he favoured and encouraged, not this leader of limited genius, but the Mameluke beys, whose return to power, he thought, would be favourable to the extension of French influence.[4] The English agent, Major Missett, suffered, excusably enough, from the same delusion.

The events of 1805 were however to illuminate the situation. Starved by the Mamelukes and plundered by the pasha, the Cairenes grew restive in their misery and turned to the Albanian leader for rescue. This, however, was the result less of instinctive recognition than of discreet instigation. Muhammad 'Ali, so the Arab chronicler of the time assures us, made friends secretly with one of the chief shaikhs, visiting him, flattering him, declaring that if he were the ruler of

---

[1] A "purse" was a sum of 500 piastres, the normal unit of large transactions, like the bag of 500 pagodas in south India.

[2] Douin, *L'Égypte de 1802 à 1804*, p. 248.   [3] *Idem*, p. 173.

[4] *Idem*, pp. 226–7.

Egypt he would govern with justice and follow the advice of the religious leaders.[1] He thus began to secure a following in the city itself, which Kurshid tried in vain to control by holding as hostages two shaikhs, but not Muhammad 'Ali's friend.[2] At the same time he sought and obtained reinforcements from Syria, to render him less dependent upon Albanian support. Their arrival brought matters to a head. Their commander proved to be a brother of one of Tahir Pasha's murderers.[3] They showed themselves to be less disciplined than either Albanians or Mamelukes. Terrible stories spread abroad of how they drove the citizens from their dwellings, raped and murdered women, and stole children. These stories, to judge from the like elsewhere, lost nothing in the telling. But their probable exaggeration in no way diminished their moral effect. The whole city of Cairo fell into panic. The gates of the great mosque of Al Azhar were closed; the bazaars and caravansarais were shut up. No man ventured out without feeling that he carried his life in his hands.[4]

At the moment of the arrival of this alarming garrison, Muhammad 'Ali had been absent from Cairo campaigning against the beys. But he speedily returned and a week later entered the city at the head of 4000 men.[5] His pretext was the demands of his men for their pay, demands with which the new-comers, like good Turkish soldiers, felt a lively sympathy. On May 9 Kurshid, quite unable to interpret portents, took advantage of Muhammad 'Ali's return to read publicly the farman conferring on him the pashaliq of Jidda. This flattering hint that his presence was no longer desired at Cairo was enough for the Albanian leader. As Kurshid was preparing to return to his residence in

---

[1] Jabarti, *op. cit.* VIII, 70.
[2] Douin, *Mohamed Ali Pacha du Caire*, p. 14.   [3] *Idem*, p. 11.
[4] *Idem*, pp. 19–20.   [5] *Idem*, p. 14.

the citadel, he was suddenly surrounded by Albanians clamouring for their pay, accusing him of having made away with the public revenues, and threatening him with instant death. One of the Albanian officers came forward to protect him from actual violence; but the populace, under the guidance of the shaikhs, were already proclaiming Muhammad 'Ali governor of Cairo.[1] Kurshid succeeded in escaping back into the citadel, from which he tried to bombard the city into submission. But Turkish gunners were unable to achieve that task, and rather excited than alarmed the inhabitants. The shaikhs, encouraged by Albanian support, put forward a great number of demands. Then as now it was regarded as sound practice in political as in commercial bargaining to begin with asking what you never expect to get. On this occasion they required that the troops should in future be stationed on the other side of the river at Ghiza, that no soldier under arms should be allowed to enter the city, and that no contributions should be levied on the citizens.[2] These being rejected, they again and more formally proclaimed Muhammad 'Ali as governor, and attempted to beleaguer the citadel. Popular enthusiasm was immense. French observers were reminded of the heady zeal with which Parisians had flung themselves into the Revolution,[3] and indeed there was this similarity that in both cases the People were busy changing one master for another. But there was a fundamental difference too. The people behind the Parisian mob did indeed aim at new institutions; the man behind the Cairene tumults was at the moment seeking nothing but personal power. The French stormed the Bastille. But the Cairenes, though they murdered Kurshid's men readily enough when they recognised them in the streets, and

[1] Douin, *Mohamed Ali Pacha du Caire*, p. 22.
[2] *Idem*, p. 27.   [3] *Idem*, p. 35.

everyone, even the children, purchased arms,[1]
t capture the citadel of Cairo. Muhammad 'Ali
a show of helping them. He had cannon dragged
e Mokattum Hills commanding the fortress, and
sharpshooters were posted in the *minar* of the Sultan
Hasan mosque. But the leader himself was in no haste
to bring the matter to a violent issue. It would perhaps
have cost him many men; his followers were not too
reliable; above all he preferred to become Pasha of
Cairo with the assent of Constantinople rather than as
an open rebel against the Sultan. The French agent
Drovetti, a far more acute observer than his predecessor
the tavern-keeping Lesseps,[2] went to the bottom of the
matter in a report which about this time he despatched
to Paris. "The measures of the enterprising Albanian
leader", he writes, "make me think he hopes to become
Pasha of Cairo without fighting and without incurring
the displeasure of the Sultan. Every act reveals a
Machiavellian mind, and I really begin to think he
has a stronger head than most Turks have. He seems
to aim at obtaining power through the favour of the
shaikhs and the people, so as to reduce the Porte to the
necessity of giving him freely the position which he will
have seized."[3]

The issue was much as he anticipated. In June an
envoy from the Sultan arrived at Alexandria with
orders to confer the pashaliq on Kurshid or Muhammad
'Ali, whichever seemed the stronger. After some delay
the envoy recognised Muhammad 'Ali, and on August
7 Kurshid quitted the citadel of Cairo and marched
down to Bulaq to take boat for Alexandria.

The political dexterity displayed by Muhammad
'Ali in the course of these events was extraordinary. He

---

[1] Douin, *Mohamed Ali Pacha du Caire*, p. 35.
[2] Missett, September 3, 1804 (W.O. 1-347).
[3] Douin, *op. cit.* p. 35.

had aided the Mamelukes to overthrow Khusrau Pasha;
he had then aided one Mameluke faction against
another; he had then helped Kurshid against the
Mamelukes; and lastly he had headed the Cairenes
against Kurshid—thus weakening in turn both Turks
and Mamelukes alike, but carefully keeping himself in
the background, never committing himself over-deeply
to any of the conflicting factions, and at last securing
for himself the sanction of the Sultan's authority. Some
have seen in this a desire to legitimise his power. But
in fact he was much too sturdy a political realist to
place excessive value on mere abstract right. As a
matter of fact, the Sultan's recognition did little to
strengthen his position within Egypt itself. He could
expect neither an accession of troops nor even consistent
moral support from Constantinople. The corrupt and
improvident Divan would turn against him as soon as
some stronger or more promising candidate appeared,
and the Mamelukes still occupied the whole of Upper
and much of Lower Egypt. But the imperial recognition did promise a temporary respite from Turkish
interference. For a few months at all events he would
only have to face the Mamelukes, and not to balance
precariously between Mameluke and Turk, unless by
chance one of the European powers intervened.

In any case the maintenance of his position remained
most uncertain. His army could be held together only
by pay or plunder; and it was therefore clear that he
would be driven into the same course of exactions as
had ruined his predecessors. Then too what were foreign
powers going to do? Drovetti might recognise the new
pasha's strong sense and Machiavellian talents, but he
did not at this time desire the continuance of his administration. Neither did the English representative,
Missett. Both in fact distrusted either his good will[1]

[1] Missett, January 1, 1806 (F.O. 24-2).

or his ability to maintain himself;[1] and both therefore set to work to encourage rival Mameluke factions. The joint hostility of both French and English thus helped Muhammad 'Ali forward, by making sure that the Mamelukes did not unite against him. Yet Drovetti at least lay under no illusions regarding the military forces of the beys. "All the chiefs combined", he writes, "have not more than 800 Mamelukes; the remainder are a mob of Greeks, Osmanlis and Arabs, attracted to their tents by hopes of pillage. The Mamelukes are no longer the brave soldiers ready to follow their masters to the death; they have no longer organisation or discipline. A bey's court, once a school of military discipline and morals, has become the source of debauch and disobedience. Their wandering life of brigandage has degraded them."[2] He concluded that Egypt would never know order or good government until the French occupation was restored.[3]

The English attitude was in most respects the converse. All our experience in the course of the expedition of 1801 had led us firmly and rightly to the conclusion that the Turks probably could never reestablish and in any event could not maintain their power in Egypt. General Hutchinson described them as deplorably feeble, distrustful of their friends, relying on their enemies, lacking the talent to form plans and the energy to carry them into effect.[4] At the same time every one believed that the French still meditated the reconquest of Egypt. As soon as the war with France was renewed, Nelson, commanding in the Mediterranean, was warned to be on the watch for any expedition eastward. For the same reason it had been re-

---

[1] Douin, *Mohamed Ali Pacha du Caire*, p. 99.
[2] *Idem*, pp. 82–3.
[3] *Idem*, p. 139.
[4] Douin, *La Campagne de* 1807, p. vi.

and asses, to carry away their effects, and bought
Venetian sequins for 14 piastres which in the ordinary
course passed for 10. The fellahin themselves were
ready to rebel, refusing provisions to parties of Muhammad 'Ali's troops not strong enough to help themselves,
and in some places even massacring them.[1] But the
failure at Rosetta entirely changed the situation. The
Albanians recovered their lost courage. The Mamelukes, instead of hastening down to join the English,
first hesitated, and then came to terms with Muhammad 'Ali. The populace sank back into submission, and
the English could no longer get intelligence of the
enemy's movements.[2]

These developments permitted Muhammad 'Ali to
assemble troops and send them northward against the
English, who in April had made a further attempt upon
Rosetta. This time they proceeded more cautiously,
bombarding the place, but deferring any actual attack
until the arrival of the Mamelukes promised by
Missett. However Muhammad 'Ali's troops appeared
instead of our supposed allies. The besiegers were
unexpectedly caught between two fires. After prolonged and confused fighting, in which we lost 400
killed and 400 more taken, our troops withdrew once
more to Alexandria.[3]

Muhammad 'Ali, at Cairo, now followed the same
temperate policy that he had employed against
Kurshid. The ordinary Turk would have been puffed
up by his success, would have killed or circumcised his
prisoners, and would have hurried on to try and push
the survivors into the sea, regardless of consequences.
The pasha so far condescended to custom as to permit

[1] Douin, *La Campagne de* 1807, pp. 179–80.
[2] Cf. Missett to Isaac Morier, May 2, 1807 (I.O., Egypt and the
Red Sea, 6).
[3] Cf. Douin, *op. cit.* pp. 73–82.

the heads of the fallen to be paraded through the streets; but he did not allow himself to forget that sooner or later peace would have to be made, that British fleets would suffer few enemy vessels to enter or leave the port of Alexandria, and above all that Britain dominated not only the Mediterranean in his front but also Indian waters in his rear. He therefore treated his prisoners well, and in May sent one of them down to Alexandria with a confidential interpreter to discuss the terms on which the English would withdraw. He offered in return for the retirement of the expedition to release his prisoners of war, to protect British trade, and to oppose any European force that should seek either to occupy Egypt or to pass through it towards India.[1] These proposals were for the moment rejected. But the Portland ministry which took office in the spring of 1807 held much sounder strategic views than Lord Grenville's ministry which it displaced. It was resolved to abandon Alexandria, which could be reoccupied at any time if necessary. On September 14 a convention was signed by which Alexandria was to be surrendered to the pasha, the English prisoners freed, and a general amnesty accorded to all who had assisted the English forces.[2]

So another crisis passed. Had it been well commanded, the expedition might have led to the destruction of Muhammad 'Ali's rising power and the restoration of Egypt to the Mamelukes or the Turks. But it was ill-conceived and mismanaged, like our abortive first expedition up the Tigris in the last war. By an extraordinary oversight it was not accompanied by any officers who had served under Abercromby and Hutchinson in the former occupation; nor was it possible to detach sufficient men from the force in

---

[1] Douin, *La Campagne de* 1807, p. 113.
[2] *Idem,* p. 164.

Sicily to achieve the object of their despatch. In all respects it seemed a complete and costly failure. But perhaps the failure was not quite so complete as it appeared, for Muhammad 'Ali's sagacious mind drew sound conclusions from the episode. He judged that the French army was a much more remote instrument of power than the British navy, and began to reflect that Great Britain might be a valuable ally in the accomplishment of schemes which he was already beginning to contemplate.

Thus little by little the situation in Egypt had begun to simplify itself. The Albanian leader was now the representative of Constantinople; French intervention was impossible; English intervention had failed. There remained only the Mamelukes to be reduced before Muhammad 'Ali could be regarded as the sole master of Egypt. But there was nevertheless a growing danger that the victor, like many a successful claimant to an estate through the processes of law, would find himself the heir of little but immoderate debt. The country itself was going fast to ruin. Upper Egypt "groaned under the iron sceptre of the Mamelukes"; Lower Egypt was "utterly unable to support the united numbers of the troops and of its population. To satisfy the demands of the government and of the more oppressive extortions of its agents, the husbandman has been reduced to the necessity of parting even with his implements of agriculture; most of the villages of the districts of the sea have been deserted; the banks of the Nile, formerly so luxuriant, are now condemned to an unnatural barrenness".[1]

The maintenance of the army was, as it always had been and as it was long to continue, "the necessary cause of great disorders".[2] In 1809, the pasha had

---

[1] Missett, January 1, 1806 (F.O. 24-2).
[2] Douin, La Campagne de 1807, p. 138.

some 10,000 effectives in his service, but, according to Turkish custom, they drew pay and allowances for 30,000.[1] Their pay and the other inevitable expenses of government greatly exceeded even in 1806 the land revenue of Lower Egypt and the customs dues on a trade that had almost vanished. The deficit could be made good only by a renewal of those levies which had been formerly made by the Mamelukes and Kurshid Pasha, but which were now more difficult and more hated than ever, because almost every one had already been stripped of his movable property. Even Europeans were obliged to contribute, and even consuls were compelled to assent.[2] The Arab annalist describes the troops as being the only people left with money to lend,[3] and indeed the Albanians at this moment in Egypt occupied much the same position as Arab mercenaries came to do at Baroda or Hyderabad. The embarrassment of the situation lay in either having to pillage and provoke the population or to displease and annoy the troops.

Muhammad 'Ali had indeed done his utmost to escape from this dilemma. He had, for instance, attached the shaikhs and chief men of Cairo to his cause by bestowing on them villages formerly belonging to the Mameluke beys, so as to separate the Cairenes from their former rulers in case their oppressions should be forgotten.[4] But, even so, difficulties broke out from time to time, and various leaders, or would-be leaders, had to be arrested.[5] More dangerous still was the attitude of his troops. As he was returning one day in October, 1807, from the citadel, a party of soldiers opened fire on him from a house as he rode by,

---

[1] Driault, *Mohamed Ali et Napoléon*, p. 34.
[2] Douin, *La Campagne de 1807*, p. 191.
[3] Jabarti, *op. cit.* viii, 182.
[4] Douin, *op. cit.* p. 111.   [5] *Idem*, p. 137.

wounding his horse and one of his companions.[1] A few days later some 500 Albanians and Osmanlis assembled before his house in the city and actually fired into his windows; and the situation was alarming enough for him to retire from the city into the citadel.[2]

Clearly a financial surplus instead of a deficit, to be attained by any means that could produce such a miracle, was the prime condition of any improvement in his position. One financial resource which occurred to him was trade. This was no very original idea. Those writers who have described the East India Company as despicable in eastern eyes because it traded have strangely misapprehended the position. The ordinary merchant was despised, not because he was a trader, but because he was defenceless. All over the East from Constantinople to Achin and Bangkok you would have found great nobles, rulers of provinces, sons and mothers of ruling kings, even emperors themselves, personally and directly interested in commerce. To Muhammad 'Ali, who had traded in tobacco before ever he had betaken himself to that life of high crime which in the East stood for politics, the step was natural, obvious, unquestionable.[3]

In this fortune favoured him. The only people with whom he could hope to do good business were the English. During the later years of the Napoleonic war the French flag practically vanished from the Levantine seas. A French vessel entering the port of Alexandria in 1808 is said to have been the first to do so for five years,[4] and another in 1811 as the first for a year and a half.[5] French ships could not be insured at Marseilles under 50 per cent. premium, and no newspapers reached Alexandria but abominable *Malta*

[1] Douin, *La Campagne de* 1807, p. 207.   [2] *Idem*, pp. 209–10.
[3] Driault, *L'Empire de Mohamed Ali* (1814–23), p. 205.
[4] *Idem*, p. 9.   [5] *Idem*, p. 137.

Gazettes, reeking, as Drovetti said, with libels on the French government.[1] But at the same time the English were eager customers for grain. The victualling of their squadrons keeping watch and ward over the Mediterranean from Malta and Gibraltar, the victualling of their ever-growing forces operating in the Peninsula, called for constant large supplies of wheat, and those years were seasons of scarcity except in Egypt where the Nile rose high and harvests were plenteous.[2] The pasha seized this heaven-sent opportunity. In true oriental style—the matter could be matched scores of times in the dominions of both the Moghul Emperor and the Ottoman Sultan—the export of grain became a monopoly, which at times was said to yield him a gross profit of 500 per cent.

Drovetti, the French consul at Cairo, did his utmost to check this growing connection. But the only satisfaction he could get consisted of assurances that the pasha was seeking his own interests only, and hints that the English might be providing money and munitions to be used against themselves.[3] However, the traffic was not limited to the sale and purchase of grain. That was paid for, partly in bullion, partly in munitions, but also, it would seem, partly in English commodities. English watches, we read, sold far better than the Geneva watches (often fraudulently marked with English names) which the French had been accustomed to sell in Egypt; and a genuine Prior would fetch twice as much as a French watch of equal quality.[4] Printed cottons too were imported and used so largely as to displace the locally made article.[5]

What was worse, from the French standpoint, was

---

[1] Driault, *L'Empire de Mohamed Ali* (1814–23), p. 26.
[2] Ghorbal, *The Beginnings of the Egyptian Question*, p. 281.
[3] Driault, *op. cit.* p. 117.
[4] *Idem*, p. 99.   [5] *Idem*, p. 189.

that political friendship sprang out of this commercial intercourse. At first Drovetti's advice and intrigues during the English expedition of 1807 had borne some fruit. He had demanded, for instance, and seems to have secured the sequestration of English goods imported under the flag of Jerusalem,[1] and waged successful war against an audacious monk who had ventured to publish at Alexandria the reported excommunication of Napoleon.[2] But when in 1811 a French privateer put in to sell prize cargoes, and when in 1812 another tried to sell an English vessel she had taken, the English agents offered a successful resistance. At their request the matter was suspended until they had obtained farmans from the Sultan, once more at peace with England, forbidding the sale of prizes or prize goods in Turkish ports by either of the combatant powers. But this, Drovetti observed bitterly, did not prevent the importation of prize goods condemned by the English court at Malta, while the French had small chance of reprisals. "What is the use", he asks angrily, "of making prizes if you can't sell them anywhere?"[3] Trade, cast into the scales, was evidently tilting the political balance heavily in the English favour, the more so as it was so rapidly replenishing the pasha's treasury.

At the same time and with the same purpose Muhammad 'Ali began to overhaul the revenue machinery. In the Turkish, as in the Moghul empire, political decay had followed the same course. On all sides public revenue had been diverted to private advantage. The modes of assessment and collection had been so elaborated as to perplex and confound enquiry. The Copts, who had long monopolised the business of public accountancy, had developed accounts as com-

---

[1] Driault, *L'Empire de Mohamed Ali* (1814–23), pp. 18, 20, 27.
[2] *Idem*, p. 63.   [3] *Idem*, p. 191.

plicated as those of the Brahmans at the Poona Daftar. A variety of coin gave opportunity for fleecing both the peasant and the government. The *feddan*, like the Indian *bigha*, did not mean the same area of land in different districts, or even in different parts of the same district. The practice of keeping officials in arrears of pay gave them an excuse (for what perhaps they would have done in any case) to impose and levy extra dues, which, as in India, were when discovered added to the public demand and at once replaced by additional impositions. Muhammad 'Ali resolved to cut his way through this forest of abuses. In 1808 he began an enquiry into landed tenures. Every oriental reformer has done so and been grievously abused for his pains; and what Akbar undertook in India, the pasha undertook in Egypt. It was indeed necessary. The pressure which he was putting on the revenue officials was not making them disgorge their perquisites but merely press more heavily on the fellah, who in consequence, weary of being plundered by the *multazim* (or zamindars, as they would have been called in India), by the officials, by the Bedouin, by the Mamelukes and by the Albanians, was abandoning his land and leaving his fields untilled. Muhammad 'Ali therefore ordered an examination of all grants by which the *multazim* claimed to hold lands, and he then annulled all which were reported to be irregular, and a little later expropriated those who were in arrears of revenue, allowing pensions to the persons thus dispossessed. Some six years later, he carried the process farther, abolishing all the immunities till then enjoyed by all religious endowments—*wakuf*; ordering the remeasurement of lands, when many were found paying revenue—*miri*—on only half their cultivated areas; simplifying the mode of assessment; and finally in 1814 expropriating the surviving *multazim*. These measures were severe, and most unpopular with the persons to whom Muhammad 'Ali owed his simulacrum of popular support. But some such measures were urgently needed. Drovetti declared that in 1808 two-thirds of the land cultivated in 1798 was lying waste. The land which the pasha thus took into his own hands (putting into practice the theory of the East India Company's servants) was not allowed to lie fallow. Fellahin were set to till it, under severe penalties if they neglected their task.[1] This interference with "the rights of property" which the English Whigs could never forgive, passed, not with that universal reprobation commonly asserted, but with only a few small gatherings in Al Azhar mosque, producing nothing but promises of alleviation which no one expected to be kept.[2]

These financial operations gradually re-established the treasury at Cairo, and the pasha's own army became a less formidable menace in proportion as it could be regularly paid.

At the same time the Mameluke question was gradually brought to a decisive settlement. In 1807, as we have seen, the beys had been induced by the intrigues of Muhammad 'Ali and Drovetti, by their own dissensions, and by the English failure at Rosetta, to neglect the last chance that fate was to offer them of re-establishing their power at Cairo and in Lower Egypt. But they still formed a very dangerous body, in occupation of Upper Egypt, successively threatening Cairo, or driven southward, according to temporary shiftings of military superiority. From time to time also there would be sudden negotiations, occasionally issuing in agreements which neither side meant to keep, and which only lasted about as long as they had

[1] Jomard, Coup d'Œil, p. 11; Driault, L'Empire de Mohamed Ali (1814–23), pp. 231, 241; Jabarti, op. cit. VIII, pp. 343, 345.
[2] Paton, Egyptian Revolution, II, 27; Driault, op. cit. p. 242.

taken to negotiate.[1] The survivors of the Elfi faction still cherished hopes of a new and more powerful English expedition to overthrow their enemy and then go away again in their ships; and the more sanguine fancied that they might extract a large sum of money from the English to enable them to buy Muhammad 'Ali's troops and then overthrow him themselves.[2] The pasha, on the other hand, was bent on their complete subjugation, and aimed at inducing them to return to dwell at Cairo under his authority. Alternate negotiations and campaigns thus occupied many months after the departure of the English; and at last, towards the end of 1809, the beys did agree to come down and settle at Ghiza.[3] They did not arrive for nearly six months, and when they did come, they came far more prepared for war than peace. For some time their force and Muhammad 'Ali's lay facing each other; and, though a group of the Mameluke leaders decided to go over to the pasha, the majority resolved on a renewal of the conflict. A series of actions followed, in which Muhammad 'Ali's artillery assisted him to success; and at last about the beginning of 1811 a majority of the survivors decided to make their submission.[4] Their power in fact was broken.

Time-honoured policy now demanded that they should be destroyed. Every good Turk held (with honest Pym) that "stone-dead hath no fellow"; and Muhammad 'Ali resolved to make an end of these fallen tyrants of the country. To achieve this it was desirable to assemble as many as possible in some secure place from which they could not escape. On March 1 the pasha's son was to be invested with a dress of honour as Pasha of Jidda and commander of the

[1] Driault, *L'Empire de Mohamed Ali* (1814-23), p. 33.
[2] *Idem*, p. 43.   [3] *Idem*, p. 54.
[4] *Idem*, pp. 69, 70, 83, 92.

troops to be despatched against the Wahabi heretics in the Hijaz. All the Mameluke chiefs were invited to the ceremony, and encouraged to bring with them as many followers as they chose. Entirely deceived, they thronged to the citadel, to take part in the procession which was to march to camp by the Gate of Victories—the Bab-al-Futuh. From the platform of rock on which the chief buildings of the citadel were erected there ran down to the Bab-al-Azab (by which you pass to the Maidan Rumeila) a steep winding passage, cut in the rock, and commanded at every point for the destruction of any enemy who should force the gate. Down this path the troops moved—first some bodies of Ottoman soldiers, then the Albanians, then the Mamelukes, and then another body of infantry and horse. But when the foremost party of the troops had reached and passed the gate, the Albanian commander ordered the gate to be shut and barred, and his men turned and opened fire on the descending Mamelukes. The passage was speedily blocked by dead men and horses. Those who survived were either shot as they sought helplessly to escape or were seized, carried before the pasha, and beheaded by his orders. One man alone is said to have survived. Nor did even this massacre terminate the business. Troops were instantly despatched to slay the remaining Mamelukes wherever they might be found. The beys' palaces were sacked. One European visitor had gone to a house near the citadel to watch the procession. Hurriedly returning home, he saw several of the unfortunate prisoners being led to the slaughter; one was cut down close beside him; he met the women of one of the beys being driven along by a party of Albanians like a flock of sheep; and everywhere he saw soldiers loaded with plunder and drunk with fury.[1]

About a year later the pasha succeeded in bringing

[1] Lane-Poole, *Life of Stratford Canning*, I, 107–9.

off a second *coup* of the like nature. A number of Mamelukes still remained in Upper Egypt. After being chased and harried for some months by a force under Muhammad 'Ali's son, Ibrahim, some 800 with 200 of their slaves surrendered, and were put to the sword.[1] These Cromwellian measures left the pasha for the first time undisputed master of the country.

Drovetti's comments on these extraordinary events are not a little illuminating. On March 4, when pools of blood were still lying in the citadel and the city still bore the marks of the sacking of the beys' palaces, it seemed to him a "terrible execution" which had deprived the English of their few remaining friends.[2] But when Missett dared to add his congratulations to those of the French, and when it became apparent that, so far from having been impaired, the position of the English was steadily improving, the French consul belatedly awoke to the moral aspect of the tragedy, and the later measures against the Mamelukes are characterised as atrocious and inexcusable.[3]

Two excuses have been put forward to palliate these massacres. One that the beys had conspired to overthrow Muhammad 'Ali; the other that he had been instigated by the Divan of Constantinople. Both may be quite true. But the real reason certainly lies elsewhere. The pasha's power was still unstable; he had been repeatedly called on to undertake an expedition into Arabia; he could not reduce his own force and leave the beys in a position to overthrow his power. The very reason which compelled Taimur to slaughter his prisoners before Delhi urged Muhammad 'Ali to exterminate the Mamelukes. Nor is there the least reason to suppose that he hesitated to act thus, once he perceived

[1] Letter to Missett, May 6, 1813 (F.O. 24-4).
[2] Driault, *L'Empire de Mohamed Ali* (1814–23), p. 113.
[3] *Idem*, p. 184.

that his personal position was at stake. He was never a bloodthirsty man, delighting in slaughter for its own sake. But neither was he ever inspired by that tenderness for human life which has grown up in the West in the last century. He recognised many reasons as entirely justifying the taking of life. Nor in this was there anything peculiar. Everyone who attended his divan, his friends and associates, his officers, his superiors, would have deemed him mad had he thought otherwise. In the very next year Jalal-ud-din, Governor of Aleppo, murdered the leaders of his janissaries *en masse*.[1] Muhammad 'Ali had after all only accomplished with wholesale success what the Capitan Pasha had attempted but bungled a few years earlier.

From the standpoint of Turkish ethics there is little more to be said, and at this time Muhammad 'Ali's views and outlook were essentially Turkish. Obviously it could not be otherwise. His birth, up-bringing, and experience had all tended to produce a vigorous but exceedingly unenlightened ruler, who would shrink from nothing for the attainment of his personal ends. The remarkable thing is not that Muhammad 'Ali set up his rule like a Turk, but that he was capable, as no other Turk of his period, of development, of absorbing new ideas, of adapting them to new and different circumstances. His keen eyes revealed to him the fundamental weaknesses of existing oriental rule; and, alongside of the perpetual weaving of a most dexterous policy for the maintenance of his own position and the assurance of his family's future, there went a constructive power, a sense of the forces by which states are built up and broken down, a ceaseless struggle for improvement, a never-dulled consciousness of the defects of his administrative machinery, such as no oriental ruler had shown since the days of Akbar. His

[1] Barker, *Syria and Egypt*, I, 138–40.

government marks a great turning-point in the history
not of Egypt only but of the Near East as a whole, for
he led the way in adapting western political ideas to
eastern conditions. We must remember this as well as
that holocaust by the Bab-al-Azab. Many years after,
a European visitor regretted that the strange episodes
of his rise to power should have remained so little
known. "I do not love this period of my life",
Muhammad 'Ali answered; "and what would the
world profit by the recital of this interminable tissue of
combat and misery, cunning and bloodshed to which
circumstances imperatively compelled me?...My history shall not commence till the period when, free from
all restraint, I could arouse this land...from the sleep
of ages."[1]

[1] Puckler-Muskau, *Egypt under Mehemet Ali*, I, 317.

Chapter II

THE PILLAR OF THE EMPIRE: ARABIA
AND THE SUDAN

Muhammad 'Ali's establishment as the real as well as
the titular ruler of Egypt was followed by a period of
some twenty years during which circumstances drove
him generally to pose as the active, zealous and
obedient servant of his august master the Sultan of
Rūm, the Caliph, "the Shadow of God upon Earth".
His obedience was indeed unreal, his zeal affected.
From the day when the idea of seizing the government
of Egypt first occurred to him as a practicable measure,
he had probably always nursed the thought of ruling,
not on behalf of another but as an independent
sovereign. His companion-in-arms, Tahir Pasha, had
dreamt of independent rule; his compatriot, 'Ali of
Janina, virtually accomplished it. He himself had
offered alliance to both the English in 1812[1] and the
French in 1810[2] if only either of them would recognise
him as ruler of Cairo; and he had actually proposed to
the Divan at Constantinople in 1810 that he should be
recognised on the same footing as the Barbary States.[3]
But both the English and the French, in view of the
European position and existing alliances of the Sultan,
had rejected his proposals; and he had under-estimated
the price at which the Divan set the favour he demanded. These rebuffs in no wise changed his views;
but they did lead to their concealment for a while.
The lack of the European alliance which he sought

[1] Missett, June 20, 1812 (F.O. 24-4).
[2] Driault, *L'Empire de Mohamed Ali* (1814-23), p. 93.
[3] Sabry, *L'Empire égyptien*, p. 37.

prevented any open breach with the Porte; and
although he seldom obeyed orders which could not be
diverted to his own aggrandisement, his public
language was always that of the loyal and devoted
vassal. Throughout this period there is an ever piquant
contrast between the professed object and the real
purpose of his conduct.

At this time the internal condition of the Turkish
empire closely resembled that of the Moghuls in the
early eighteenth century. Both were rotten to the core.
The Divan of Constantinople, like the durbar of Delhi,
was engrossed by the private interests of individual
ministers. The pashas of the Turkish provinces, like
the nawabs of the Moghul subahs, were bound by so
slight a thread to the central government as to be
almost independent. Baghdad and Cairo, like Hyderabad and Lucknow, were almost separate capitals. But
there was a vital difference in the political environment of the two decaying empires. The Moghul's
neighbours, Marathas and Afghans, were too remote
one from the other, and their political conduct guided
too much by the law of nature, for either to be tempted
to uphold Delhi for fear of the other's getting the lion's
share of the spoils; whereas the Sultan's territories
touched a whole group of closely inter-knit European
states, inspired by a most watchful jealousy of each
other's expansion. So that while the Moghul empire
was left to dissolve by natural process into chaos, the
Turkish dominions were held together by pressure
from without long after they had ceased to possess any
internal coherence. Muhammad 'Ali's conduct as a
pillar of the empire was dictated by this situation.

He had small cause for gratitude. The position of the
Divan had been consistent only in its hostility. It had
first accused him of conspiring with the beys to his
private benefit and the injury of the state; and when he

sent their heads to be set up at the Great Gate of the
Seraglio, he was reproached with having murdered the
Sultan's most reliable supporters.[1]

Even while he had been struggling with the Mamelukes for the mastery of Egypt he had been repeatedly
called upon by the Porte to undertake the suppression
of the sect of Wahabis in Arabia, but until 1811 he had
constantly pleaded the dangers arising from "these
miserable Egyptian chiefs", their encouragement by
the neighbouring pasha of Syria, or the difficulty of
procuring shipping in the Red Sea.[2] So in acceding at
last to the demands of Constantinople, Muhammad
'Ali certainly was not inspired by any empty sentiment
of obedience. He resolved to undertake an expedition
into Arabia on the solidest of grounds. It would keep
busy those turbulent soldiers who had fired upon him
even when the Mamelukes were still unsubdued and
living, and who might be yet more turbulent when no
force remained in Egypt capable of resisting them; and
it would raise high his repute in the world of Islam if he
drove the heretics from the Holy Cities.

The Wahabis were a sect that had sprung up in
Arabia about the middle of the eighteenth century.
Their founder, Muhammad ibn Abdul Wahab, after
studying in the schools of Damascus and Baghdad, had
dwelt for a while at Mecca. There continued contem-
plation of the lives and manners of the pilgrims
strengthened and confirmed his rising belief that Islam
had been corrupted from and should be restored to its
early purity and simplicity. He therefore began to
attack the luxury of his age and the dialectical subtleties by which deviations from the plain intention of
Koranic texts were excused or justified. He began to

[1] To Nakib Effendi, Rajab 5 and 19, 1226 (Abdine Archives).
[2] To Nakib Effendi, Zilhaj 5, 1225, and Muharram 1, 1226
(ibid.).

expound these puritan doctrines in his native village in Najd; but having no honour in his own country, and being moreover at this time an unarmed prophet, he fled, like his prototype, and found refuge with Amir Muhammad ibn Saud at Darayyah. The amir adopted the new doctrines, and there rose in Najd a barbarous theocracy warring ceaselessly on the corrupt Muslims who surrounded it, renouncing the Turkish caliphate, and defying the neighbouring pashas of the empire. In the enfeebled condition of the state, the movement for some time met little effective opposition; and it was able to display its impartial hatred of both Shiah and Sunni by sacking the most sacred shrines of either sect at Karbela and Mecca, and Medina, and slaughtering devotees by the hundred within the holy precincts themselves.

Their occupation of the Hijaz produced great commotion in the Muslim world, for it completely interrupted the annual pilgrimages to the Holy Cities. In 1805 and again in 1806 the great Syrian caravan was turned back. On this the Pasha of Damascus was disgraced and superseded. Indeed this was well merited. The *miri*, or land revenue, of the provinces of Damascus and Syrian Tripoli had been specifically assigned (according to Turkish methods of finance) for the cost of conducting and protecting the caravan of pilgrims; and the Wahabi occupation of Hijaz had seemed to the pasha a heaven-sent chance of allowing the pilgrim caravan to lapse and of diverting the miri into his own coffers. He had not therefore made any very serious efforts to disturb the Wahabis in their occupation of Mecca and Medina.[1]

The Sultan had for some years been issuing unavailing orders to the Pashas of both Baghdad and Damascus to expel the invaders from the sacred territory. Indeed

[1] Burckhardt, *Nubia*, p. xxxiii.

the protection of the Holy Cities was traditionally regarded as a great honour, and the expulsion of the Turks as a great disgrace. The Porte turned therefore to the rising Pasha of Cairo. It would be a great stroke if he could be induced to exhaust his resources and use up his troops in destroying the Wahabis, for this would restore not only the Hijaz but Egypt as well to the effective control of the Sultan. So the Sultan and pasha were at last united (though for the most different reasons in the world) in a common desire to reconquer the cradle of Islam.

Accordingly in the latter part of 1811 the pasha's son Tussun, whose earlier setting-out had been so tragically attended by the beys, really began his march. This time it was followed, instead of being preceded, by a tragedy. The expedition embarked at Suez and landed at Yambo, but was caught in a narrow defile on the way up to Medina early in 1812, and the survivors fled back to Yambo, after three days' fighting, with the loss of all their artillery.[1] The retreat had been begun by Tussun's principal lieutenant, who indeed reached Yambo in safety, but was at once beheaded by Muhammad 'Ali's orders to promote fortitude among the rest. Advantage was also taken of this disaster to get rid of certain Albanian leaders whose turbulence had caused a good deal of anxiety to the pasha. Discredited by their defeat and disgusted with the hardships of Arabian campaigning, where the booty at best amounted to no more than a few camels as against strong risks of getting one's throat cut, they were not unwilling to comply with the pasha's proposal that they should seek more profitable service elsewhere.

These measures, with the preparations for a new campaign, filled up the hot weather of 1812. The preparations included the seduction of Arab tribes in

[1] Missett, February 16, 1812 (F.O. 24-4).

the Hijaz, by methods familar to us in recent times, in order to facilitate the advance on Medina. These measures succeeded. The Wahabis were driven from Medina in November, from Mecca and Jiddah early in the following year, so that the Hijaz came into Muhammad 'Ali's possession, and the caliph was once more prayed for in the mosques of the Holy Cities.[1]

Later in the year Muhammad 'Ali in person visited Mecca "for the purpose of establishing order" in his new conquests.[2] The event showed that his plan was to set up a new 'sharif' in Mecca, since the old one was believed not only to have sympathised with and encouraged the Wahabis but also to be possessed of a large treasure. The deposition was successfully accomplished. The sharif and his three sons were seized and sent off to Cairo.[3] But this transaction alarmed a number of Arab tribes and the Wahabis began to gather once more in the desert. More men were summoned from Egypt to meet this reviving danger. The pasha ordered 10,000 to be sent with the least possible delay. As there were not many more than 12,000 in Egypt, the demand could only be met with vigorous recruitment. Moors from the Barbary states, Sudanese slaves, Greeks and even Armenians were enlisted and gradually sent off.[4] But this new campaign of 1814, like Tussun's, opened with disaster. A detachment two days' march beyond Taifa was suddenly attacked by the Arabs. Ten out of the twelve chief officers fled at the first onset, carrying their men with them. Muhammad 'Ali mounted a dromedary and hastened to meet the fugitives, but neither threats nor promises could induce them to rally. As a consequence

---

[1] Missett, November 4, 1812 (F.O. 24–4).
[2] The same, October 14, 1813 (*ibid.*).
[3] The same, January 12, 1814 (F.O. 24–5).
[4] The same, April 9, 1814 (*ibid.*).

seven commanders were degraded and sent back to
Cairo; it is said that the other three were beheaded.[1]
A further defeat occurred in an attack on Taraba
under Tussun. The force was misled by its guides,
and its camp was rushed by the Wahabis at night.
All the Egyptian baggage and artillery was lost.[2] The
result was widespread discouragement. "An intelligent
traveller"—by which term Major Missett seems to
disguise the famous Burckhardt—who was at Jidda in
August, observed that "in general the soldiers are
broken-spirited, sickly, discontented on account of the
expenses of living which are at least double what they
are in Egypt, without any hopes of gain or plunder,
there being here neither fellahs to fleece nor villages to
sack. Their enemies are naked Bedouins, and a starved
camel is the most valuable booty they can hope to
make."[3]

However at this moment fortune turned. In April,
1814, ibn Saud had died and his three sons could not
agree among themselves.[4] Reinforcements were procured, tribal chiefs conciliated and bribed, and the
pasha in person took the field after celebrating the
Bairam festival at Mecca. The Wahabis had assembled
a great force (40,000 men, it is said) at Biselah, twelve
hours' march west of Taraba. Muhammad 'Ali
attacked, and after a most bloody conflict (the descrip-
tion is his own) the Wahabis fled, pursued for an hour
and a half by the Egyptian cavalry. Their camp, 5000
camels, and much baggage fell into the victor's hands.[5]

This success ought to have led to the complete
overthrow of the Wahabis, but for various reasons

---

[1] Missett, April 9, 1814 (F.O. 24–5).
[2] The same, June 6, 1814 (*ibid.*).
[3] Encl. of August 7 in Missett, December 7, 1814 (*ibid.*).
[4] Missett, July 9, 1814 (*ibid.*).
[5] Muhammad 'Ali to Missett, 7 Safar, 1230 (F.O. 24–6).

failed to do so. The pasha had now been over a year absent from Cairo; on at least one occasion the Porte had attempted to remove him from the pashaliq of Egypt,[1] and the return of Napoleon from Elba promised renewed confusion in Europe from which political profit might be secured.[2] He therefore entrusted the completion of the campaign to his son Tussun, and Tussun, as before, exhibited his incapacity. He began an advance which should have conducted him to the Wahabi capital of Darayyah; but found himself running short of stores and provisions. The Wahabis under their old leader would probably have inflicted a heavy defeat on the Egyptian invaders. But Abdullah, the new amir, had been severely shaken by the victory of Biselah. He hesitated to attack, while Tussun shrank from advancing. They therefore made a peace, by which the Wahabis renounced all rights over the tribes in the area occupied by Muhammad 'Ali. As this left the Wahabis in possession of districts north and east of Medina and between Medina and Mecca,[3] the arrangement was a mere truce to be continued until one side or the other should choose to renew the war.

Early in January, 1816, when exhausted Europe had relapsed into a long-unaccustomed peace, news was received, or at all events given out in Cairo, that some of the Arab tribes had broken into rebellion at Wahabi instigation. Tussun had fortunately died, from the zest with which he gave himself to the joys of Egypt after his desert campaigns. The command of the new expedition was therefore entrusted to the pasha's second son, Ibrahim, "the lion of the brave, whose counsel hath always proved fortunate".[4] The new commander was

[1] The conspiracy of Latif Pasha. Missett, November 13, 1813 (F.O. 24-4).   [2] Cf. Burckhardt, *Arabia*, I, 149.
[3] Missett, January 13, 1816 (F.O. 24-6).
[4] The same, March 8, 1816 (*ibid.*).

to play a great part in the events of the coming years. He had been born at Kavala in 1789, and was now twenty-six.[1] Of low stature but powerfully built, he enjoyed abundant energy and could resist alike the fatigues of pleasure and of war. He had clear blue eyes, a high forehead, a fair beard. He was very active in both mind and body. Uneducated, like his father, he possessed, like his father, a rare combination of courage and prudence. He lacked his father's charm of manner and his insight into men and situations. He was austere and would overawe where his father charmed. He would never have raised himself so high out of obscurity as Muhammad 'Ali had done, but in any event he would have been a soldier of mark, and he became his father's right hand, regarding him with filial awe and obedience, and carrying out his orders with scrupulous fidelity. He possessed too his father's love of looking into matters for himself, instead of implicitly trusting the reports which were made to him.[2]

His early measures were directed, not so much at securing any particular military success, for which he judged the time was not yet ripe, as at winning over to the Egyptian side a number of the principal chiefs, who had begun to weary of Wahabi control. "The talents...which he has evinced", writes Missett's successor, Henry Salt, early in 1817, "in managing the different tribes of Bedouin Arabs give some promise of his ultimate success."[3] The same agent rightly ascribed his success to "an undaunted firmness, or rather cruelty, to those who oppose him, to his having a

[1] The story was put about that he was the son of Muhammad 'Ali's first wife by a former husband. But this was untrue. Campbell, July 30, 1839 (F.O. 78–375).
[2] Lane-Poole, *Stratford Canning*, I, 469; Campbell, Report on Syria (F.O. 78–283).
[3] Salt, April 28, 1817 (F.O. 78–89).

command of money, and being celebrated for scrupulous adherence to his word—three qualifications peculiarly requisite to gain influence over the Arabs".[1] At the same time his control over his subordinates was a very different thing from Tussun's loose command. An incident related by Salt illustrates this very effectively. Hasan Aga, in charge of the Hijaz frontier, fell into an ambush. Instead of being the first to flee, "the Aga shot his horse in front of the line and shared the fate of his men".[2] If Ibrahim could inspire his followers with this noble sense of duty, he deserved to succeed.

Abdullah ibn Saud had felt the completest security in his desert fastness of Darayyah. But, when all his plans had been laid and his preparations completed, Ibrahim began his advance. He moved as a friend and protector, not as a conqueror. Every skin of water, every date, every piece of wood, was promptly and generously paid for. His severe discipline kept his troops in a wholly unaccustomed way from pillage and insult. This ensured him something of the support which British armies in India had usually encountered on the march. But even so his expedition, based on the distant Red Sea port of Jidda, almost sank under the difficulties that beset it. No less than 80,000 camels were employed on his line of communications,[3] and he arrived before Darayyah with less than 6000 men. For three months he lay before the place able to accomplish little, and then his magazine was destroyed by fire. Many leaders would have spiked their guns and led their troops to massacre and starvation on the long road back. But Ibrahim held his ground, and repulsed the enemy's attacks, until he received fresh supplies of powder and reinforcements of men. Then

[1] Salt, June 6, 1818 (F.O. 78–91).   [2] *Ibid.*
[3] *Ibid.*

he pressed the siege, and at last stormed the place, in September, 1818. Two shaikhs, the leaders of the Wahabi sect, were captured. Ibrahim shaved their venerable beards, plucked out their teeth, and so exposed them to the derision of the populace.[1] At the same time a large number of the ruling family was deported to Cairo,[2] and Abdullah ibn Saud sent on to make his peace if he could with the Sultan.

For the moment the Wahabi peril had been crushed. The strong arm of Ibrahim, the organising energy of Muhammad 'Ali, had accomplished what the pashas of Syria and Baghdad had lamentably failed to achieve in spite of their relative proximity to Darayyah, and in spite of Ibrahim's neglect of earlier schemes for persuading the sectaries by peaceful argument that they had wandered from the path of salvation. The Sophy of Persia sent Muhammad 'Ali a precious scimitar, its hilt and scabbard encrusted with precious stones.[3] Even the Sublime Porte was gratified by an unaccustomed degree of success which enabled it to behead the principal rebel, and named Ibrahim wali of the provinces of the Hijaz and Abyssinia,[4] while the English consul-general at Cairo rejoiced at the destruction "of a band of robbers who had proved themselves more bigotted, intolerant, and far greater enemies to the progress of civilization than the very followers of that religion which it was their object to supplant".[5]

The Turkish empire, like that of the Moghuls, the Marathas, the Persians, or even the Chinese, rejoiced in the most elastic of boundaries, which enabled the imperial government to resent or to ignore, to profit by

[1] Salt, October 8, 1818 (F.O. 78–91).
[2] Douin, *L'Égypte de 1802 à 1804*, p. 46.
[3] Driault, *L'Empire de Mohamed Ali*, p. 176.
[4] The Abdine records contain a copy of the farman, Rabi-al-awal 4, 1237.
[5] Salt, *ut supra*.

or to disavow, the aggressions of neighbouring rulers or
of its own provincial governors. Beyond the provinces
under the actual or nominal administration of the
Sultan, there always stretched vague areas where
Turks had once appeared as conquerors, where local
chiefs had been frightened into a temporary submission,
or where, in accordance with the universal ideals of
Islam, the Caliph ought to be recognised. These vague
claims, which could not for a moment stand the tests of
European jurists, extended down the Red Sea and
beyond it to Aden, and across it to the small ports like
Massowa and Suakin on its African shore. Hence the
inclusion in Ibrahim's pashaliq of titular authority over
Abyssinia. It meant in fact no more than the power of
appointing governors at the ports in order to collect
tolls on the produce of the Sudan—gum, ivory and
slaves—carried down by caravan for sale to the Guja-
rati traders frequenting the Red Sea ports.[1]

Muhammad 'Ali, however, was far from content with
this restrained authority. He desired to control the
trade himself. He believed that the Sudan and
Abyssinia abounded in gold. He knew that from the
south came those dark-skinned stalwart slaves who had
always been greatly prized in Egypt. All three motives
were strong. But at the moment it would have been
hard to tell whether he was more attracted by the idea
of discovering mines of gold that would enable him to
win over the whole Divan at Constantinople or the
hope of levying and training whole armies of Sudanese,
who would enable him to dispense with mutinous Albanians and Turks and to defy the Sultan and all his hosts.

Accordingly in 1820 preparations were made for a
great southward expedition, ostensibly to resent some
insult said to have been offered by the Sultan of Sennar

[1] Valentia's observations enclosed in his letter to Canning,
September 13, 1808 (F.O. 1–1).

and to clear the way for the trading caravans once more to descend the Nile to Cairo. By the middle of the year 5000 troops had been assembled at Wadi Halfa, beyond which the pasha's authority extended no great distance, and the command of the expedition was entrusted to Ismail, a third son of Muhammad 'Ali, sent to acquire experience of war and government.[1] He succeeded speedily in overrunning the territory of Sennar, the eastern portion of the Sudan, subduing the *maliks* or chiefs of that area with little resistance. In this there was small credit, for the Sudanese were entirely unacquainted with the use of firearms and they were besides divided among themselves under two rivals who aspired to the chief authority. One murdered the other, and then fled to Abyssinia, while the nominal king at once submitted. The Egyptian army then moved farther south, ultimately reaching a point between the 10th and 11th degree of north latitude.[2] But this proved much less successful than the earlier part of the invasion. The broken jungles were difficult to penetrate and were easier to defend. The invaders suffered from dysentery and the fevers of the country. Their supplies of provisions gave out. Ismail found himself obliged to retire again into Sennar.

Meanwhile another body of troops under the pasha's son-in-law, the Daftardar Bey, had advanced into Kordofan, the western half of the Sudan. After a much severer resistance than was met with in Sennar, Al Obeid was taken and pillaged. The Sudan was thus conquered. But its administration was confided to inexperienced hands. Muhammad 'Ali had intended that Ibrahim should organise the province, but he was seized by dysentery soon after his arrival and returned to Egypt. The expected gold mines were not discovered.

[1] Salt, June 30, 1820 (F.O. 78–96).
[2] Deherain, *Le Soudan égyptien*, p. 86.

By March, 1822, only 500 negroes capable of bearing arms had reached Assouan,[1] instead of the army that had been expected. And Ismail himself proved a bad governor. Muhammad 'Ali had found it constantly necessary to admonish his son to employ gentler methods, to act with justice, to conciliate the people.[2] But at the same time he was perpetually demanding fresh supplies of slaves, who could only be obtained by repeated raids upon a terror-stricken people. It is difficult simultaneously to conciliate and to enslave a population, and Ismail doubtless considered the demand for slaves the more urgent matter of the two. Late in 1822, returning down the river, he landed opposite Shendy, and demanded of the local malik within three days the payment of 15,000 dollars and the delivery of 6000 slaves. The malik declared that he could not do so. "Will you insult me, slave?" cried Ismail, and struck him across the face with a small Indian riding-switch. On this another malik interposed with promises of obedience, and they then retired. But their object was only to collect their followers. As soon as this was done, Ismail's troops on one side of the river were pinned to their ground by a night attack which broke on them quite unexpectedly, while Ismail on the other awoke to find the house in which he was sleeping had been set on fire, and he and his suite were cut to pieces.[3]

But the unfortunate maliks had forgotten the Daftardar Bey in Kordofan. The news of Ismail's murder brought him back in hot haste to Sennar, and there he took a most bloody vengeance. He is said to have massacred 30,000 persons. Other troubles sprang up.

[1] Salt, May 30, 1822 (F.O. 78–112).
[2] Letter to Ismail, Rabi-us-sani 9, 1236.
[3] Salt, December 14, 1822, and May 3, 1823 (F.O. 78–112 and 119).

A mahdi arose and obtained a considerable following. The European consuls were informed that he had been taken and beheaded, but a couple of months later he was still at large and reinforcements were being sent from Assouan to suppress him.[1] But these movements also were gradually crushed, and by 1826 the Sudan was quiet enough for Muhammad 'Ali to be taking measures for its development. Eight of the most notable village head-men of Lower Egypt, with a hundred and ten other persons, were to be sent to the Sudan to teach the natives the Egyptian manner of cultivation.[2]

This measure seems to have had no particular result. Hunger is probably the sole motive strong enough to make primitive races, like the Sudanese, industrious; and they seem to have learnt nothing from their Egyptian instructors, who moreover cannot be supposed to have been exceedingly zealous in their enforced task. In the next ten years the only notable change was the rise of Khartum from a petty village into a town of over 500 brick-built houses, with barracks, storehouses, and many gardens growing excellent figs and grapes. This was the work of Kurshid Pasha, who for several years ruled the province and made the place his capital. Its growth was the consequence which has always followed (especially in the East) the establishment at any point of the seat of government.

But Muhammad 'Ali was most dissatisfied with the stationary condition of production in the province. In 1838-9 he spent some six months inspecting it, partly in the never-dying hope of finding gold, but principally,

[1] Salt, April 28, 1824 (I.O., Egypt and the Red Sea, 7). Also letter to the General of Kordofan, Shawal 17, 1239 (Abdine Archives).
[2] Letter to the Mudirs of Lower Egypt, Rajab 11, 1241 (*ibid.*).

no doubt, in order to promote and extend the cultivation of the land. The accounts of his tour exhibit at once
the slight results which had been obtained and the
ideas of development which the pasha cherished. In
spite of or perhaps because of the high yield which
could be obtained—60-fold was the current estimate—
agriculture was still neglected, and the ground was only
scratched, by way of cultivation, with large pieces of
wood. Another experiment was therefore decreed in
order to promote the growth of sugar-cane, cotton and
indigo. A number of Arabs who had been trained at
the School of Engineering were offered grants of 100
feddans of land tax-free for five years, with an assignment of a number of young Sudanese who were thus to
be taught the more advanced methods of Egypt. At
the same time the pasha exhorted the chiefs to seek and
promote improvement. "If you follow the example of
others", he said, "you too will rise from the level of
beasts to that of men; you will acquire wealth and
learn to enjoy pleasures which your ignorance does not
allow you even to imagine." But for this labour was
needed, and without it nothing could be secured. His
audience is said to have been so moved by the prospects
held out to them that they begged to be taken to Egypt
to learn its arts; but they were told that they had better
send their sons.[1] Since this occurred at the close of the
active period of Muhammad 'Ali's career, we must
conclude that his conquest of the Sudan had for the
time being established Egyptian authority there, had
provided the pasha with a certain number of slaves,
but had not affected the primitive culture of the people
or (what was of much higher interest to Muhammad
'Ali) their material production, just as the overthrow of
the Wahabis had done no more than reopen Mecca and
Medina to the pilgrims.

[1] Campbell, No. 28, May 8, 1839 (F.O. 78-373).

In another direction, however, the expansion of Muhammad 'Ali's power eastwards and southwards had produced important results. The French had remained mere spectators; but the English were more directly interested, and to this period, 1811–22, may be traced the origin of their distrust of Muhammad 'Ali's policy. His military action in Arabia and the Sudan affected three regions in which they were already interested—the Red Sea, the Persian Gulf, and Abyssinia. Much of the trade of those areas passed through the hands of Banyan merchants—mostly Gujaratis—sailing from Surat and other ports of western India. Even at the height of its power the Moghul empire had never been able to protect Indian ships at sea. Akbar had been forced to seek passes from the Portuguese; later emperors had obtained Dutch or English convoy. In the middle of the eighteenth century, six years before the Company obtained the diwani of Bengal, it had acquired the office of admiral of the empire, with the revenues and districts thereto annexed, and for seventy years afterwards the Bombay marine regularly convoyed Indian shipping to Basra and Jidda, flying the Company's colours at the peak and the Moghul's at the main.[1] The decay of Persian and Turkish power rendered convoy indispensable. Piracy grew rapidly, and was not at all discouraged by the strange leniency with which captured pirates were released, or the folly with which merchants were allowed to export timber from Bombay to repair and build the craft which preyed upon them.[2] This rising evil was encouraged morally, politically, and practically by the Wahabi movement. The Wahabis themselves formed a pirate fleet at Kamfuda, south of Jidda, and on occasion were joined by the pirates of the Gulf.[3] In 1808 a British-

---

[1] Low, *Indian Navy*, I, 151.   [2] *Idem*, I, 319, 336.
[3] Burckhardt, *ap.* Missett, March 9, 1815 (F.O. 24–6).

owned ship was captured, and the throats of her crew ceremonially cut; and in the same year the Company's armed sloop *Sylph* was taken.[1] A punitive expedition destroyed a considerable number of pirate vessels in the Gulf; and finally a strong expedition equipped at Bombay in 1819 not only captured the pirate stronghold of Ras-al-Khaima with the help of the Imam of Maskat but forced nearly all the maritime Arab tribes of the Gulf to enter into treaty relations with the Company, obliging themselves to abandon not only piracy but the slave trade as well.[2] In this measure the Company's Government had hoped to obtain the co-operation of Ibrahim after his capture of Darayyah; but at that time Muhammad 'Ali did not care to look so far afield, and the Company's proposals came to nothing.[3]

Matters had followed a less troubled course in the Red Sea. Napoleon's conquest of Egypt had directed attention thither, a flying survey had been made of it in 1795, and in 1804–5 Lord Valentia insisted on returning that way at the end of his Indian tour. He had two objects in view. One was the best method of blocking the Red Sea against any hostile advance from the West, the other the increase of Indian trade. He therefore visited all the principal ports from Aden onwards, and collected information about the course of trade. He inclined towards the occupation of Aden, and an alliance with the Wahabis and Abyssinia as the best means of securing both objects.[4] But his proposals remained without effect, except that Henry Salt, who had accompanied him on his eastern voyage and who

[1] Low, *Indian Navy*, I, 320.　　　　[2] *Idem*, I, 342 *sqq.*
[3] Sadleir's instructions, April 13, 1819 (Sadleir, *Diary*, pp. 138 *sqq.*).
[4] Valentia, Observations, enc. in letter Sept. 13, 1808 (F.O. 1–1).

was afterwards to become consul-general at Cairo, was sent on a mission to Abyssinia in 1809 in the hope of developing trade between that country and Bombay.[1]

At this time the East India Company was represented by an agent at Mokha with an assistant—Belzoni, who played a part of some note afterwards in the early history of excavations in Egypt—who was moved about to Aden or elsewhere as circumstances required. At the moment, as has been already shown,[2] Muhammad 'Ali's principal aim was the restoration of the Egyptian finances, mainly by means of trade. He not only supplied grain to the English victuallers in the Mediterranean, but also made proposals to the Company's government in India for the development of trade eastwards.[3] Those suggestions were thought important enough for Belzoni to be sent up to Cairo, where a provisional treaty was arranged and signed on May 28, 1810. It declared that the Turkish capitulations should form the basis of intercourse with India; that in the event of an Anglo-Turkish war the pasha would under no pretext whatever molest British subjects or property, but on the contrary afford them every protection; that deserters from English vessels should be restored, even if they had embraced Islam;[4] that travellers with their personal baggage should pass free of duty; that caravans of merchandise should be escorted to and from Suez at a charge of 3 Spanish dollars the camel-load; and that customs-dues should be levied at the *ad valorem* rate of 3 per cent.[5]

This agreement was never ratified, no doubt for fear of impairing British relations with Constantinople.

[1] Salt, Report, March 4, 1811 (F.O. 1–1).
[2] See p. 29 *supra*.
[3] Anni, September 28, 1808 (F.O. 24–3).
[4] A provision hitherto invariably refused by the Turks. Cf. Abbott, *Under the Turk*, p. 29.
[5] Briggs, May 30, 1810, and enclosure (F.O. 24–3).

About the same time the English government refused to allow the pasha's corvette, the *Africa*, to proceed to the Red Sea by way of the Cape.[1] For the time therefore the pasha hesitated, uncertain how to invest the alliance he desired with sufficient attraction to induce assent on the part of the English. At one time we find him prohibiting (in ironical obedience to the Sultan's standing orders) Bombay vessels from proceeding further north than Jidda.[2] But he ultimately resolved upon embarking personally in the Indian trade, appointing Forbes and Company his agents at Bombay, and despatching thither a considerable quantity of European goods as well as a million dollars in specie.[3] At the same time he urged again upon the English consul, in view of the growing depredations of the Wahabi pirates, the need of having "some sort of naval force there to repel their insults, since otherwise it would be no longer safe for even his sons to pass to and from the Hedjaz". The consul, Salt, now supported this request. "It undoubtedly would be far better", he wrote, "that His Highness should have a preponderating influence there than that such pirates as the Wahabees should have possession of the sea. With regard to Egypt the pasha has become so complete a merchant that he has placed himself entirely at our mercy, his revenue now so vitally depending upon commerce...that he could not support his government many months without it. The admiral commanding in the Mediterranean might in my opinion at any time bring him to our own terns, in the event of a rupture, without any additional force than that always under his command, by simply anchoring at Aboukir and

[1] Missett, February 16, 1812 (F.O. 24–4).
[2] The same, June 6 and September 7, 1815 (F.O. 24–6).
[3] The trade proved very disappointing and was soon abandoned. Salt, April 28, 1817 (F.O. 78–89).

blockading the coast. The same thing might be done in the Red Sea, as two frigates stationed between Jedda and Suez would cut off all their communication by sea and soon reduce him to terms."[1]

As a result of these arguments, the objections to the pasha's sending his corvette round to the Red Sea were withdrawn.[2]

So far then English relations with the pasha ever since his rise to effective government had been decidedly amicable. Nor, as we have just seen, were they affected by his progress against the Wahabis, although individual Englishmen may have been disposed to back the latter.[3] Missett had indeed regretted Muhammad 'Ali's success in Arabia, but only because he feared the pasha would be lured on to destruction, "convinced as I am that were he to meet with a premature death this country [Egypt] would again relapse into that state of revolution from which he drew it";[4] and Captain Sadleir had been sent to congratulate Ibrahim on his success at Darayyah and propose joint action in the Gulf.[5] In like manner, when Salt feared that the expedition into the Sudan might be designed to embrace also the conquest of Abyssinia, and informed Muhammad 'Ali that such an event would be unwelcome in England, the pasha at once declared emphatically that though the country were full of gold and jewels, and its conquest certain, he would relinquish it rather than compromise his relations with Great Britain. "I have never known him give his word to us", Salt adds, "on a point which he did not mean to keep."[6]

[1] Salt, June 15, 1816 (F.O. 24–6).
[2] To Salt, May 3, 1817 (F.O. 78–89).
[3] Memorandum by R. Dundas, January 3, 1809 (F.O. 1–1).
[4] Missett, March 9, 1815 (F.O. 24–6).
[5] *Vide* p. 56, *supra.*
[6] Salt, November 20, 1820 (F.O. 78–96).

But such relations in the eyes of the Divan were fraught with danger. They feared that sooner or later this over-strong pasha would win the English alliance which he sought and shake himself entirely free from control. They therefore seized every occasion that offered of stirring up trouble. They had, for instance, endeavoured to commit Muhammad 'Ali to a support of the pirates of the Persian Gulf—protégés worthy of their protectors. More serious difficulties arose out of the conduct of the governor of Mokha. In 1817 an Arab was detained for a short time at the British factory. He was released at the governor's request, but the small factory guard, the captain of a merchant vessel by chance there, and the resident were seized, beaten, and abused, while the factory itself was plundered. After a considerable delay spent in ascertaining and deliberating upon the facts, it was resolved to send a force to obtain satisfaction.

The dependence of Mokha upon the Turkish empire was peculiarly tenuous. It was the chief port of the Imam of San'a, over whom the Sultan exercised neither influence nor authority. But in the course of 1818 Muhammad 'Ali had handed over to him certain districts round the northern port of Hodeida, on condition of his supplying annually a certain quantity of coffee for the use of the Sultan. This was reckoned as tribute, and the country was thereafter "considered as in some degree under the protection of the Porte".[1] Such views however could scarcely be accepted by European powers which did not recognise rights unaccompanied by effective control. Accordingly the East India Company demanded reparation from the Imam of San'a. He followed the usual policy of delay. Mokha was therefore bombarded; the forts were

[1] Salt, November 19, 1820 (I.O., Egypt and the Red Sea, 7).

attacked and destroyed;[1] and the imam then yielded to force what he should have conceded to the former unarmed demands. A treaty was made by which the British resident was to have a guard as at Baghdad or Basra, and to be allowed to appear in public on horseback; a cemetery was to be allotted for the burial of Christians; the Surat merchants were admitted to be under British protection; and the customs dues payable by British traders lowered to the rate paid by the French.[2]

Thus fell a stronghold of Islam in which till then Christians had been exposed to unpunished insult, had been condemned to walk, had been forbidden to pass a certain gate, and had been obliged to see the corpses of their countrymen thrown out to be eaten by dogs and jackals, and where Indian merchants had been coerced into payment of large sums by being half-stifled with the smoke of brimstone.[3] Such an odious change as was involved in the new treaty produced a flood of sapient rumour. A chain-cable happened to be landed for the use of one of the Company's cruisers. The story spread abroad that each link bore magic characters, and that it was to be used either to draw the whole city into the sea or to pluck up mountains so as to open a passage to San'a itself.[4] At Constantinople whither these stories spread, strong remonstrances were addressed to the British ambassador, while Muhammad 'Ali was severely reproached for his neglect and enjoined to occupy all the Red Sea ports as far as Aden in the name of the Sultan.[5]

The defeat of the Wahabis and the conquest of the

[1] Bruce to Salt, January 20, 1821 (I.O., Egypt and the Red Sea, 7).
[2] The treaty was signed Jan. 15, 1821. A copy occurs *loc. cit.*
[3] Salt to Strangford, August 16, 1822 (I.O., Egypt and the Red Sea, 7).
[4] Hutchinson to Bombay, January 25, 1823 (*ibid.*).
[5] Salt to Strangford, August 16, 1822 (*ibid.*).

Sudan were immediately succeeded by a remarkable reorganisation of Muhammad 'Ali's military forces. The troops by whose aid he had climbed to power, were hardly more than an armed rabble, impatient of discipline, to be kept in check only by regular pay and ferocious punishment, and as great an obstacle to the pasha's maintenance of his position as they had been an indispensable aid to its creation. In 1816, for instance, Missett reported that a considerable part of the army had been cantoned along the coast, and that on his enquiring the reason for this measure Muhammad 'Ali had explained "that finding himself unable to repress the excesses of which for the last few months his troops have not ceased to render themselves guilty, he had had recourse to the expedient of ordering them out of the city...in the hope that, when divided into small bodies they would be more easily brought back to discipline and subordination".[1]

For these reasons Muhammad 'Ali resolved upon establishing a Nizam jadid—a new-model army—with a European mode of organisation, discipline and control. His retention of power would certainly depend upon his success in this project; and yet it was undoubtedly a measure of the greatest difficulty. Quite recently Sultan Salim had been deposed and murdered for having dared to introduce the manners of infidels into Islam by attempting to enrol his janissaries in new corps. The pasha however was not the man to turn aside from an enterprise merely because it was difficult and dangerous. He did not believe either that military reform was unwelcome to the rank and file but only to the chiefs who could not endure the detection of their long-established frauds upon the public treasury.[2] The justice of this view was

[1] Missett, March 8, 1816 (F.O. 24-6).
[2] Burckhardt, *Arabia*, I, 146.

immediately demonstrated upon his first attempt to introduce the European mode of military exercise. This took place after his return from the Hijaz. He began with the bodies under the command of his own immediate relatives; but when he extended it to the troops over whom he did not possess the same degree of influence, discontent at once began to show itself. The pasha proclaimed that any who were indisposed to obey orders might draw any arrears of pay due to them and depart from the country. But no one took advantage of this offer, and then one afternoon a party of soldiers, assembled in the Usbekiah Square at Cairo, before the pasha's palace, began suddenly to plunder the shops with cries that there was no God but God. The next day the mutiny spread. Many shops and warehouses were plundered. The Frank quarter was several times assaulted, and Europeans could not venture out except in Turkish dress.[1] For the moment therefore the new plans were dropped.

But opposition, instead of weakening Muhammad 'Ali's purpose, set him upon devising other ways of carrying it into effect. As has been observed, one great object of the Sudan expedition was to secure supplies of slaves, who could be trained to war in whatever way he pleased. Hence the urgency with which Ismail was ordered to collect and send Sudanese slaves to Assouan. And since such persons could not be expected to provide material for officers, a body of over 300 young Mameluke slaves, Muhammad 'Ali's personal property, were sent up to Assouan to be trained as well.

The charge of this new military school was confided to a French officer, Colonel Sève. He had fought his way up from the ranks, gained a well-deserved Cross of the Legion of Honour, and after Waterloo retired with the rank of Captain. In 1819 he had come to Egypt,

[1] Missett, August 24, 1815 (F.O. 24–6).

where he was completely conquered by the charm and character of the pasha. He renounced his faith, but in him the act betokened none of that lightness of character which we associate with the renegade. He became and remained one of the most attached and trustworthy servants of Muhammad 'Ali. Twenty years later, when Great Britain was bent on restoring Syria to the Sultan's tyranny, great offers were made to Sulaiman Pasha (as Sève was then called) to bribe him into desertion. But neither the offer of a hereditary pashaliq nor the consciousness of a failing cause could move him. He answered that he was bound not only by the duty of gratitude but also by an unlimited devotion to his master.[1]

The early organisation of the Nizam jadid was probably the most difficult task that Sève was ever called upon to undertake. Military discipline administered by a European was so strange and so unnatural a thing in Egypt that at first Sève's life was in frequent danger. He would exercise a party in musketry, and hear shots whistle by his head.[2] On one occasion he is said to have met a conspiracy among the Mamelukes by assembling the conspirators, informing them of their designs, and offering to fight with his sabre single-handed as many as chose to attack him.[3]

At first the training camp at Assouan comprised only the young Mamelukes and the Sudanese slaves. The latter proved disappointing. They were strong and docile enough, submitted patiently to military discipline and learnt their drill. But they refused to be kept alive. Trivial ailments, which would hardly have laid up a European or an Arab, in them ended fatally. They died like sheep with the rot. Some 20,000 were

[1] Medem to Nesselrode, September 26–October 8, 1840.
[2] Douin, *Une Mission militaire*, p. xiii.
[3] Salt, February 8, 1824 (F.O. 78–126).

thought to have been collected and sent up to Assouan by 1824, but in that year not 3000 remained alive.[1] This failure, which contrasts so pointedly with our own experience, was perhaps mainly due to the fact that Muhammad 'Ali's recruits were not free men but slaves.

The failure of this expected military resource led, on the advice of Drovetti, the French consul-general, to the application of a similar method of recruitment to the fellah population of Egypt. The idea was perhaps originally suggested by the great success which had attended the application of European discipline to the sepoys of India. But any comparison is impaired by the fact that till now no one had dreamt of employing the despised fellah as a soldier, whereas in India the sepoy had practically always belonged to a military caste. The proposal was warmly taken up; its unusual character led to a rebellion in various districts,[2] but about 30,000 fellahin were taken and sent up to Assouan, and Sève was allowed to increase his cadre of European instructors. These received a very bad character from the French officer who later was placed over them. He describes them as Spanish, Piedmontese, and Neapolitan refugees, void of truth, faith or honour; in short the worst set of rascals to be found anywhere in the world.[3] But under Sève at all events they seem to have done their work well. Salt, who visited the training camp with Muhammad 'Ali in 1824, thought the pasha had reason to be delighted with and proud of his new army—an opinion amply borne out by its coming service under Ibrahim in the Morea and in Syria. The most noticeable deficiency was the lack of an organised medical service. A school of medicine

---

[1] Salt, February 8, 1824 (F.O. 78–126).
[2] Driault, *L'Expédition de Crète et de la Morée*, p. 13.
[3] Douin, *Une Mission militaire*, p. 22.

could not (as Salt said) be planted like a melon-bed, and Arabs could be made into soldiers quicker than into hakims.

In another direction also a very significant beginning had been made. Salt had called repeated attention to the manner in which the pasha's power and commerce was limited and overshadowed by British naval power, which both in the Mediterranean and the Red Sea could place him under irresistible pressure. Muhammad 'Ali was as acutely aware of this fact as was the British consul-general. It was and remained throughout his active career the chief reason for his consistently seeking to secure an alliance with Great Britain in preference to any other power. But he was also intelligent enough to draw from it very valid conclusions as to the advantages of sea power itself. It is in the last degree unlikely that he ever contemplated any attempt to rival Great Britain on the seas; but he did seek to secure a naval preponderance over every state with which he expected to be drawn into conflict. He seems indeed to have been the only eastern ruler who recognised the importance of sea power and who set himself deliberately to cultivate it.

These views first unmistakably exhibited themselves in the course of his Arabian campaigns. The Wahabi pirates had threatened his sea communications between Suez and Jidda, and he had therefore been anxious to send his armed corvette the *Africa* round into the Red Sea. When he was disappointed of this by the English refusal of a pass, he ordered a frigate to be built for him at Bombay;[1] he sought to induce a notable Arab pirate chief to take service with him;[2] and he actually built a ship of war mounting sixteen guns at Suez.[3]

[1] Burckhardt, *Nubia*, p. xciii.
[2] Burckhardt, *Arabia*, I, 282 n.
[3] Enc. *ap*. Missett, March 9, 1815 (F.O. 24-6).

Altogether he must have assembled in the Red Sea a flotilla more than capable of holding its own against the Wahabis.

A little later he applied the same ideas to the Mediterranean. He began to purchase such vessels as could be picked up in the Levant or built at Genoa or Venice. He then sought to strengthen himself by obtaining vessels of a superior type. In 1821 he applied to both France and Great Britain, desiring each country to supply him with a couple of frigates of the latest model.[1] Both powers declined. Canning wrote: "It is entirely out of the power of His Majesty's Government to comply with this request, inasmuch as it would be a direct violation of the neutrality which the King has declared it to be his intention to observe during the present unhappy contest between the Ottoman Porte and the Greeks".[2] Muhammad 'Ali then sought (and obtained) permission to build two frigates and a brig-of-war at Marseilles. He was therefore beginning to provide himself not only with an army framed and trained like those of Europe, but also with vessels which would enable him to meet the Greeks, and perhaps one day, which he could not too clearly foresee, the fleet of the Sultan.

[1] Salt, November 6, 1821 (F.O. 78–103).
[2] To Salt, January 31, 1822 (F.O. 78–112).

Chapter III

THE PILLAR OF THE EMPIRE:
THE GREEK WAR

The successful invasions of Arabia and the Sudan had thus led to the reorganisation of Muhammad 'Ali's army, to the foundation of a naval force, and to a considerable extension of the pasha's authority. But so far his progress had not brought him into collision with any European power. French policy at the moment was far from aggressive; and though individual Englishmen might view the employment of French officers with a jealous eye, London exhibited no trace of anxiety, while Calcutta was much more disposed to co-operate with than to resist the establishment of public order in important areas of Indian foreign trade.[1] The endeavours of the Sublime Porte to embroil Muhammad 'Ali with England had so far failed.

Then in April, 1821, the Greeks in the Morea, taking advantage of the rebellion of 'Ali Pasha at Janina, themselves broke into rebellion. There were some 20,000 Muslims scattered through the country districts. They were suddenly attacked. Those who could escaped into the Turkish garrisons. The remainder were massacred. The garrisons were then beleaguered. Some surrendered under promises of safety, others surrendered at discretion. It made no difference. All alike were put to death. Near Tripolitza 3000 Greeks defeated 5000 Turks. The result was the surrender of

[1] M. Sabry's view (*L'Empire égyptien sous Mohamed Aly*) that England was hostile from the first seems based on ignorance of, or a failure to understand, the documents he cites.

that place and Navarino. At neither did the insurgents carry out the terms of capitulation, and at Tripolitza they slaughtered 8000 Muslim men, women and children. As a matter of course these events were followed by like massacres of Greeks at Constantinople and elsewhere. The Greek patriarch and four of his bishops were hanged, and it was believed that at least one Greek life was taken for every Muslim that had perished in the Morea. The Shaikh-ul-Islam—the head of the theologians of Constantinople—was removed from his post for his unworthy conduct in seeking to stay the course of this revenge.[1]

The movement spread naturally to the islands of the sea. The small shipping that carried a great part of the Levantine trade was owned by island Greeks and manned by a considerable number of Greek sailors. A war fleet was formed, and developed the use of fire-ships. These tactics filled Turkish sailors with horror and alarm. Control of the sea meant power for the insurgents ashore. A national government was formed; a popular assembly was convened. The Sultan might exact blood for blood in Smyrna and Constantinople, but he could not recover his lost territory. He was as impotent against infidel Greeks as he had been against heretic Wahabis.

Muhammad 'Ali seems to have observed these events with benevolent detachment. In true opportunist vein, he had got rid of Albanian troops whom he did not want by encouraging them to leave his service for that of the rebel of Janina. He was informed of the activities of the Greek revolutionary societies which had been established at Cairo and Alexandria, but took no measures against them. He did nothing to hinder the embarkation of Greek volunteers at Alexandria. He even set free a party of Greek slaves sent to him by the

[1] Driault, *L'Expédition de Crète et de la Morée*, p. 5.

Dey of Algiers.[1] In 1822, however, the Sultan offered him Crete if he would reduce it to submission. The island had been the scene of reciprocal massacre. Hasan Pasha, who had married one of Muhammad 'Ali's daughters, and on his death Husain Bey, were accordingly sent. The Cretan rebels were numerous and bold, but were reduced by measures of undeviating severity. This process occupied nearly two years; but in 1824 Muhammad 'Ali was able to report that their last refuge, Sphakia, had been cleared, and that the rebel chiefs had been executed; in proof of his assertion he sent a bag of ears to be nailed to the Great Gate of the Seraglio.[2] Even better evidence of Husain Bey's success was however to be found in the fact that he was able to extend his operations. Not far to the north-east of Crete lie the islands of Kasos and Scarpanto. The former was the home of numerous mariners who had enthusiastically supported the cause of Greek independence by preying upon Turkish trade. Husain Bey equipped an expedition against these islands. The Kasiotes rejected his summons to surrender. Their stronghold was carried by storm; and the troops were then given twenty-four hours' plunder, in which about 100 men were killed, 900 women and children taken prisoners, and great quantities of coffee, silk and other goods—the results of the islanders' privateering—made booty. As a further punishment 500 men were picked to serve at the usual rate of pay on the Egyptian vessels. The people of Scarpanto, on the contrary, surrendered on the first summons, and were only required to pay the three years' tribute that they owed to the Turkish government.[3] The episode very fairly displays the policy of Muhammad 'Ali. Obstinate rebels should be relent-

---

[1] Politis, *L'Hellénisme et l'Égypte moderne*, I, 187 *sqq.*
[2] To Nakib Effendi, Shaban 19, 1239 (Abdine Archives).
[3] Salt, June 24, 1824 (F.O. 78-126).

lessly destroyed but others admitted to favourable terms, so as to keep equally alive the sentiments of hope and fear.

Success in pacifying Crete led of course to further demands on the pasha. Very early in 1824 the Sultan Mahmud II issued a farman graciously bestowing the pashaliq of Morea upon him. It is unlikely that this *damnosa haereditas* was accepted out of fear of the Sultan's displeasure. But there was the Nizam jadid, which had done so well in Crete, to be tried out on a larger scale. Great Britain was still neutral, and the factors which were shortly to transform her into an active participant were still beyond the range of even the keenest eye at Cairo. Above all, there was the thought that the conquest of the infidel following on the conquest of the heretic would raise the conqueror's name high in the world of Islam, wholly obliterating the ill-effects of eating Christian-wise with a knife and fork in private, of drinking Christian liquor, and of protecting with a firm hand the lives and goods of Christians within his government. The subjugation of the Greeks would mark him out as the leader of the age, enable him if he pleased to defy the orders of the Sultan, and (he fancied) entitle him to the respect, the friendship, even the alliance of one or other of the great powers.

Six months were spent in preparing the expedition. On July 10 it set sail from Alexandria. It consisted of at least 16,000 soldiers, 100 transports, and 63 armed vessels.[1] The command was entrusted to Ibrahim, but it was not as complete as his father had desired. He was named Wali of the Morea, with authority over all the troops and over certain vessels;[2] but with its usual and

[1] A letter to the Grand Vazir, Zilkaidah, 1239 (Abdine Archives), states that the expedition comprised 30,000 men and 196 vessels.
[2] Letter of Shaban 15, 1239 (*ibid.*).

indeed justified, but fatal, habit of dividing authority, the Porte gave the chief naval command—the office of Capitan Pasha—to Khusrau Pasha. Even in the West, it has almost invariably happened that when the command of the army has been given to one man and of the fleet to another, the commanders have been too busy quarrelling to defeat the enemy. In the present case that result was completely secured by the selection of Khusrau as Capitan Pasha. He and Muhammad 'Ali had been declared enemies ever since the former had been so unceremoniously driven from the pashaliq of Cairo. So that while the Sultan might rest assured that his general and admiral would never unite to overthrow their master's power, he had every reason also to expect that they would never lay at his feet the trophies of a combined victory.

The due consequences followed. The plan of campaign had been for the Turkish fleet and the Egyptian expedition to rendezvous off Rhodes, to capture the island homes of the Greek privateers, and then to reconquer the Morea. The plan was Muhammad 'Ali's and displays his acute sense of the importance of the command of the sea. Khusrau had begun well enough. On July 3 he had captured Psara, a nest of corsairs just west of Chios. Samos was to be the next place of attack; but Khusrau spent a month celebrating his victory, with the result that off Samos he encountered a squadron of Greek vessels. In the action that followed on August 16 he lost two frigates and a corvette, and the Turkish squadron fled, "its sails filled with terror". Meanwhile Ibrahim had arrived off Rhodes on August 13, and on the 29th he joined the Capitan Pasha off Budrun, near the site of the ancient Halicarnassus. In September a number of conflicts followed with the Greeks, who invariably took the offensive, and invariably had the best of the engagement, while the

Turkish portion of the Muslim fleet displayed the greatest anxiety to avoid a close encounter. At the end of the month Khusrau was temporarily recalled to Constantinople. Ibrahim, left alone, stood naturally on the defensive, but by the close of the year managed to concentrate his ships and men at Suda Bay, on the north-west of Crete, without having undergone any considerable loss. In face of the hastily improvised character of his squadron, this negative result must be considered highly creditable. The Egyptian squadron, strong in the resolute character of its commander, had not yielded to the panic that Khusrau had failed to overcome; and Muhammad 'Ali in Egypt was the last man living to give way to defeatism. "I know very well", he said, "that I can't form a navy in the sands of the Pyramids, and that I can't help incurring losses. But in the long run I shall have a navy, and then I shall be able to meet and overcome the Greeks."[1]

In this admirable constancy of purpose, the pasha busied himself in enlarging his naval forces. Four vessels which he had ordered from Italian shipyards arrived. Five more were bought (indirectly) from the Greek rebels. He sent a French officer back to France to obtain leave to build two frigates and a brig in the king's dockyard under the superintendence of French officials.[2] These vessels were accordingly begun at Marseilles.[3] Greek merchants were found to lay down other vessels on account of Muhammad 'Ali, although their parents had been massacred at Chios and they themselves incurred by their conduct the greater excommunication.[4] Other vessels were built at Venice and Leghorn.[5]

Meanwhile the Greek fleet had been compelled to

[1] Douin, *Une Mission militaire*, p. 7.   [2] *Idem*, pp. 25–6.
[3] Douin, *Les Premières Frégates de Mohamed Aly*, p. 28.
[4] *Idem*, p. 31.   [5] *Idem*, p. 65.

quit their watch over the Egyptians, by the demands of the sailors for their pay. Ibrahim was thus enabled in January, 1825, to cross without opposition from Suda to Modon, in the south-west corner of the Morea. From the first the Greeks were no match for him in the field. A considerable body of them was defeated before Navarino and that place surrendered on May 18, and next month he was able to occupy Tripolitza in the centre of the peninsula. This event was followed by a guerilla war in which the Greeks had a better chance of success. However this was met by the burning of the villages concerned, the destruction of their crops, and the driving off of their cattle; so that even here the Greeks began to weary of the war.

Nor did they seem able to use their superiority at sea. The one notable attempt which they made was a raid on Alexandria where they tried to burn the Egyptian ships lying in the harbour. In the afternoon of August 10 a vessel ran in under Russian colours, and as she was nearing one of the men-of-war, she was fired, and the crew dropped into a boat astern and rowed off in safety to another vessel near the entrance of the port. The attempt wholly miscarried. The sails of the fireship taking fire, she fell off her course and drifted safely away from the anchored vessels. Muhammad 'Ali chanced to be sitting in the Ras-al-tin Palace, overlooking the harbour. He at once jumped upon his mule and rode to the battery at the point, hoping to be able to catch the enemy before they got out of range. Failing in this, he ordered several vessels to proceed in chase of the Greeks, and one which was unlucky enough to be ready for sea was obliged to sail at once alone. Next day three more sailed. On the 12th news came that the Greeks had burnt a boat bringing wood from Sataliah, within sight of the ship that had put out on the 10th. This was too much for the pasha. In unbearable anger, he

hurried aboard a corvette on the first boat he could find
at the water-side and immediately put to sea, where he
remained for a week, seeking in vain both the Greek
vessels and his own.

Had he met the Greeks, he would almost certainly
have perished. But he nearly fell into another even
greater danger. The day after his departure all Alexandria was alarmed at seeing a fleet of forty sail, which
were thought to be the Greeks coming to renew their
attack in full force. They actually proved to be the
squadron and transports of the Capitan Pasha, forced
by lack of provisions and ammunition to abandon the
besiegers of Missolonghi, whose operations he had been
covering from the sea. It is doubtful whether his arrival
at Alexandria much reduced the anxiety of either the
populace or the ministers. A hurried council was held;
the French and English consuls-general were consulted;
and it was decided to admit the Turkish fleet into the
harbour, but under no circumstances to allow the
Capitan Pasha to land. The story reached Cairo that he
had detached seven of his vessels to block the entry into
Rosetta and Damietta, and that he was resolved to
seize Muhammad 'Ali if he could.[1] Both French and
English consuls-general were aghast at the recklessness
with which the latter had put to sea in a single vessel
when most of his troops and his ablest commanders
were in the Morea. Great was the relief when on
August 20 it was learnt that he had entered the harbour
under cover of darkness and had reached the Ras-al-tin
Palace before anybody was aware of his return.

Whatever had been Khusrau's designs on finding his
ancient enemy absent, they were instantly covered by
bland congratulations on his return and polite requests
in the name of the Sublime Porte for assistance in
money and munitions. He hastened to be the first of

[1] Douin, *Une Mission militaire*, p. 61.

the two to pay the other a visit of compliment. He was met at the water's edge by Muhammad 'Ali. They went together to the palace. Reaching the hall of audience each used gentle violence to place the other in the seat of honour. Each tried to seize the fly-swish to keep flies from settling on the other's revered face. Supplies were ordered for the fleet, and Khusrau was given 80,000 dollars with which to pay his people.[1] When at last in October he went away, the two pashas parted like brothers. With him went Muhammad 'Ali's new vessels, and a considerable body of men—1500 horse and 8000 infantry—intended to enable Ibrahim to hold his position in the Morea and at the same time to co-operate in the siege of Missolonghi which the Turks had been vainly attacking for the last six months.[2] The measures proved successful. Leaving Colonel Sève to command the Morea, Ibrahim moved across to Misso-longhi, and his aid enabled the Turks to storm it early in 1826. This was followed by the siege and capture of Athens. The Greek cause was visibly sinking. They had routed the Turks; but they were being crushed by Ibrahim and the regular troops that his father had organised and the naval force that his father had gathered together.

These successes first in Arabia and then in Greece had something of an intoxicating influence. For the moment perhaps it seemed to the pasha that no limit need be set to the expansion of his power. He dreamt of raising his disciplined forces to 100,000 men. As soon as the Morea had been completely subjugated, he saw him-self handing over this uninviting territory "to its legiti-mate master, the Grand Signor", recalling his troops, filling up the gaps in their ranks, conquering Yemen, holding the Red Sea and the Persian Gulf, and occupy-

[1] Salt, September 15, 1825 (F.O. 78–125).
[2] The same, October 22, 1825 (*ibid.*).

ing the pashaliqs of Acre and Damascus. Then,
Alnashar-wise, having reorganised those unfortunate
provinces, with redoubled power he would move on the
Tigris and Euphrates, and there consider what further
conquests would be most profitable. "The sword", he
said, "has delivered power into my hands, and I should
be indeed ungrateful if I did not continue to employ it
for the service and salvation of the Turkish empire."—
"But", said the French officer to whom these con-
fidences were addressed, "will the English give you
time to accomplish these great designs?"[1]

The truth was that they could not be carried into
effect at all unless the pasha could reach an understanding with Great Britain and obtain English co-
operation. Probably he himself was as fully convinced
of this as anyone in the world; and the time was indeed
approaching when he was perhaps nearer to securing
his object than at any other point in his career. Two
conditions had to be fulfilled in order to make a treaty
seem worth while in English eyes. The first was that our
relations with the Sultan must be severely strained, if
not absolutely broken, before the separate political
existence of Egypt could possibly be recognised. The
second was that the pasha must have some clear advantage to offer or withhold, commensurate with the obligations implicit in an alliance. One attempt had
already been made by way of a treaty with the Company's government in India; but in 1810 the development of trade along the Suez route had seemed of
dubious advantage to the English authorities, and the
treaty had never been ratified. But Ibrahim's conquest
of the Morea had perhaps provided a pledge of greater
value.

The Greek revolt had excited great interest in
Europe. Poets and liberals hailed it in prose and verse

[1] Douin, *Une Mission militaire*, pp. 79–80.

as the rebirth of liberty. Even musty scholars in their closets were stirred by the fancied repetition of Marathon and Salamis. When it began to seem likely that the rebellion would be drowned in blood, indignation ran high. All the misdeeds of the Turks were multiplied and exaggerated. Every hint that the Greeks were a trifle less heroic than the heroes of classical literature was angrily rejected. Stories spread that Ibrahim contemplated the wholesale enslavement and removal of the Greek population and the resettlement of the Morea by Turks or Arabs. Even George Canning, indisposed as he was to romantic policies, thought the situation demanded intervention. "The selling into slavery", he wrote to his cousin, the ambassador at Constantinople, "the forced conversions, the dispeopling of Christendom, the recruiting from the countries of Islam, the erection in short of a new *puissance barbaresque*—these are facts...new in themselves, new in their principle, new and strange and hitherto inconceivable in their consequences, which I do think may be made the foundation of a new mode of speaking, if not acting,... and one which, I confess, I like the better because it has nothing to do with Epaminondas nor (with reverence be it spoken) with St Paul."[1]

The agrarian character of the war in the Morea and the traditional practice of all Muslim armies had indeed produced something like the conduct that Canning so indignantly described. As we ourselves had found, and were again to find, in Ireland, it was impossible to discriminate between the peasant and the soldier, for the characters were instantly interchangeable. Then too by ancient custom, while men prisoners might or might not be claimed by the general, women and children became the personal slaves of their individual captors.

[1] Lane-Poole, *Stratford Canning*, I, 395. His information came from a suspect Russian source. Bulwer, *Palmerston*, I, 290.

When the Turks were warring in Hungary, Constantinople abounded in Hungarian slaves; when Ibrahim
was fighting in the Morea, Greeks filled the slave
market of Cairo. This naturally shocked a generation
which had so recently become alive to the horrors of
the slave trade. But individual blame can scarcely be
attached to Muhammad 'Ali or his son. "It must be
remembered", our consul-general wrote with complete
but unwelcome truth, "that this is not a particular
feature of the present contest. It is the same course that
has been practised by the Turks in every war they have
carried on....Nor let it be supposed that it has been in
the power as yet of the pasha to effect in this respect a
change. It has only been by strict conformity with
certain of these deeply rooted prejudices of his subjects
that he has been able to accomplish so much." Nor was
the number anything like the myriads of gossip. About
3000 had been brought to Cairo, mainly by speculators
who had bought them from the troops, and of these
about half had been liberated by various agencies.
Some had been ransomed by European residents in
Egypt; others had been released by their purchasers on
the petition of their Greek servants; and Muhammad
'Ali himself had aided in this, sometimes by the issue of
orders, sometimes by advances of money.[1] Such
methods of war were barbarous; it was high time they
were suppressed; but they were not personal or deliberate, and not nearly so extensive as was imagined. However the truth of a story has small relation to its influences
upon the feelings, and the belief that the whole Greek
race was being sold into bondage played a considerable
part in leading the western powers to intervention.

A better established fact led also in the same direction. The Greeks of the islands had in general succeeded
in repelling the attacks of Khusrau, the Capitan Pasha.

[1] Salt, August 12, 1826 (F.O. 78–147).

But lack of money had created the greatest difficulty in keeping the Greek fleet together. Greek sailors were indisposed to serve even their country for nothing. Since they could not be paid, they must be suffered to plunder. They took to wholesale piracy under a thin disguise of blockade, seizure and condemnation. French ships bound for Candia with coin with which to pay for oil, were seized and their crews tortured to make them say where the money was. Hydra and Spezzia were the chief piratical centres. At Hydra the French admiral de Rigny sent an officer ashore to demand restitution of goods seized on a French vessel; the populace at once gathered together, threatening to slay whoever dared betray the pirate. At Napoli was a so-called prize court. It was attended by the captors, pistol in hand, threatening to burn down the houses of judges who would not condemn their prizes. The commander of an Austrian squadron had to seize Greek vessels at Hydra and Spezzia to make good the losses of Austrian subjects. An English commander, similarly unable to obtain justice, entered and seized in the port of Hydra the pirates that he found there.[1] The Greek navy, which at first had displayed plenty of skill and gallantry, had thus dissolved into a disorganised body of corsairs, much more concerned with plundering European vessels than with destroying the Turks.[2] It was clear that if rebellion in the Turkish empire involved such interference with the freedom of the seas, and the Turks themselves could not keep Greek pirates in order, the powers whose trade was thus affected would be likely to intervene, in order to set a limit to the conflict.

[1] Douin, *Navarin*, pp. 3 *sqq.*
[2] They only made one attempt on Alexandria in 1827 and were easily repulsed. Driault, *L'Expédition de Crète et de la Morée*, pp. 255–6.

The actual impulse however came neither from the outcries of the humanitarians nor from the piratical outrages of the Greeks, but from the political ambitions of Russia. The Emperor Alexander had always viewed his natural championship of the Orthodox Church as a convenient pretext for intervening in Turkish affairs. But in 1823-4 he was unwilling to break away from the other powers by any separate action, and accordingly planned, under cover of a European congress, a settlement which would have made Russia predominant in Greece. The projected congress was successfully evaded by Canning. But when at the end of 1825 Alexander died and was succeeded by Nicholas, other measures were needed to prevent the outbreak of war between Russia and Turkey over the Greek question. In these circumstances a joint Anglo-Russian mediation was proposed and accepted, and France was also induced to join. The result was the agreement of July 6, 1827, by which the three powers were to make combined efforts to induce the combatants to accept an armistice, and, in the event of their refusal, to "use all the means which circumstances may suggest to their prudence" in order to prevent further collision between them. The actual method contemplated was the blockade of the Morea, in order to starve Ibrahim out, by the naval forces of the three powers.

Repeated representations had already been made to the Porte by the ambassadors, but had elicited no other answer than that the Greek rebellion was a purely internal matter of no legitimate interest whatever to the European powers. On August 16 the three dragomans carried to the Reis Effendi—the Foreign Minister—a note which he refused to receive. On the 29th they repeated their visit, and were assured that the Sultan would never accept any proposals regarding the Greeks and that he would persist in his resolve until the day of judgment. On the 31st they were sent again with a further declaration, which the minister, after a childish pretence of not understanding, again refused to accept.[1] The only course then remaining open to the allied powers was the use of force.

The cause of this demented decision was certainly a belief that Europe was too divided to intervene effectually, and that Russia would resent any action by the French and English squadrons. This belief seems to have been based in part on the difficult history of European coalitions; in part on the conduct of the Russian ambassador;[2] and in part on the deliberate suggestions of Austria. Metternich regarded the Greek rebels in the same light as Italian revolutionaries, and at the same time was convinced that the other powers would benefit more than Austria by intervention. The internuncio's first dragoman held long and mysterious conferences with officials about the Sultan's person;[3] and we now know enough about the conduct of Austrian agents elsewhere to be certain that the internuncio's object was to urge the Sultan to make an end of the rebels as soon as possible. This of course jumped with Sultan Mahmud's own instincts. The first hint of collective intervention had thrown him into an ungovernable passion in which with tears of rage he had sworn to burn and ruin every province and city he had in Europe rather than submit to such intolerable humiliation.[4] And he had ordered his servants to declare that interference would only assure the extermination of the Greeks. "We will slay every Greek in all our territories, and when blood has begun to flow, so much the worse if the Armenians, our other rayas, and the Franks themselves mingle theirs with the blood of the

---

[1] Douin, *Navarin*, pp. 111 *sqq.*
[2] *Idem*, p. 117.   [3] *Idem*, p. 121.
[4] *Idem*, p. 119.

guilty."[1] Mahmud had yet to learn that he was not Sulaiman the Magnificent.

Ideas of this kind certainly had no place in the plans of Muhammad 'Ali. His one purpose all along had been to strengthen his position either inside or outside the Turkish empire, with a decided preference for the second alternative if circumstances should permit. He had been much disturbed by the news that Lord Cochrane, that volatile admiral, had joined the Greek service;[2] and he had listened in a very different manner from the Reis Effendi's to the English remonstrances. He fancied indeed that he had found the lever needed to move the European world.

Before ever the Greek revolt had begun he had made tentative overtures to England. In 1820 Salt was desirous of visiting London, partly for reasons of health, but partly also for reasons of state, "our great man here having pressed me to make communications which I cannot commit to paper".[3] Nothing came of this advance. But in 1826 the obvious reflection occurred to Stratford Canning at Constantinople that the easiest way of shaking Ottoman obstinacy would be to enlist the aid of the Pasha of Cairo. Would not, he wrote to Salt, a share in the tribute which at that time it was proposed that the Greeks should pay the Porte, and a pashaliq for Ibrahim in Syria be far more profitable to Muhammad 'Ali than exterminating the Greeks at great cost to himself?[4] Salt at first thought that so flagrant a violation of Muslim sentiment as supporting the Greek cause could not possibly be looked for.[5] But a fortnight later began a series of conversations in

---

[1] Douin, *Navarin*, p. 122.

[2] Salt, November 1825 (F.O. 78–135), and August 4, 1826 (F.O. 78–147). [3] Salt, August 20, 1820 (F.O. 78–96).

[4] S. Canning to Salt, June 10, 1826 (F.O. 78–147). Cf. Lane-Poole, *op. cit.* I, 409.

[5] Salt to S. Canning, August 31, 1826 (F.O. 78–147).

which the pasha gradually developed his views. He at once brushed aside all possibility of assisting the English cause at Constantinople. The Divan was too wavering, the Sultan too bigoted. But there were other ways of favouring our policy, and he would like to know what the British government would be prepared to offer him. A week later he reminded Salt that he had never put on his seal any other inscription than his name alone. "I have little left, as you may see, of the Pasha except my chiaoushes[1] with silver sticks and my divan." He then dwelt upon the fact that geographically and commercially "England and Egypt might be of use to each other—there is nothing that I desire more". And when Salt broached the evacuation of the Morea, "That is not so easy a matter", he answered; "it wants the assistance of some able helmsman to bring it about. But if there are those who desire it, they will be able to accomplish it." In the last conversation of the series, on September 26, he became more explicit. "I now have my foot in two stirrups...", he said. "Everything shall remain in balance as it now is until the spring. If in that time I find your government has any propositions to make that may please me, I shall be ready to embrace their offers, and will find means altogether to withdraw my troops from Greece. If not, I will collect all my force and through the influence I have at the Porte get the command of the whole Ottoman fleet—for by that time the Capudan Pasha will have been disgraced; and then I will put myself at the head of it and so finish the business." Salt asked what services he expected from England in return. Muhammad 'Ali mentioned help in enlarging his marine, and liberty to expand in Arabia; but (Salt adds) "I am persuaded that he has at heart the gaining from our government some general assurance of sanc-

[1] Corresponding with the Chobdars of Indian courts.

tion to his independence, should any circumstances drive him into a rupture with the Porte, but he carefully abstained from touching on this point".[1]

Shortly after these conversations an Austrian diplomat reached Alexandria on a mission from Metternich. This was Prokesch-Osten, who was to make at a later time another peculiar visit to the pasha. On this occasion he was sent to spur on Muhammad 'Ali's flagging activity and especially to press him to undertake a winter campaign against the Greeks, in order to secure their overthrow before Russia and the western powers should have time to intervene. He urged the danger of Greek independence to Egyptian commerce. He expatiated at length upon English desires to keep Egypt weak and averred that, however beneficial English advice might appear, its real object would be to paralyse, not to assist, the viceroy. But this argument failed to convince Muhammad 'Ali that any alliance could be nearly so beneficial to him as English friendship, or that any advantage could compensate for the hostility of English naval power. "If England does not wish me to, what can I do?" he bluntly asked the Austrian.[2]

But as the weeks passed, and no response was made to his overtures, his mind naturally recurred to his alternative plan of securing from the Porte the whole control of the Greek war, and the more so because success at Constantinople would in no wise prevent him from coming to terms with the English, and would at the same time involve his personal enemy, Khusrau, in humiliation. He had already sent complaint on complaint of Khusrau's misconduct in command of the Turkish fleet.[3] Now, on January 7, 1827, he wrote two

[1] Salt, October 1, 1826 (F.O. 78–147).
[2] Sabry, *L'Empire égyptien*, pp. 120 *sqq.*
[3] E.g. to the Grand Vazir, Ramzan 5, 1241 (Abdine Archives).

letters, one to the Grand Vazir, one to his personal agent[1] at Constantinople. In the first he said he had spared neither wealth nor men in the Sultan's service; but his resources were now exhausted, he himself was smitten by advancing age, and he therefore begged to be excused from further demands in order that he might spend his remaining years in peace, praying for his master's health and prosperity. The significance of this humble petition was made clear by the second letter. It said, "Khusrau Pasha's participation in affairs having been such as to produce neglect and inaction, if he is maintained in his office I shall cease from all cooperation with him and shall demand to be released from this service".[2] It so happened that shortly after these letters reached Constantinople, Stratford Canning made very unwelcome proposals to the Porte about the Greeks. In such circumstances procrastination was impossible even in the Turkish Divan. Almost at once an aga of distinction was ordered to proceed to Egypt on a secret mission. He sought a passage by a British man-of-war, being mortally afraid of being captured by the Greeks. Stratford Canning refused, being persuaded that the mission would be unwelcome to the viceroy.[3] He need not have been anxious. The aga carried the news that Khusrau was no longer Capitan Pasha, and farmans investing Muhammad 'Ali with the sole conduct of the war.

But with his customary prudence he was in no haste to withdraw a foot from either stirrup. He began leisurely preparations for the renewal of the campaign, but even at mid-June following his ships were still

[1] In the Turkish as in the Moghul empire, every great official at a distance from headquarters maintained an agent at court to watch over his interests.
[2] Douin, *Navarin*, p. 19.
[3] Stratford Canning, February 8, 1826 (F.O. 78–152).

lying at Alexandria, his reinforcements for Ibrahim still incomplete. But he began to press our consul-general for an answer to his proposals, for his fleet could not be delayed for ever. Besides the Divan at Constantinople had observed that the change of command had made no difference to the slow progress of operations, and the wily Khusrau had already regained Mahmud's favour and received the pelisse and sabre of investment as *sar-'askar*, commander-in-chief of the Sultan's forces. On June 11 Muhammad 'Ali assured Salt of his desire to comply with the wishes of the British and French governments. He suggested that, if the powers really intended to intervene, the British and French fleets had better appear before Alexandria "to make a demonstration of compelling His Highness to desist from the war, and in that case, if they would show it to be to his advantage, he would immediately withdraw his troops and son from the Morea, His Highness assuring me that he wanted only a fair pretext for taking such a step".[1] For nearly eight weeks longer he delayed despite the urgency of the Porte, despite the incitements of the Austrian consul.[2] At last, on August 6, the fleet put to sea. Two days later arrived an English envoy on a special mission.[3]

The new-comer was Major Cradock, whom Canning had sent specially to communicate the decision of the allies at London and to induce the pasha to abandon the Morea without more ado. He was to point out that the great powers were now agreed, that no intervention on behalf of the Turks could be expected, and that ample forces were being despatched to the Levant. If the Turks chose to resist, "the consequences of the Pasha's identifying himself with the Porte in so unequal

---

[1] Salt, June 11, 1827 (F.O. 78–160).
[2] Douin, *Navarin*, p. 150.
[3] Salt to Stratford Canning, August 12, 1827 (F.O. 78–160).

a struggle might be fatal to those plans of maritime and commercial improvement which have hitherto been pursued by him with so much success". These considerations, Canning thought, would be decisive with a man "wary, astute, neither a fanatical Mussulman nor a devoted servant of the Porte".[1] But though Cradock was expressly ordered to avoid the use of threats, his was not the most gracious of missions. As Salt observed, "we have to ask from him a neutrality which may compromise him altogether with the Porte, and have nothing specifick to offer in return".[2]

A week[3] was spent at Cairo in discussions. The pasha was as amenable as could reasonably have been expected. Salt pressed him to seize this opportunity of explaining his wishes to the British government in precise terms, since "if such an opportunity of ingratiating himself with the European powers were once permitted to slip by", he could never expect another equally good. Muhammad 'Ali then advised that the allied admirals should formally require Ibrahim not to proceed to the attack of Hydra, which was the next projected operation, hinting that he himself would send corresponding orders. "Let England stand by me", he continued, "and I shall be repaid. I have long wished ardently...to form a lasting league of commerce and amity with her, and she must, I should hope, now feel that she is bound to aid me." In reply Salt gave it as his private opinion "that when the occasion came, should he carry this business successfully through, England would not desert him". The pasha then burst out with his hopes of the future. His face lit up, his eyes flashed. "Syria and Damascus and Arabia are in fact at my disposition....If your government

[1] Cradock's instructions, July 14, 1827 (F.O. 78–182).
[2] Salt to Stratford Canning, August 12, 1827 (F.O. 78–160).
[3] August 15–21.

support me, as I hope, if it will acknowledge me, when occasion comes, as an independent prince, I shall be satisfied."[1] Before his departure Cradock himself, in conversation with Boghoz Bey, the pasha's most confidential servant, gave it as his private opinion that if Egypt established and could maintain her independence, it would be recognised by England.[2]

The discussions thus ended with no formal undertakings on either side. The viceroy hinted that his troops should be kept inactive in the Morea; the English agents said they thought that in that case he might rely on the benevolence of the British government. The pity was that Cradock had not been able to reach Alexandria in time to induce the pasha to defer the despatch of his fleet. His position had become most difficult. Pressed by the Sultan to exterminate the Greeks at once, pressed by France and England to withdraw at once from the Morea, it seemed that he could not but mortally offend one side or the other. He was himself convinced of the futility of further opposition to the wishes of the allies. But he was linked to a court too ignorant and proud to admit that the days were gone when the Sultan's anger could safely confine western ambassadors in the Castle of the Seven Towers and when the Turks could meet the united force of Christendom on equal terms. On October 5 he made a strong endeavour to open the eyes of the Divan to the real position. He ordered his agent to observe that the demands of the powers might be mere bluff, but might also be enforced; that the wise prepare against misfortune instead of promising themselves prosperity; and that if the allied squadrons resorted to force, in his humble judgment the Ottoman fleet would be destroyed

[1] Salt, Memorandum, August 19, 1827 (F.O. 78–156).
[2] Cradock to Stratford Canning, August 21, 1827 (F.O. 78–182). Cf. Temperley, *Foreign Policy of George Canning*, pp. 148 *sqq.*

and 30,000 or 40,000 souls perish. "It is wrong", he continued, "in affairs of war to rely solely upon God. It is needful also to do all that can be done by man. Assuredly victory comes of God, and He alone controls all power and might. But in the Koran He has said: Strive and I will help you to win the victory."[1] Faith, in short, was no remedy for damp powder or ill-found ships.

His prevision was unhappily justified. The allied admirals, Codrington and Rigny—the Russian squadron did not enter on the scene before October 13—at once began to put pressure on the combatants. The Greeks of course immediately agreed to an armistice. But since the Sultan refused, they considered themselves released from the engagement, planned an expedition to Albania, and destroyed a Turkish flotilla at Galaxidi. Meanwhile the admirals themselves had had a personal interview with Ibrahim, who then agreed to suspend operations for a month until he could receive instructions from the Porte and his father. But when he learnt of the continued Greek operations, he took action to revictual Patras and to clear the country in his occupation of potential enemies. The admirals tried to hold the balance even. If on the one hand Codrington compelled the Turkish fleet to retire to Navarino without relieving Patras, so also on the other he forbade the Greeks to undertake their projected expedition into Albania. But he and his fellows were desirous of preventing further devastations in the Morea. They had nothing but naval force at their disposal. They therefore sought to achieve their end by a combined demonstration against the Turkish and Egyptian fleets.[2] On

[1] Douin, *Navarin*, pp. 243–5.
[2] *Idem*, chapters ix–xi. An account differing in some particulars from this will be found in Temperley, *Foreign Policy of Canning*, pp. 406–9.

October 20 they sailed into Navarino Bay. The Turks
inevitably distrusted their intentions, and when armed
men fear attack the guns fire themselves. Musketry was
opened on a British boat's crew and it was answered
with ship's guns. From half-past two till nightfall a
fierce action followed, in which the whole Muslim fleet
was destroyed.

This event was hailed with enthusiasm by all good
Grecophiles. But it surprised the allied governments.
They had in fact tried to do with naval force more than
naval force alone can possibly accomplish. Its effect on
land operations is slow, constrictive, gradual; and what
the allies wanted was an immediate cessation of arms.
They were giving the admirals an impossible task.
Again their instructions were faulty and incomplete, as
a result of the illogical position which they had
assumed. While they posed as intervening between the
Sultan and his rebel subjects, they were in fact intervening to save the Greeks; so that while the action
certainly went beyond the expectations of the western
powers, it also with equal certainty helped strongly
forward the accomplishment of their purpose. But to
Muhammad 'Ali it must have been a double blow. He
had been ready to negotiate with the allies, and, had
Cradock only arrived two days earlier, his fleet, as
Canning expected, might never have sailed, and
Navarino would never have been fought. Ibrahim and
the Divan at Constantinople were at first in favour of
retirement northwards out of the Morea and beyond
the immediate influence of the allied vessels. But
Muhammad 'Ali was in no mind to continue the fruitless conflict. The day after the news was received he
informed the English consul that even if war broke out
between Turkey and Great Britain, British subjects in
Egypt should be unmolested. "I know well", he said,
"how to appreciate and to maintain the reputation I

have acquired for justice and liberality."[1] The same day he wrote to his son declaring that the Divan's stupidity had been the cause of the misfortune, and that he was to remain in camp without making any attempt upon the Greeks.[2] When he heard of the proposal to move Ibrahim's army to the northward, he protested strongly and effectually.[3] Ibrahim therefore remained in the Morea until the debarkation of a French force made his position so desperate that even the Porte could not but recognise the cogency of his capitulation. On August 6, 1828, Codrington visited Alexandria and signed the convention with Muhammad 'Ali by which the Morea was finally evacuated.[4] Since the Sultan still remained obdurate, the Russians proceeded to employ military force, and in the following year, when they forced him to sign the Treaty of Adrianople, he at last acquiesced in the views which the viceroy of Egypt had submitted to his ministers two years before.

This excursion into European politics had strained Muhammad 'Ali's resources to the utmost. The money he had lavished on his ships, the victuals and munitions which he had poured into the Morea, the men whom he had levied, trained, and sent, had been wasted. Ibrahim's army returned starved, crippled and miserable. Many were so worn by privations that they could not march.[5]

So far the Divan at Constantinople had succeeded in putting the Greek rebellion to good use. The strong pasha was less strong than he had been before he undertook the office of champion of Islam. But he had not been satisfactorily embroiled with the western powers,

---

[1] Barker, *Syria and Egypt*, II, 58.
[2] To Ibrahim, Rabi-al-awal 13, 1243 (Abdine Archives).
[3] To Najib Effendi, Jumadi-al-awal, 1243 (*ibid.*).
[4] Convention dated August 6, 1828 (F.O. 78–170).
[5] Barker to Sir P. Malcolm, September 24, 1828 (*ibid.*).

though they had burnt his fleet and starved his army. He had unluckily had sufficient insight to lay these misfortunes at the door of the "pig-headed Sultan" and "ass-like Vazirs" who had rejected his advice. He had withdrawn from the struggle and looked on unharmed while the conquering Russians had been daily expected at the very gates of Constantinople. He was justly filled with contempt for the impotence and malice of the Sublime Porte, and more resolved than ever to establish his complete freedom from its blighting influence. He was more convinced than ever of the efficacy of sea power, and especially of British sea power. The possession of the Morea indeed had not proved to be the pledge which would purchase for him a British alliance because in a single afternoon sea power had torn it from his grasp. But the necessary pledge he still might find. Might it not be the mastery of both the overland routes to India? Might it not be the threat of an alliance with Britain's great Mediterranean rival?

Chapter IV

THE ALGERIAN INTERLUDE AND
THE CONQUEST OF SYRIA

Along the north African coast from Mogador to Ben-
ghazi lay the Barbary states, piratical principalities
that once had formed part of the caliphate, but with the
break-up of the Islamic world had attained a virtual
independence. The rise of the Ottoman empire had
left them almost free, though attached by ties of envious
veneration and respect for the great barbaric power
which had seated itself at Constantinople. All through
the sixteenth and seventeenth centuries they had
carried on a ceaseless war against all Christian mariners.
They had provided the excuse for ship-money, and
every English boy was familiar with the capture and
enslavement of Robinson Crusoe by the Moors of
Sallee. The rise of the western navies in the eighteenth
century had somewhat abated their predatory activities; but their inclinations remained quite unchanged,
and though they became somewhat shy of meddling
with French or English vessels, they still preyed freely
enough on Spanish, Genoese or Neapolitan ships that
fell within their reach. Between 1805 and 1815 they
took some ninety ships, and though discouraged by
Lord Exmouth's bombardment of Algiers in 1816, they
nevertheless captured twenty-six more in the ten years
that followed. In 1824 Algiers, the chief offender, was
again visited by an English fleet. The time was evidently drawing near when these upholders of medieval
tradition would be brought to a sharp reckoning.

Like all good Muslims, the Barbary Moors had been

deeply moved by Christian interference in the affairs of Greece and had lent the aid of their shipping to the Sultan, resenting the lost freedom of the seas and by no means foreseeing the catastrophe of Navarino. In their sore, irritable frame of mind they were disposed to defy the Occident and all its fleets. In April, 1827, Husain, the Dey of Algiers, in the course of a stormy interview with the French consul, Deval, struck the consul with his fly-whisk. Reparation was demanded and refused. The consul was withdrawn, and Algiers was blockaded by a French squadron. As the Dey remained impenitent, and the general situation (especially the outbreak of the Russo-Turkish war in 1828) did not permit of more vigorous action, attempts were made by the Sardinian consul and then by a French naval officer to persuade him to accept easier terms than at first had been demanded. This convinced the Dey that the French were weakening and made him more obstinate than ever. Then in the middle of 1829 the *Provence* was sent under a flag of truce with new proposals, coupled with threats of an expedition if they should not be accepted. But Husain still refused. When threatened with attack, "I have powder and guns," he said, " and since we cannot agree, you may depart". On August 3, therefore, the *Provence* still flying her flag of truce set sail. The wind carried her past the town batteries. The Moors, perhaps fancying that this was a deliberate insult, opened fire on her and maintained it as long as she remained within range. With an expenditure of eighty rounds they actually succeeded thrice in hitting her.

When this news reached Paris, public opinion, already indignant at the delay in bringing the Dey to terms, ran dangerously high. But the moment was strangely embarrassing. The Russians had just occupied Adrianople, the collapse and partition of the Ottoman empire seemed at hand. Could a prudent minister at such a moment commit the naval and military forces of France to a campaign in northern Africa? Besides Polignac, who had become minister for foreign affairs in August, had just formulated a scheme which, could it but be effected, would restore all the popularity of the tottering throne of Charles X and undo the work of the allies on the overthrow of Napoleon.[1] He assumed that Russia and Austria would divide between them most of the Turkish provinces in Europe, and so open the way for France to demand an equivalent for the disturbance of the balance of power. His project was that France should receive the Belgian provinces up to the line of the Meuse and Rhine. The assent of Prussia might be secured by letting her annex Saxony and the northern Dutch provinces. The King of Holland should be compensated for this partition of his kingdom by being sent to reign at Constantinople over such of the Turkish provinces in Europe as were not absorbed by Russia and Austria, while Great Britain should be offered as the price of acquiescence the Dutch colonies which would by this arrangement have become *res nullius*. This plan was to be carried into action by a secret treaty between France and Russia; that signed, Prussia would be invited to join; Austria then would have no choice but to fall in with the scheme, and Great Britain could accept or reject Java and the Moluccas as she pleased. As soon as the treaty had been signed, the agreeing powers would assemble their troops, so as to confront Europe with such a force as none of the remaining states could think of resisting. Polignac thought of putting 200,000 men into the field. But such ideas absolutely ruled out all possibility of any

[1] He was no doubt deeply influenced, not only by the unpopularity of the king, but also by the active discontent of the Southern Netherlands.

immediate expedition to chastise the peccant Dey of Algiers.

In these circumstances the French minister resolved to adopt a plan which had been suggested by Drovetti, who had long served as consul and consul-general in Egypt, and who in 1829 had just returned to France. This new plan was to punish the Dey by the hand of Muhammad 'Ali, who would organise a great expedition to conquer and annex the three Barbary regencies of Tripoli, Tunis and Algiers. A direct French expedition, Drovetti argued, would provoke English jealousy and opposition, whereas the extension of the pasha's authority along the African coast would not offer the same opening to diplomatic protests, and besides that (Polignac may well have thought) the proposed revision of the European map would keep the English cabinet too busy for it to spare a thought to what became of Tunis and Algiers, while every other European state would certainly welcome the establishment in those regions of the good order and discipline which reigned in Cairo and Alexandria.[1]

This plan seems to have originated with Drovetti himself. He had urged on Muhammad 'Ali the advantages of co-operating with the French in Algiers instead of alarming all Europe with adventures in Syria;[2] and he seems to have assumed that the advantages of his proposal would be as evident to the English as they were to himself. By 1829 he was so full of the plan that it had become his favourite subject of conversation, even with the English consul-general, Barker. The latter, in the seclusion of his own office, judged the project to be wholly chimerical; but while he was listening to the enthusiastic speeches of Drovetti all difficulties vanished, and French support in ships and

[1] Douin, *Mahomet Ali et l'Expédition d'Alger*, pp. 1 *sqq.*
[2] *Idem*, p. 6.

men seemed merely to be making success doubly
certain.[1] Muhammad 'Ali's own attitude was perhaps
not entirely that which he led Drovetti to suppose. He
was not really interested in the Barbary states, and
probably was well aware that an extension of his
authority in that direction would be a source of weakness rather than of strength. He fully realised the
strategic importance of the area comprising the pashaliqs of Syria and Baghdad, and well knew that if he was
to rise to the position of weight and power which he
coveted, Syria and Baghdad would be far more valuable
than the north African littoral. But at the same time he
never liked to let chances slip away unused. If the
French proposals ever came to anything, they might
afford him two advantages—an opportunity of re-
building his vanished fleet, and the possibility of an
alliance either with the French themselves, or, if that
prospect was sufficiently alarming to the English, then
with Great Britain. He was in fact willing to undertake
the conquest of Algiers if it was made worth his
while or to lay aside the scheme if that would pay him
better.

Drovetti, it seems, was too deeply enamoured of his
plan to read aright the pasha's intentions; while
Polignac was eager to adopt any plan which would at
once placate French opinion by inflicting due punishment on Algiers and conserve French forces for the
much more momentous European project simmering
in his mind. He therefore laid the matter before the
king, secured the royal assent, and then, apparently
without consulting his colleagues, issued instructions to
Guilleminot, the ambassador at Constantinople, and
Mimaut, the new consul-general at Alexandria. The
first was ordered to obtain farmans authorising Muhammad 'Ali to subdue the three Barbary regencies; this

[1] Barker, August 18, 1829 (F.O. 78–184).

demand was to be supported by the arguments, first
that if the French themselves despatched a punitive
expedition they would probably be obliged to keep the
territory which would thus be lost for ever to the Porte,
and secondly that Muhammad 'Ali would pay tribute,
which the Deys never did.[1] The second was instructed to
inform the pasha that France approved of his views and
favoured his designs against the Barbary states, that if
he wished it the French fleet should co-operate with his
forces, and that he should receive an advance of ten
million francs if the expedition set out without delay.[2]

But the discussions at Constantinople and Alexandria
did not go so smoothly as Polignac had over-hastily
assumed. Muhammad 'Ali strongly deprecated opening the matter at Constantinople at all, urging that the
Sublime Porte would never willingly permit any extension of his power, and might seek the assistance of an
English fleet to counteract his operations, whereas if it
were not consulted beforehand it would bow easily
enough to an accomplished fact.[3] These objections
proved well founded. In vain did Guilleminot, the
ambassador, make the most of all the advantages of the
French plan. As the viceroy had foreseen, the Porte,
though not of course avowing it, had the most rooted
objection to anything likely to increase its ambitious
vassal's power or prestige. It put forward a counter-
proposal. All that was needed to end the dispute
between the French and the Dey, declared the Reis
Effendi, was the interposition of the Sultan's exalted
authority, and for this purpose he offered to despatch
an agent of his own, Tahir Pasha, a known and bitter
enemy of the French, who would without question

---

[1] To Guilleminot, October 10, 1829 (Douin, *Mahomet Ali et
l'Expédition d'Alger*, pp. 9 *sqq.*).
[2] To Mimaut, October 19, 1829 (Douin, *op. cit.* pp. 14 *sqq.*).
[3] Mimaut, November 27, 1829 (Douin, *op. cit.* pp. 23 *sqq.*).

bring the Dey to reason without any need of force.[1] And while this obstructive suggestion was under discussion, the Turkish minister informed the English ambassador, Sir Robert Gordon, of what was going forward, shrewdly calculating that this was the best method of defeating plans which the Divan intensely disliked.[2]

At Alexandria Muhammad 'Ali declared he was willing to despatch 20,000 regular troops, and a like number of Bedouin, under the command of his son Ibrahim, but he required an advance of at least twice as much as the consul-general, Mimaut, had been empowered to offer, and above all he demanded as an essential part of the bargain that the French should give him under cover of a pretended sale four 80-gun men-of-war, which he declared essential to the prompt success of the expedition and the avoidance of inconvenient foreign intervention. All the efforts of Mimaut and of Huder, who had been specially sent to aid Mimaut in the negotiations, failed to induce him to depart from his demand of four ships, which he said had formed an integral part of his discussions in the past with Drovetti.[3]

Huder returned therefore to Paris to lay these requirements before Polignac, who was made acquainted with them on December 26. At this time, although the Peace of Adrianople had put the general plan for the modification of European boundaries out of the question, Polignac still hoped to secure Russian support for the annexation of the Belgian provinces.[4] He therefore decided to accept the proposals of Muhammad 'Ali,

---

[1] Guilleminot, December 9, 1829 (Douin, *Mahomet Ali et l'Expédition d'Alger*, pp. 53 *sqq.*).
[2] Gordon, December 15, 1829 (F.O. 78–181).
[3] Mimaut, November 27, 1829 (Douin, *op. cit.* pp. 27 *sqq.*).
[4] Douin, *op. cit.* p. xxviii.

and laid them before his colleagues. But here he met with strong opposition. More than one member of the cabinet felt it would be equivocal and perhaps dishonourable to transfer vessels flying the French flag to another state. The Minister of Marine was obstinately opposed to any such weakening of the French navy, and threatened to resign should the proposal be accepted. Bourmont, the Minister of War, saw prospects of personal glory in a possible expedition to Algiers and was most unwilling to allow himself to be replaced by Ibrahim Pasha. After repeated efforts Polignac could not induce the cabinet to go further than to consent to an advance of twenty-eight millions—twenty to be handed over to Muhammad 'Ali in accordance with his demand, and eight to be devoted to building expressly for him four men-of-war such as he desired. But a French squadron was to be held in readiness to support Ibrahim's operations in case it was required. Huder therefore returned to Alexandria with these revised terms, the commander of the French squadron in the Levant was ordered to prevent the Turkish fleet from threatening Alexandria or attacking any Egyptian transports proceeding against the Barbary states, and, since the time of overt action was now drawing near, Polignac at last opened the matter to the states of Europe.[1]

In spite of the secrecy which had been observed at Paris, the English cabinet was not ignorant of the projects that had been formed. Barker had reported Drovetti's conversations in 1829. Gordon at Constantinople had sent home the interesting communication which he had received from the Reis Effendi. Metternich had intercepted French despatches from Guilleminot and made haste to favour our ambassador, Lord Cowley, with copies. Meanwhile the French ministry

[1] Douin, *Mahomet Ali et l'Expédition d'Alger*, pp. xxx *sqq.*

had replied to all the English enquiries with absolute denials. This conduct was little likely to induce Aberdeen and Wellington to accept the statements at last made to them or to acquiesce in the ostensible policy at last declared. On January 23 the Duc de Laval (the French ambassador at London) called on Wellington and read to him an ostensible despatch from Polignac. The ambassador was received with marked coolness. It was observed that Muhammad 'Ali could not legitimately take up arms against the Barbary states except on behalf and by order of his master the Sultan, and a hope was expressed that the French ministry would abandon its plan of common action with the viceroy of Cairo.[1] Aberdeen immediately wrote to the English representatives at Cairo and Constantinople. To the latter he declared that whether the Sultan had or had not authorised the project, we could not view with indifference such a change in the possession of important African territories effected by French means, under French influence, and presumably in order to promote French interests.[2] To the former, after dwelling on British objections to seeing the pasha undertaking such a scheme under French patronage, Aberdeen added that he hoped Muhammad 'Ali would not doubt the friendliness of the motives which impelled the British government "to counsel him on this occasion to weigh well the serious consequences of the enterprize in which he seems disposed to engage".[3]

This opposition to the French project could have surprised no one. The establishment of French influence in Algiers, either directly or through some third party acting on their behalf, would change the position in the Mediterranean and the question of protecting

---

[1] Douin, *Mahomet Ali et l'Expédition d'Alger*, pp. xli *sqq.*
[2] To Gordon, January 25, 1830 (F.O. 78–188).
[3] To Barker, January 29, 1830 (F.O. 78–192).

British interests would arise. But there were much greater possibilities involved in the proposal. Beyond the status of Algiers loomed the whole Eastern Question. If Muhammad 'Ali conquered Algiers for the French, that could mean nothing else than that he would be taken directly under French protection. His position as regards his sovereign the Sultan would be affected. The status of Egypt would be tacitly modified. The tottering walls of the Turkish empire would receive another shock, and the Ottomans would become less than ever capable of opposing their Russian neighbours. To the French government, now as in the past, such events might be welcome as affording a possible opportunity for the expansion of French power; Polignac had just been seeking to turn them to the advantage of the monarchy. But in English eyes they were pregnant with danger. One of our major interests demanded that no European state should be suffered to establish itself on the routes to India. To France then the maintenance of the Turkish empire was an open question to be decided in the light of interests mainly continental; but to Great Britain it was the only alternative to developments which no one could forecast and which therefore it was but wise to retard as long as possible. The position in 1830 thus anticipates and points on to the much sharper clash of French and English policy that was to come ten years later.

But at the moment this firm declaration of English disapproval coincided with the complete failure of Polignac's plans to recover the Rhine frontier. His secret and obscure discussions with St Petersburg—a special cipher was used and destroyed afterwards[1]— came to nothing. Prussia bluntly answered that nothing would induce her to let France advance to the left bank of the Rhine. The forces that till then had been

[1] Douin, *Mahomet Ali et l'Expédition d'Alger*, p. xxviii.

immobilised by the possible need of supporting the European project were thus set free just when it became clear that the whole weight of English influence would be thrown into the scale against Muhammad 'Ali's occupation of the Barbary states. Polignac therefore resolved once more to change his plan, to limit Muhammad 'Ali's part to the conquest of Tripoli and Tunis, and to send a French expedition against Algiers. Thus the viceroy of Egypt would still be made an active ally of the French, ready to be recognised (as Polignac himself wrote) at a convenient time *pour le lieutenant du Roi de France.*[1]

But in this he was reckoning without his proposed ally. From the first Muhammad 'Ali had never intended to move unless he secured advantages, naval and political, which would make it clearly worth his while. Nor can he have been favourably impressed by the wavering conduct of French policy at this time. Resolute himself, he thought slightly of those who shifted their designs from day to day. The inconstancy of French plans probably led him to distrust the value of a French alliance, which, whatever advantages it might secure, would assuredly be accompanied by an unwavering English hostility. Before the despatch of Aberdeen had been communicated to him, he had already rejected the French proposals.[2]

A few days later he received in audience the English consul-general who had gone up especially from Alexandria to Cairo to inform him of Aberdeen's views. The viceroy objected that the English warning was superfluous, and then proceeded once more, as he had done to Salt, to expound his views and declare his desire for a friendly understanding with Great Britain. "Do you not

[1] Douin, *Mahomet Ali et l'Expédition d'Alger*, p. lviii.
[2] Mimaut, March 2, 1830, and Huder, of the same date (Douin, *op. cit.* pp. 191 *sqq.* and 197 *sqq.*).

see that it is impossible to maintain the Porte?" he demanded. "You may prop here and prop there, but all will be to no purpose. What can you do with a government that has lost the confidence of the people both within the capital and in the provinces?..." It was therefore idle to look to the Turks for any effective resistance to future Russian aggression. Yet that was a matter in which English interests were most deeply involved. "The only way to strengthen the Sultan is to support me. By supporting me, he would soon have at his disposal a disciplined army of 125,000 men, ready to form a barrier against the Russians both at Constantinople and in Persia. In Persia, it is there after all that England must fight the Russians." What is the use of peeping through your fingers and pretending to see nothing? "The Porte is gone, and England must prepare to raise a force in Asia to meet the Russians. And where can she find it but with me and with my son after me?"

He then dwelt at length on the ease with which the Ottomans would join his standard "if the English would but come forward and support me", and upon the extent of his resources, which he said with truth the English ministry underrated. And then he burst out, "With the English for my friends I can do anything: without their friendship I can do nothing....I foresaw long ago that I could undertake nothing grand without her permission. Wherever I turn, she is there to baffle me".[1]

Statesmen seldom utter more of their inner thoughts than they think well to make known to their audience, and Muhammad 'Ali was no child to blurt out more than he intended. But he was undoubtedly sincere in his statement of his attitude towards England. She enveloped him on every side. No other power could aid him so effectually. There was great truth too in his

[1] Barker, March 8, 1830 (F.O. 78–192).

estimate of his own position and opportunity. He represented at the moment the one live progressive force in the world of Islam. He might with English aid have built up under the shadow of the Turkish caliphate such a power as our own East India Company had built under the shadow of the Delhi empire. But once more what advantages could he offer to induce English statesmen to abandon their declared policy and co-operate to establish a new power in the Near East? Support against Russian designs? Perhaps. But were he once firmly entrenched on the borderlands of Persia, with his power stretching from Cairo to Baghdad, might not the Russians have something to offer which would induce him to forsake his English friends? And then our position would be dangerous indeed. Only some most pressing motive could warrant our supporting Egypt in a career of conquest. Probably a great European crisis alone could provide such a motive. In any case the trend of English policy was decidedly opposed, not, as some writers have thought, to Egyptian greatness, but to Egyptian intrusion into areas beyond the natural limits of the country.

Muhammad 'Ali had long coveted the four pashaliqs of Syria. Their possession would cover his Egyptian territory from attacks by the Turks; would give him the rule of Jerusalem, another of the Holy Cities of Islam, and so enhance his prestige in the Muslim world; and as he supposed, though the event proved otherwise, increase his resources in men and money. It would give him Damascus, one of the leading centres of Islamic culture. It would give him control of territory rich in timber and save his buying it at high prices in Trieste. And it would demonstrate to the world at large his favourite thesis of the vanished power of the Porte and his unique capacity for reorganising and rejuvenating Turkish power.

The pashaliqs were in a miserable condition. They were so disturbed that couriers could not pass through them with any certainty of safety.[1] They had long been governed by pashas whose rapacity had been limited only by their power. No one ventured the least parade of wealth. Everyone was or at all events seemed miserable, and the mixed population with its various sects and creeds was seamed with ineradicable feuds and quarrels.

This land of misrule had been desired by the viceroy for many years. As early as 1812 he had spoken to the English consul of his intention to conquer Palestine as soon as circumstances should permit.[2] For the time being, however, he found too many obstacles in the way. The chief one was perhaps the need of reorganising his army so as to render it a trustworthy instrument of his will. And then also the spiritual influence of the Sultan had to be considered, especially in those years of rising fanaticism which coincided with the Greek revolt. "Such are the religious prejudices of these people", he said to Salt so late as the year of Navarino, "that they all desert a pasha when once under interdiction of the head of the Church." To oppose the Sultan with effect, he added, a pasha "must be strong enough to command publick opinion and that is not an easy matter"; and this view he supported by the example of a rebel pasha in Kurdistan, whose troops fell from him "like sand from a pilgrim's feet".[3]

But in 1830 the Egyptian army had been reorganised; Ibrahim had been proved to be a skilful and resolute leader; while conscription promised as many men as should be wanted. At the same time the disasters

---

[1] Cartwright to the East India Company, November 9, 1822 (I.O. Egypt and the Red Sea, 7).
[2] Missett, June 20, 1812 (F.O. 24-4).
[3] Salt, Memorandum, January 20, 1827, enc. in despatch of February 10, 1827 (F.O. 78-160).

which had befallen the Turks at the hands of the infidels, afloat at Navarino, and ashore in the Russian
campaign, showed even to thick-headed Turks that
Sultan Mahmud was no certain guide to victory. The
empire needed indeed only one good push to overthrow it altogether.

And while the negative reasons which had earlier
held Muhammad 'Ali back had vanished, an additional and positive reason had appeared. The bait by
which he had been lured into taking part in the Greek
war had been the four pashaliqs of Syria. They had been
promised; but with the revival of Khusrau's influence
at the Porte the promise had been cast aside. At the
close of 1827 the viceroy was still demanding in vain the
farmans of investiture.[1] He had therefore lost his fleet,
and imperilled his army and his son for nothing. He
made up his mind to occupy Syria before anyone else
did.

Pretexts were of course not lacking. He had been
called upon by the Porte to provide assistance in suppressing the rebellion of Mustafa Pasha Iskudarli in
Rumelia. This demand covered his military preparations; and when he was informed that help was no
longer needed, he proposed to use his assembled forces
to attack Abdullah Pasha of Acre, who had been levying
exactions on Egyptian merchants.[2] Another excuse
was the welcome which Abdullah gave to the fellahin
who fled to Acre to escape Muhammad 'Ali's conscription. In the course of 1831, 6000 are said to have
escaped thus. Abdullah refused to return them. Muhammad 'Ali replied that he would come and take
them.[3] He set his troops in motion in October, 1831.

[1] Salt, August 27, 1827 (F.O. 78–160). Muhammad 'Ali to the
Shaikh Effendi, Jumadi-al-awal 23, 1243 (Abdine Archives).
[2] Grand Vazir to the Wali of Damascus, Rabi-al-awal 3, 1247
(ibid.).   [3] Sabry, op. cit. p. 191.

A singular commentary on the incompetence of the
Divan at this time is afforded by its reception of
Muhammad 'Ali's proposal to attack Abdullah. The
Grand Vazir was aware that he was preparing to
occupy the Arabic-speaking parts of the empire, to
organise their affairs, and proclaim his independence,
but no better expedient could be devised to meet the
danger than to warn Abdullah to be circumspect and
avoid provoking a quarrel, while a bland letter was
addressed to Muhammad 'Ali himself, telling him that
a few merchants' complaints did not justify a declaration of war and that disputes between neighbouring
pashas should be determined, not sword in hand, but
by the mediation of the Sublime Porte.[1] But nothing
was done, no preparations were made, no orders were
issued, to guard against the impending danger.

In accordance with the Egyptian plans Acre was
besieged by sea and land. But the Egyptians encountered a stout resistance. Abdullah may not have
been very honest or very wise, but he was a brave and
resolute man, while the siege in its early stage was conducted with great want of skill. On December 9 an
attempt was made to overwhelm the place with a combined bombardment from the shipping and the land
batteries. But the ships suffered considerable damage
and the land batteries made small impression. After
three months more of effort a determined attempt was
made to storm the walls. It almost succeeded. A party
of the stormers penetrated to the market place, but
finding themselves unsupported had to withdraw.
Ibrahim's position began to appear critical.[2] Various
bodies of troops were assembling to relieve the town,
and the Porte, gathering courage from its protracted
defence, ventured to strike out the names of Muham-

[1] Grand Vazir to the Wali, *ut supra*.
[2] Barker, *Syria and Egypt*, II, 179–80.

mad 'Ali and Ibrahim from the list of the pashas of the empire published annually at the Feast of Bairam, which in 1832 fell at this moment. A feeling of unrest spread through Cairo and Alexandria. Men began to murmur against the viceroy's government. On March 14, and again on the 21st and 23rd, men found exposed by the Bab-uz-Zuwaila at Cairo the newly beheaded bodies of three Turks, two of them soldiers and the third one of the ulema, with labels on their breasts declaring, "This is the fate which awaits those who cannot govern their tongues".[1] And on April 7 two new corpses were exposed, with the grim warning, "This is the punishment that awaits those who speak against the government in secret".[2]

The malcontents, however, were reckoning not only without the spies of Muhammad 'Ali but also without the unskilled commanders of the Turkish forces. After the failure of his attack on March 9, Ibrahim determined to leave some 5000 men to blockade Acre, while with the remainder he moved against his gathering enemies. After scattering 12,000 Turks who had concentrated near Homs, Ibrahim then returned to renew his attack upon Acre. At dawn on May 27 he directed the storming party in person. A long struggle ensued. Ibrahim is related to have cut down with his own hand several officers who had fallen into the rear of the storming columns, and after great efforts he had by nightfall succeeded in capturing the place, which was then, in strict accordance with western rules of war, given up to plunder.[3] Abdullah proudly declared: "I had walls, men, and money, with which to defend Acre. When Ibrahim took it the walls had been destroyed; of my 6000 men 5600 were dead, and of my

[1] Barker to Stratford Canning, March 29, 1832 (F.O. 78–213).
[2] Same to same, April 11, 1832 (ibid.).
[3] Barker, June 4 and 27, 1832 (F.O. 78–214).

treasure nothing remained but a few jewels". He laid
with good reason the blame of his defeat upon the
Sultan who had done nothing to relieve him. "The
Porte", he said bitterly, "has the honour of a dancing-
girl".[1]

Acre having fallen, Ibrahim once more advanced
northwards. He entered Damascus without opposition
on June 13. On July 8 he unexpectedly attacked the
Turkish forces at Homs, and after a brief action completely routed them, capturing their artillery and
baggage. On the 15th he occupied Aleppo. On the
29th he defeated another Turkish force in the Beylan
Pass. With that for a while action was suspended.

Clearly enough two courses were now open to the
viceroy. He might proclaim his independence and
press his advance against the demoralised Turks in
order to force the Sultan to recognise the position; or he
might pause in the hopes of obtaining by western intervention such a settlement as he desired. There were
grave dangers attached to either plan. A direct advance
on Constantinople, which was advocated by Ibrahim,
was disagreeably likely to provoke a hostile intervention in favour of the Sultan. When Ibrahim proposed to
strike coin and have the Friday prayers read in his
father's name, Muhammad 'Ali refused. He had
attained to power by moderation, he declared, and
would have no new titles or honorifics.[2] While Ibrahim,
carried away by his triumphs, fancied that everything
they wanted could be secured by defeating the Turks,
his father shrewdly remembered that other and more
powerful states than Turkey had to be dealt with if his
success was to be consolidated. Ibrahim's advance to
Constantinople would be the certain signal for action
by the powers that had already intervened in Greece.
A pause in the advance would certainly allow the

[1] Sabry, *op. cit.* pp. 197–8.   [2] *Idem*, p. 205.

Turks to recover from their panic, to reassemble their forces, and to guard the road to Constantinople. But the Turks had been beaten once and could be beaten again. Muhammad 'Ali, reckoning Turkish soldiers a much less formidable enemy than France and Britain, preferred therefore to pause and negotiate.

Indeed at the moment the attitude of both powers was friendly. The monarchy of July desired to see Muhammad 'Ali's power strengthened, so long as that involved no convulsion at Constantinople serious enough to raise prematurely the question of the partition of the Turkish empire. Accordingly from the middle of 1832 all the French influence was directed towards inducing Muhammad 'Ali, not to recede from his conquests, but "to limit his ambition at the point at which he has admitted it should be satisfied, and to prefer an arrangement with the Porte to the continuation of the war...".[1]

The attitude of the English ministry was not dissimilar. Barker, the consul-general, who was probably influenced by consular opinion in Syria where he had served and where the advantages of the corrupt Turkish régime were fully understood, disapproved of Ibrahim's victories, refused to pay Muhammad 'Ali a visit of congratulation on the fall of Acre,[2] and delighted after the promulgation of the viceroy's removal from office by the Porte to refer to him as "the ex-viceroy" or "the rebel". But this by no means represented the views of the London Foreign Office. Palmerston, who had accepted the Secretary's seals at the close of 1830, not only gave Barker a sharp rebuke for thus venturing to take for granted the decision of His Majesty's government,[3] but shortly afterwards replaced

[1] Douin, *Mission du Baron de Boislecomte*, p. iii.
[2] Barker, June 13, 1832 (F.O. 78-214).
[3] To Barker, October 3, 1832 (*ibid.*).

him by Colonel Patrick Campbell,[1] by far the ablest
and most understanding of all the British representatives
in Egypt in Muhammad 'Ali's time.

In order to render his aggrandisement less alarming
in western eyes, the viceroy, as he still was, however
much his sovereign might disclaim him, proceeded to
develop a somewhat paradoxical thesis which he had
already pressed upon Great Britain. That was the view
that he remained at heart a humble servant of the
Turkish empire, if not of the Turkish Sultan, that he
was acting only for the advantage and glory of the
Sublime Porte, that he had no views of independence,
and that he was conquering Syria merely in order to
consolidate Turkish power.[2] But, since Sultan Mahmud
had been proved by experience incapable of guiding
the Turks anywhere except to defeat, and since the
Divan was incurably hostile to the only man—that is,
Muhammad 'Ali himself—who could save the empire
from ruin, it had become his clear duty as a patriotic
and loyal Turk to dethrone Mahmud and set his young
son, Abdul Majid, up in his stead with such a Divan as
would ensure the wise conduct of affairs.[3] A tentative
move was made in August and September to abolish
the only visible sign in Egypt of Mahmud's sovereignty.
Under cover of the fact that the Turkish coinage had
long undergone a steady course of debasement and was
becoming worse, its currency was prohibited throughout Egypt, in order to prevent it from replacing the
European and Egyptian coins in use in the country.[4]
This had in reality no connection with Gresham's
famous law. It was an ingenious attempt under the
guise of an economic reform to proclaim to the people

[1] To Campbell, January 7, 1833 (F.O. 78–226).
[2] Barker, June 25, 1832 (F.O. 78–214).
[3] The same, August 12, 1832 (*ibid.*).
[4] The same, September 19, 1832 (*ibid.*).

of Egypt that they were no longer governed in the name of Sultan Mahmud.

Meanwhile discussions had been continuously proceeding between Alexandria and Constantinople. The Sultan had sent commissioners at the end of 1831, who had been received with much graciousness; but the discussions were prolonged over the next two months,[1] and ended in nothing more lasting than the fumes of the chibouques they puffed day after day in the viceroy's palace. Then followed an indirect negotiation conducted through the Turkish Capitan Pasha. In September Muhammad 'Ali told Barker that as he had had no satisfactory answer, there was nothing left for him but to march on Constantinople and that he had secret news from that place that "there is now nothing to prevent my doing so".[2] But in November he was still ready to negotiate with any agent whom the Porte chose to send to Alexandria,[3] and directing Ibrahim not to proclaim the abolition of the Sultan's authority in Syria unless he could first obtain *fatwas* from the local religious leaders declaring Mahmud deposed as unfit to rule.[4]

But under cover of these palavers, the Sultan was preparing a final effort to drive the rebel's forces out of Syria. Indeed his negotiations were apparently designed to throw the enemy off his guard and divert him from either advancing on Constantinople or increasing his forces until the Turkish preparations had been completed.

Ibrahim with his army had advanced as far northward as Koniah—the ancient Iconium—where he had been detained by his father's fear of provoking inter-

[1] Barker to Mandeville, January 2, and to Hotham, February 28, 1832 (F.O. 78–213).
[2] Barker, September 20, 1832 (F.O. 78–214).
[3] Sabry, *op. cit.* p. 208.   [4] *Idem*, p. 212.

vention. At the close of the year 1832 the Grand Vazir
himself, Rashid Muhammad Pasha, advanced against
him. Rashid had a numerous army, stiffened with
large levies from Bosnia and Albania. On December
21 the armies met close to Koniah. The Turk cavalry
early left the field; the infantry were drawn on into an
attack in the course of which they suddenly found
themselves fired on from either flank. They were
utterly routed; the Grand Vazir was taken prisoner;
and the way to Constantinople lay open and defenceless. Ibrahim resolved to advance at once, in the hope
of confronting Europe with the accomplished fact of
the Sultan's overthrow. But at Kutahia he received a
letter from his father directing him to halt, wherever
he might be.

This decision was brought about by the very intervention that Muhammad 'Ali had always feared. On
January 12, 1833, rumours had already reached Alexandria that the Turks had accepted a Russian alliance.[1]
The news in fact was premature, for though the
Emperor of Russia had offered the Sultan armed
assistance against Muhammad 'Ali, the offer had not
yet been accepted; but almost immediately afterwards
a Russian officer, Lieutenant-General Muravief, had
reached Constantinople with orders to proceed at once
to Alexandria and require the viceroy to desist from his
attacks on Turkey. He reached Alexandria on January
13. Early next morning he had a short audience. He
presented no written document to the viceroy; and it
was announced that he had come as a mediator of
peace. But it was generally believed that his mission
was to call upon Muhammad 'Ali to retire from Cara-
mania and Syria, to give up his fleet to the Sultan, and
to reduce his army to 20,000 men. Two days later, and
again on the 18th, he had two more conversations with

[1] Barker, January 17, 1833 (F.O. 78–231).

the pasha, prolonged and secret. Muhammad 'Ali gave way, promised to submit to the Sultan, and, as a pledge of good faith, to suspend hostilities.[1]

The Turkish Divan had naturally looked for help in its distressing circumstances to England, its traditional ally, rather than to Russia, its traditional foe. A special envoy had been sent to London to seek the aid of English men-of-war. But Palmerston was not prepared for such definite action. He refused. This rebuff determined Mahmud, sorely against his will, to make terms with the rebellious viceroy. On January 21 therefore Khalil, the Capitan Pasha, reached Alexandria, with offers of peace.

The meeting of the two pashas was ceremonious in the extreme. Khalil was assisted up the staircase of the Ras-al-tin Palace by two of Muhammad 'Ali's principal officers. The viceroy himself advanced half-way down to meet him, would not allow the other to kiss his hand, but embraced him and kissed him on the cheek. They proceeded to the audience chamber hand in hand, Khalil's disengaged arm clasping the viceroy's portly waist. When they took their seats, Khalil respectfully doubled up his legs under him. So much etiquette was a natural prelude to prolonged, tedious, insincere discussions.

What terms of peace could Muhammad 'Ali hope to secure? Ibrahim from his army headquarters at Kutahia suggested a list of demands. In the first place he set independence—"a vital question for us, dominating all the rest". Then Anatolia and Cilicia, for the sake of the timber they might supply—an article which Egypt must obtain from abroad, if the fleet was to be maintained. Lastly Cyprus, as a base for the fleet. Baghdad he thought of small moment; it was too distant and too poor.[2] From the Egyptian point of

---

[1] Barker, January 17 and 19, 1833 (F.O. 78–231). Sabry, *op. cit.* p. 223.   [2] Quoted *ap.* Sabry, *op. cit.* pp. 227–8.

view all were most desirable. But the only claim which could be laid to any of them was the claim of the conqueror. Such claims can be made good only by superior force; and there could be no reason why Europe should acquiesce in such demands if they seemed politically undesirable.

An instructive contrast to Ibrahim's view is afforded by the instructions which at almost the same time Palmerston was drawing up for Colonel Campbell. "His Majesty's Government", he wrote, "attach great importance to the maintenance of the integrity of the Ottoman Empire, considering that state to be a material element in the general balance of power in Europe, and they are of opinion that any considerable encroachment upon the Asiatic territories of the Sultan, and any consequent defalcation from the resources which he might bring to bear for the defence of his European dominions, must operate in a corresponding degree upon his relative position with respect to neighbouring powers, and must thereby have injurious bearings upon the general interests of Europe. His Majesty's Government therefore deem it of importance to prevent not only a dissolution but even a partial dismemberment of the Turkish Empire." It was obviously impossible to re-establish the former state of things, but in the circumstances the best solution was to assign Syria to Muhammad 'Ali on such terms of tribute and military aid as would leave the Porte's revenues and resources undiminished.[1]

And the fact was that Ibrahim's impatience, his reliance on the sword despite his experience in the Morea, had turned the scales decidedly against his own and his father's ambitions. The news of his decision to advance upon Constantinople, arriving just after the despatch of Khalil to Alexandria, had filled the Divan

[1] To Campbell, February 4, 1833 (F.O. 78–226).

with wild, but not exaggerated apprehension. There were no troops but the broken fragments of the late Grand Vazir Rashid's army to bar the way. All had gone on that most unlucky throw at Koniah. Ibrahim's approach would arouse every smouldering ember of discontent; Muhammad 'Ali's agents would fan them into a blaze. The empire would collapse, the Sultan would fall, the ministers would lose office and perhaps life. In their panic they turned to Russia who already had offered military aid. They begged her to send men-of-war and at least 20,000 men to save Constantinople. And Russia eagerly agreed. Even when Muravief returned from Alexandria with the news that Ibrahim's march had been stayed, and when both English and French representatives assured the Porte that military aid was no longer needed, the Divan still refused to withdraw its request, and a Russian force encamped on the Asiatic side of the Bosphorus. Ibrahim in fact had committed a ruinous blunder. For it was not merely the Russians who were roused. The western powers, who had been mere spectators in the earlier phases of the war, were now drawn into inevitable action. It had become necessary to end the Syrian war, to free Constantinople from fear, to get rid of the Russians as soon as possible, to protect the Turks, if fate permitted, from the consequences of their own misconduct, lest the partition of their empire should set all Europe by the ears. In vain Muhammad 'Ali sought to retrieve Ibrahim's slip by urging once more his pet theory of regenerating the empire by way of rebellion. He had never dreamt of independent power, he assured Campbell, and, by supporting him, France and England would be supporting the Sultan in the most effectual way possible.[1] "Cool and clear-sighted observation", ran a memorandum which he gave to Campbell,

[1] Campbell, March 31, 1833 (F.O. 78–227).

"shows that the Turkish government is worn out on every side, with its foundations cracking beneath it, having exhausted its physical and moral resources, abandoned and despised by the nation,[1] discredited and distrusted at Constantinople itself, incapable of defending either itself or the nation; it has in short abandoned itself to its fate and lies a helpless prey in the Russian talons...."[2] But while the pasha's assertions corresponded not unfairly with the facts as they appeared to contemporary Europe, western statesmen were indisposed to admit that Muhammad 'Ali was the sole possible regenerator of the empire. The western nations themselves might come to the aid of the Sultan, and the maintenance of the Sultan's position as little weakened as might be seemed to them to promise better chances of gently edging out the Russians from their extraordinary and unprecedented attitude of champions of the Turk, than all the forces which Ibrahim had at his disposal.

Another argument which the pasha strove to introduce was the principle (as we should call it nowadays) of self-determination. The case offers a delightful example of the false facility with which the political principles of the western world may be employed to mask action essentially different in character. Muhammad 'Ali claimed to be acting on behalf and in the name of the "nation" of Islam. He had urged on Ibrahim the need of obtaining from the learned men of Syria declarations that Sultan Mahmud was or should be deposed as incapable of rule. In reply Ibrahim had pointed out to him the patent absurdity of expecting the ulema of Damascus to renounce the Sultan's sovereignty before another had laid claim to it and proved his right by force. And a further difficulty lay

[1] *Scilicet*, the world of Islam.
[2] Campbell, *ut supra*.

in the fact that the western nations had consular agents all over Syria, so that it would be hard to obtain declarations without knowledge leaking out of the means by which alone such declarations could be secured. But what could hardly be got in Syria without certain exposure of the coercion or bribes employed might of course be asserted of more distant regions where there were no consular agents. A declaration was produced purporting to have been made by a group of Kurds bordering on the Black Sea, renouncing their allegiance to the Sultan and offering their obedience to the Pasha of Cairo. It was not a little singular, as the French consul-general remarked, that such a declaration should come from a province which, at the moment at all events, Muhammad 'Ali could not possibly protect against the Sultan's agents, and that the persons bearing it should have been able to travel by Angora undisturbed.[1]

In European eyes, at all events, such arguments carried little conviction. The pasha might claim to be regarded with the same sympathy as Europe had accorded to the Belgians and the Greeks, but even his persuasive tongue could not disguise the fact that he was fighting for his own hand. He did not represent any nation struggling to be free. His military superiority over the Turks could give no moral claim to special consideration. His only moral claim—if so it can be called—lay in the superior order, justice and regularity which it might be expected he would introduce into his new conquests as he had introduced them into Egypt. But even then, since his methods would certainly be those of oriental administration, western statesmen would still find opportunities for criticism and doubt.

[1] Mimaut, December 25, 1832, quoted *ap.* Sabry, *op. cit.* pp. 230-1. M. Sabry, I think, misapprehends the significance of the concluding part of the despatch.

Political expediency was therefore the only standpoint from which the matter could reasonably be discussed at Paris and London.

France and England were at least thoroughly agreed on the necessity of eliminating the suddenly arisen Russian influence at Constantinople, and on the need of arresting Ibrahim's advance in order to quiet the extraordinary alarm which had seized upon the Porte. They therefore called upon Muhammad 'Ali to withdraw from Asia Minor, and even threatened to blockade Alexandria unless he complied with their demand.[1] But while Palmerston was entirely indisposed to admit any alteration in the pasha's theoretical position of vassalage to the Sultan, the French were inclined to toy with the idea of recognising him some day as virtually independent, like the Barbary deys, and to use this as a means of inducing him to accept unpalatable terms with a minimum of ill-feeling. They even sent a minister plenipotentiary to Alexandria. This diplomatic blunder provoked the Austrian representative to enquire to what court the plenipotentiary was accredited, and the French consul-general was obliged to declare that the minister claimed no rank above that of envoy on a special mission.[2]

While the western powers were thus seeking to cajole or to alarm the viceroy into withdrawing his troops, the Porte suddenly yielded to Muhammad 'Ali's demands so far as to grant him Crete and the four Syrian pashaliqs, withholding only the district of Adana. The news arrived on April 16. The messenger was received in the presence of the English and French consuls-general. On the delivery of his message, "the pasha started up with tears of joy in his eyes, and, laying aside anything like Turkish gravity, burst into a sort of hysterick

[1] Campbell, April 9, 1833 (F.O. 78–227).
[2] The same, May 3, 1833 (*ibid.*).

laugh ".[1] He doubtless assumed that this was a sign
that the Porte was weakening and would in a little
concede Adana as well. But both England, France
and Austria continued to press on him the need of
yielding. He was indeed brought to declare "that he
was ready to give up all claims to the government of
Adana, and to promise besides to all the great powers
to remain for ever the faithful vassal of the Porte and
not to disturb his sovereign in any way, provided the
Porte would declare on her part to the representatives
of those powers that she (the Porte) would never
attempt to withdraw the rights which she had granted
to him ".[2] A few days later, in conversation with the
French "plenipotentiary", he observed in a like spirit:
"I am a peaceable man, who aims at nothing else but
to consecrate the rest of his days to the prosperity of the
countries that I have to govern. They ask me the proof
of this disposition. I give it by begging of Europe to
guarantee Turkey from all aggression on my part, and
at the same time to guarantee me from all aggression on
her part ".[3]

These negotiations however proved otiose, except in
giving the pasha an opportunity of developing his
views, for on May 3 the Porte had already given way on
Adana as well. Thus the various points had now all
been settled, except the question of the tribute to be
paid the Porte for the ceded provinces. That was agreed
in the following September, on the basis of 30,000
purses a year for the governments of Egypt, Syria,
Adana, and Tarsus.[4]

The Syrian war thus ended to the satisfaction of no
one. The Sultan had suffered the vexation of defeat by

---

[1] Campbell, April 17, 1833 (F.O. 78–227).
[2] The same, May 9 (P.S. May 10), 1833 (*ibid.*).
[3] The same, May 13, 1833 (*ibid.*).
[4] The same, September 13, 1833 (F.O. 78–228).

a contumacious pasha; Muhammad 'Ali had secured
neither independent status nor a controlling influence
at the Porte; the western powers were annoyed at the
opening which Ibrahim's victories had offered to the
Russians; while the Russians were disappointed at
having been unable to entrench themselves more
securely at Constantinople. However, they did not
withdraw until they had obtained by the secret clause
of the Treaty of Unkiar Skelessi, which was signed on
July 8, the right of closing the Dardanelles against any
foreign man-of-war. Here is perhaps to be found the
source of that unconquerable distrust with which
Palmerston came to regard the policy of Muhammad
'Ali. Even before the conclusion of the treaty, Palmerston, though not actively hostile, had been unfavourable
to Muhammad 'Ali's plans. "His real design", he had
written, "is to establish an Arabian kingdom, including all the countries of which Arabic is the language.
There might be no harm in such a thing in itself; but as
it would necessarily imply the dismemberment of
Turkey, we could not agree to it. Besides Turkey is as
good an occupier of the road to India as an active
Arabian sovereign would be."[1] Such an attitude was
natural towards the schemes of one whose ambition
had just raised the most difficult question of European
politics in a most acute form. That Anglo-Egyptian co-
operation, which the viceroy had hoped to secure, as a
consequence of Turkish feebleness, or of European
jealousies, had quite definitely become less probable.
A political principle—the assertion of national independence or the substitution of political liberty for des-
potism—might form a reasonable ground for political
disturbances and could at least be reckoned on to evoke
considerable popular sympathy. But the mere substitution of an efficient for an incompetent autocrat

[1] Bulwer, *Life of Palmerston*, II, 144–5.

aroused no particular sentiment in the whig or liberal breast. The process of reform which Muhammad 'Ali had undertaken, the beneficent consequences of a stern, regular, and highly despotic government, the infusion into heterogeneous peoples of that common consciousness without which nationality is impossible, the civilising influences which his administration was gradually spreading—all these were obscured by stories of the severity of his conscription, the ferocity of his punishments, the oppressiveness of his monopolies. Palmerston must not be too severely blamed if he failed to grasp the significance of Muhammad 'Ali's career. In his eyes Muhammad 'Ali was above all the man whose inordinate ambition had almost established the Russians in a dominant position on the Bosphorus.

Chapter V

THE IDEA OF AN ARAB EMPIRE AND
THE OVERLAND ROUTES

Palmerston had already, as has been seen, attributed to Muhammad 'Ali the project of establishing "an Arabian kingdom", embracing all the countries in which Arabic was the common form of speech. Such an ambition came very naturally to the viceroy. The conquest of Syria, following on the conquests of Egypt, of the Hijaz, and of the Sudan, left him with comparatively few further acquisitions to make in order to bring that plan within sight of realisation. There remained only 'Iraq and the Persian Gulf, together with southern Arabia, in order to complete such a territorial expansion. From a financial point of view, none offered any particular advantages except perhaps the pearl fisheries of Bahrein, while in a military sense all were inhabited by nomadic or quasi-nomadic tribes, who would bitterly resent regular government, especially when accompanied by the imposition of taxation or the establishment of conscription. But while these areas might be of small value in themselves, their occupation did in fact promise certain advantages. 'Iraq would bring the viceroy's territories into touch with Persia and through Persia with central Asia. Southern Arabia would render him master of those two great inlets of the sea, the Red Sea and the Persian Gulf, at all times of great strategic importance, and perhaps enable him to allow or deny their use to the British squadrons in the East. Such an expansion therefore, though adding little to Muhammad 'Ali's material resources, might greatly increase his political weight and influence.

He was convinced, and with good reason, that southern Arabia could offer no sustained resistance to any well-organised force, and that Baghdad in all probability would offer none at all. The general condition of the pashaliq is described as wretched in the extreme. "In their misery", wrote Colonel Taylor, the East India Company's agent, "the people look to Ibrahim."[1] Merchants at Baghdad could see no limits to the rapacity of the Turkish government save its fear of the despatch of troops from India, and they deplored the decision of Palmerston to prevent the addition of the province to what they had already begun to call "the Egyptian caliphat".[2]

Indeed, could Muhammad 'Ali have asserted his independence, the Egyptian caliphate would certainly have been revived. He controlled and protected the Hijaz; and, whatever subtleties theologians might have spun around the caliph's holy office, the popular view was that the Sultan's caliphate could not survive the disappearance of his nominal authority at Mecca and Medina. As Ibrahim wrote to his father, the Sultan could no longer be prayed for in the mosques as the Servant of the Holy Places.[3] Even before the Syrian war it had been common talk in Egypt that the sharif of Mecca was about to publish a declaration "that he who is the possessor and defender of the Kaba is the true head of the Mahometan church".[4]

But besides the possession of the Hijaz, Muhammad 'Ali controlled another source of influence. Mecca might be the spiritual metropolis of Islam, but it was not a centre of Islamic culture or learning. It possessed

[1] Taylor to Campbell, November 6, 1833 (F.O. 78–288).
[2] Tod to the same, November 27, 1833 (*ibid.*).
[3] Sabry, *op. cit.* p. 281. Cf. Ponsonby, No. 305. November 7, 1839 (F.O. 78–360).
[4] Barker to S. Canning, February 23, 1832 (F.O. 78–213).

no considerable school. It had no great libraries. It had neither bookshop nor bookbinder. True, lectures were delivered in the great mosque, but they were never delivered by any of the great *literati* of Islam, and were attended only by a few ignorant Indians, Malays, and negroes.[1] Cairo and Damascus were the true homes of Muslim learning at this time; and now Muhammad 'Ali governed both. This gave him great weight in the Muslim world; and could he have developed those cities into conscious centres of Arab, as opposed to Muslim, culture, and stood forth as the champion of Arab against Turk, he might perhaps have created in his territories some stronger bond of union than subjection to a common master. He was indeed reproached for his failure to achieve this idea.[2] But such criticism seems to ignore essential factors in the situation as it was. Islam is a faith that has never encouraged the growth of nationality. Its universal character has toned down, rather than accentuated, racial and cultural differences that might have hardened into national qualities; and it is noteworthy that even a century afterwards, even under the prolonged influence of western education and ideas, nationalist rulers have been rather hindered than assisted by its unlimited, catholic claims. Nor was that all. The only common factors in the Arab world were unity of language and unity of subjection. The Syrian and the Egyptian, the nomad and the fellah, the learned and the populace, were too much divided by custom, by ideas, by tradition, to be at all willing to recognise anything common but religion. So that Muhammad 'Ali found himself obliged to pose as the champion of the Muslim "nation", not of an Arab nation, which indeed he could not even imagine. As Ibrahim was to find, the

[1] Burckhardt, *Arabia*, I, 389–391.
[2] Puckler-Muskau, *op. cit.* I, 210.

differences between Syrian and Egyptian were far too strong and deep for any assimilation to be possible; and the attraction for Muhammad 'Ali of the territories occupied by the speakers of the Arabic tongue lay in his just sense of their strategic importance rather than in any anticipation of conditions which in his day were scarcely conceivable. The idea of an Arab nationality has been begotten and brought forth only in our own day, under the pressure of western influence, of the spread of education, of a popular press, and above all of an extraordinary development of com- munications.

His idea, therefore, was not to create an Arab unit within the circle of Islam, but to become, and be ac- claimed by all, the foremost leader of Islam itself. This, however, would involve either the overthrow of the Sultan and the dismemberment of his dominions, or the overthrow of the Divan at Constantinople and the substitution of Muhammad 'Ali's for Khusrau Pasha's influence. His position, always anomalous, had be- come yet more evidently so after the Syrian war and Ibrahim's victorious campaign. "He is", wrote Camp- bell with truth, "*de jure* a vassal and *de facto* he is inde- pendent; and although he makes professions of his being a vassal and subject of the Sultan, it is in such a manner as to lead me to think that he would not wish anyone else to suppose so."[1] Both French newspapers and official French communications nourished in him the belief that a declaration of his independence would meet with much sympathy and support. The evident (and natural) ill-will displayed towards him by the Sultan and his ministers pressed him strongly in the same direction. "These late menaces and hostile demon- strations of the Porte", Campbell wrote again a week later, "will doubtless tend to confirm Mehemet 'Ali in

[1] Campbell, August 15, 1834 (F.O. 78-246).

his desire of independence and in the object which I
feel almost certain that he contemplates eventually, of
forming an Arab caliphat....He is naturally very
ambitious of power and glory, and unlike the generality
of Mussulmans he is actuated by the strong desire of
handing down his name to posterity in the page of
history. Success has ever attended him...."[1]

The Sultan's policy in calling in Russian aid had
intensified at once Muhammad 'Ali's scorn and his dislike
of the conduct of affairs at Constantinople. It had of
course introduced an unexpected element into the
game. It was a thrust for which he commanded no
suitable parry. Hence one strong reason why he should
condemn it openly and bitterly. But, quite apart from
that, it violated Muslim sentiment and threatened
Muslim unity. It had alienated the affection of the
whole people, he declared, and the newly arrived qazi of
Cairo, whose appointment was one of the few relics of
Turkish dominion in Egypt, said—it was of course
worth his while to conciliate the pasha's good opinion—
that he had been assured by many of the chief people at
Constantinople that they looked to Muhammad 'Ali
"as the chief support of the empire in the event of any
future war with Russia".[2] If the Turko-Russian
alliance could be countered by an Anglo-Egyptian
understanding, all the dreams which the viceroy had
cherished in his heart for years might yet come true.

Accordingly an interesting memorandum was given
to the English consul-general for transmission to
London. It was the viceroy's first object, it asserted, to
root Russian influence out of Turkey, and to organise
such a force as would compel the Russians to respect the
independence, not only of Turkey, but of Persia as well.
"The viceroy's desire of possessing Syria was inspired

[1] Campbell to Ponsonby, August 21, 1834 (F.O. 78–246).
[2] Campbell, June 25, 1833 (F.O. 78–227).

by that single purpose; and after the battle of Koniah
he had hoped to bring about such a change in the
government and policy at Constantinople as with the
help of England and France would have speedily dis-
concerted the designs of Russia." He would (the
memorandum continued) soon have an army of 150,000
men ready to co-operate with England in the glorious
task of delivering Turkey and Persia from the Russian
yoke. Meanwhile he demanded of British equity and
justice whether he would not be justified in declaring at
once his independence, as he had resolved on doing
should the Porte's hostility continue.[1]

At the moment the English agents in the East were
much disposed to assent to these views. In 1833
Ponsonby had written to Campbell, "If Russia should
look to selfish ends, it is to be hoped that the strength
of Mehemet Ali may be found efficient where it seems
certain it must be his interest to exert it, viz. in driving
from Asia and the Ottoman territory a power, which, if
allowed to spread its roots there, will easily ere long be
great enough to destroy the new-born energies of his
Egyptian and Arab population".[2] Campbell himself
in the next year thought "that so far as regards the
resistance to Russian encroachments and aggrandize-
ment on the side of Asia, perhaps the establishment of
an Arab caliphat under Mehemet Ali would be a better
barrier and more likely to afford effectual opposition to
Russia than the Porte could now ever be expected to
offer, and in case of need Mehemet Ali could give great
assistance to Persia (supposing him to rule over Baghdad etc.) in any struggle of Persia against Russia".[3]

To some extent these views may have coincided with
Palmerston's dislike of Russian policy and aims. He

[1] Boghoz Bey to Campbell, September 3, 1834 (F.O. 78–246).
[2] Ponsonby to Campbell, May 24, 1833 (F.O. 78–227).
[3] Campbell to Ponsonby, August 21, 1834 (F.O. 78–246).

regarded her as the only European power with which
we were likely seriously to quarrel, and he complained
of her system of universal aggression, inspired alike by
the personal character of the emperor and by the permanent character of her government.[1] He was, too,
receiving at this time information from persons in no
way under the command of Muhammad 'Ali's power
or the spell of his persuasion that the Russians were
seeking to strengthen themselves in the critical area of
'Iraq. Once their influence was established at Baghdad,
our agent wrote, "its central position and its navigable
streams and natural resources will afford the highest
advantages to future advances...or the establishment
and continuation of intrigue more fatal than war".[2]
Might not the threat of Russian intrigue, the fear of
Russian advances through Persia towards India, secure
at last for the viceroy that British recognition and aid
which neither the evacuation of the Morea nor the
project of alliance with France had been able to
obtain? Had not the British government in India
sought the alliance of the Sikhs, the Afghans, and the
Persians when it feared that Napoleon might advance
overland upon India?

But these calculations left out of account the position
of Great Britain and the character of her foreign
minister. At this time she was fully conscious, it may
have been over-conscious, of her power and her re-
sponsibilities. For five generations she had lost one war
only, when her arm had been weakened by the knowledge that those she fought were of her own household.
Her last war had been not only the fiercest but the
most triumphant of them all. Was she then likely to
change the whole basis on which her European policy

[1] Palmerston to W. Temple, December 3, 1833 (Bulwer, *op. cit.*
II, 176).
[2] Taylor to the India Board, March 14, 1834 (F.O. 78-245).

was built in order to buy an alliance against a possible foe who had never in an offensive war beaten anyone but Turks and Persians? Nor was Palmerston ever the man to seek the prop of a foreign alliance instead of developing the power and resources of his own country. His limitation lay in bluntness of intellect, not in any defect of courage; and he was bent on hindering the progress of Russia by other means than those which Muhammad 'Ali was suggesting.

He therefore returned the most uncompromising answer. Campbell was ordered to express regret and surprise at proposals so at variance with Muhammad 'Ali's former professions and incompatible with the honour and good faith of the British government. Muhammad 'Ali desired "that Great Britain should either consent to an attack to be made by the pasha upon the Sultan or she should sanction an attempt on the part of the former to throw off his allegiance to the latter and to declare himself the independent ruler of the provinces which he at present administers as the vicegerent of his sovereign". How could we sanction rebellion and usurpation directly against a crowned head in alliance with His Majesty?[1]

In this language there was doubtless an element of absurdity and perhaps of falsehood. Palmerston was writing of Muhammad 'Ali's attitude towards the Sultan much as though the relations of that derelict monarch and his ministers were those familiar in the West. The Secretary of State indeed approached the matter as he would have expected the United States to treat similar offers from the Governor-General of Canada, or France the like suggestions from the Governor-General of India. Acceptance or even encouragement could be justified only by a state of war or at the least a state in which war was confidently antici-

[1] Despatch to Campbell, October 26, 1834 (F.O. 78-244).

pated, while the minister capable of seeking foreign aid against his sovereign was clearly guilty of the blackest treason. But such views evidently took for granted conditions which were notoriously non-existent. The Governor-General of Canada could rest assured that the success of his administration would not expose him to the hatred and vengeance of his king; the Governor-General of India could rely on the prime minister's not seeking his disgrace and execution. The political ideas of the West were therefore being applied to a world in which they were imperfectly apprehended and completely ignored.

But the recognition of this does not perhaps invalidate Palmerston's general attitude. Turkey had become a part of the state system of Europe. Alliance with her carried the same obligations as alliances with other powers—obligations which could not really be affected by the chaotic state of her internal affairs. So much was completely undeniable. And in this case the guidance of political principle was strengthened by considerations of political expediency. It would have been entirely permissible to denounce our long-standing alliance with the Sultan and then to support Muhammad 'Ali in his projects against the Turkish empire and the Ottoman caliphate. But the art of foreign policy consists in pursuing national interests within the limits imposed by a due observance of political principle. The latter would have been violated by any secret countenance afforded to the viceroy of Egypt; the former would have been threatened by an open union with him. The withdrawal of our support from the Sultan would have meant an instant scramble for the inheritance of his empire,—a contingency which we could not view with composure, for we should scarcely have been benefited by seeing the Adriatic become an Austrian lake, or Constantinople a Russian port. What advantage could Muhammad 'Ali offer to make it worth while to turn Europe upside down, or why should we gratuitously aid the ruler of Egypt to extend his power by military conquest into new areas to which he could not allege the least shadow of a rightful claim? Out of these considerations emerged a policy of supporting the maintenance of Muhammad 'Ali's authority in the territories already ruled by him but of opposing consistently any further expansion of his power. Palmerston sensibly preferred to strengthen our own position on the newly developing routes to India rather than help to build up a new state in the hope that some day that new state would throw in its lot with us in a possible war with Russia.

As matters stood, the two possible overland routes to India—by the Euphrates and by Suez—had by no action of our own fallen from under the control of a single political authority. The rise of Muhammad 'Ali's power in Egypt had given him the Suez route, while the Euphrates valley still remained under the government, however nominal, of the Sultan. It would indeed have been an act of great folly to have assisted, without any moral or political obligation, in placing both under Muhammad 'Ali's command at the very moment that they were coming into high political importance.[1] The primary cause of this development had been the application of steam-power to shipping. So long as the Red Sea route had been closed during several months of the year by the prevailing winds, and so long as the passage up the Euphrates could be accomplished only by the tedious method of tracking, those ways to the East, while of undoubted military importance, could not rival the long sea voyage round the Cape. But before the close of the Napoleonic wars

[1] Cf. Palmerston to W. Temple, March 21, 1833 (Bulwer, *op. cit.* II, 144).

steamboats were in use on English rivers and canals, and a few years later they were already employed in channel crossings. By 1820 men were anticipating their introduction on to the great ocean routes. But here progress was more difficult. The early marine steam engine was feeble and wasteful. It consumed enormous quantities of coal, and so was closely tied to the coastline where alone it could renew its stores of fuel. The clumsy paddle-boxes were liable to be torn away by high seas, and the engines themselves had to be stopped frequently for cleaning and repair. In these circumstances their earliest use was evidently destined to be limited to regions offering a continuous chain of ports—the Channel, the Mediterranean, the Red Sea, or the Persian Gulf.

The importance of these possible developments was rapidly grasped in India. In 1823 the Calcutta merchants formed a committee to investigate the matter. This led to the voyage of the *Enterprize*, which spent 113 days half-steaming, half-sailing, from London to Calcutta round the Cape. This comparative failure demonstrated the disadvantages of the long sea route for these primitive steamers and turned public attention to the more appropriate route by Suez and the Red Sea. This had been advocated by Mountstuart Elphinstone at the time when the Calcutta committee had begun its campaign. His successor in the government of Bombay, Sir John Malcolm, took up the idea with enthusiasm. In 1829 he attempted to send the *Enterprize* from Bombay to Suez. He had a new vessel, the *Hugh Lindsay*, specially built, and in 1830 she accomplished the first steam voyage up the Red Sea. Although at this moment the East India Company could not be induced to complete the plan by chartering steamers to Alexandria and back, to meet the mails and passengers from Suez, other experimental voyages were made, admiralty packets sailed from Malta to Alexandria, a select committee was appointed to report on the whole question of steam communication with India, and merchants began largely to use the Suez route for letters even before any regular service had been established.[1] Thomas Waghorn, who had been active in promoting the scheme, established himself at Alexandria and began to act as an agent for forwarding correspondence, although the East India Company still refused to make use of the route. Auckland, the Governor-General of India, in 1836 drew a lively picture of the condition of affairs. "The merchant", he writes to Hobhouse, "receives at the India House bills upon our treasury at so much after sight, which at the Court's rate of travelling [i.e. via the Cape] should be four or five months after date. He sends them to Alexandria.... The indefatigable Waghorn gets into a boggoora [a dhow] with the letter-bags, finds his way to Mocha, puts them on board a trader, and they are at Calcutta a little more than two months after leaving England. The merchants here have all their letters; their bills for 20 lacs are paid at our treasury to their profit and our loss; private correspondence flourishes; newspapers pour in; and the government upon public business has not a single line from any authority. As far as I, as governor-general, am concerned, I would rather have the communication by the Cape of Good Hope than the Red Sea and by Cape Horn than either; but if the short path is open, it is strange and inconsistent that all should use it except those who have a paramount interest in India."[2]

But these conditions were rapidly passing. The French established a line of steamers between Marseilles and Alexandria in 1835, and under pressure from the

[1] Hoskins, *British Routes to India,* chapter v, *passim.*
[2] Auckland to Hobhouse, October 7, 1836 (Brit. Mus. Add. MSS, 36473 A, f. 91).

Board of Control the East India Company ordered the building of two new steam vessels for the Bombay-Suez service. The development of the route, in accordance with the recommendation of the select committee, was therefore assured.

This, however, was not the only possible route. In the past Basra had been an active competitor of Suez, and steamers had proved so much more reliable on inland waters that men naturally wondered, in an age which had recently seen England covered with a network of canals, whether the best solution might not be found in joining the waters of the Orontes and the Euphrates, which, it was generally thought, would be a much simpler matter than cutting through the isthmus of Suez. In 1830–1 this route was being simultaneously surveyed by Chesney from Syria and by a party of the Company's officers from India. The latter were seriously interrupted, and some of them were murdered, by the unruly Arabs who occupied the banks of the Euphrates. Chesney succeeded in the face of great difficulties in completing a preliminary survey. In 1834 he was sent again with an expedition, carrying two flat-bottomed river steamers, which were to be put together on the upper waters of the Euphrates, to convey the expedition down to the Persian Gulf. The Sultan's farman was obtained, permitting the navigation of the Euphrates. After overcoming many obstacles, Chesney succeeded in assembling his two vessels on the Euphrates. One was sunk in a cyclone. The other actually reached Basra. But though the leader of the expedition remained enthusiastic about the possibilities of the route he had so laboriously surveyed, almost everyone else was convinced that, whatever its political importance and ultimate development, the Euphrates route could not compete with the Suez and Red Sea way to India.[1]

[1] Cf. Hoskins, *op. cit.* chapter VII.

However, the expedition had been inspired by a definite political object. Since the progress of Russia and the development of Muhammad 'Ali's plans, the area had acquired a great importance; and a knowledge of the facilities of transport which it offered was of the utmost political interest. It seems to have been opposed by the Russians as well as by Muhammad 'Ali. Ponsonby learnt at Constantinople that the Russian minister had conveyed a message to the Porte that the viceroy was ready to throw every possible obstacle in the way of the expedition, if that were the Sultan's wish.[1] Campbell at Alexandria believed that the Russian consul-general had endeavoured to prejudice the viceroy against the undertaking.[2] Great difficulties arose about work-people and supplies. Such opposition was but natural. The Russians did not want British influence established on the Euphrates, Muhammad 'Ali feared we meant to build forts and occupy the river,[3] while from a revenue point of view he desired the Red Sea route to be developed rather than that of the Persian Gulf. Perhaps, too, he hoped that his opposition in a matter which the British seemed to have at heart would render them more amenable to his suggestions of independence. While therefore Ibrahim in Syria did all that could be done underhand to hinder Chesney's progress, Muhammad 'Ali declined to send any orders to his son, until he should have received express orders from the Sultan.[4] Palmerston was very much annoyed. He wrote two stiff despatches, in the second of which he observed that "His Majesty's government are determined that the undertaking...shall not fail in consequence of the

[1] Ponsonby, November 6, 1835 (F.O. 78–256).
[2] Campbell, July 30, 1835 (F.O. 78–257).
[3] Sabry, *op. cit.* p. 299.
[4] Campbell, September 28, 1835 (F.O. 78–258).

obstacles which bad faith in any quarter may oppose to it".[1]

While Muhammad 'Ali was thus seeking to check British schemes for the survey of the 'Iraq rivers, the British Foreign Office was keeping a sharp lookout against any encroachments on the Sultan's remaining territories. Muhammad 'Ali had, for instance, sought to add the district of Orfa to his Syrian territory, on the grounds that it had never been occupied by the Turks, that it was in a state of brigandage, that its inhabitants raided the country round Aleppo, that he would pay tribute for it, and that it had always formed part of the Aleppo pashaliq.[2] He was induced to withdraw from the district. In 1835 he occupied Deir on the Euphrates, doubtless with a view to control Chesney's expedition more effectively. His excuse was that the nomad tribes of those parts raided his settled territories.[3] He was firmly warned not to encroach on the pashaliq of Baghdad.

Whatever were the viceroy's intentions about Baghdad, that city and Basra were regarded by the British as places of great moment. The occupation of Deir coincided with military activity in southern Arabia threatening to extend on to the Persian Gulf. "Great Britain", Palmerston wrote, "would...think her interests directly concerned in preventing the authority of the Sultan from being shaken or interfered with at Baghdad"; and again, with regard to any movement towards Baghdad or the Gulf, "You will state frankly to the pasha that the British government could not see with indifference the execution of such intentions".[4]

[1] To Campbell, July [ ] and November 2, 1835 (F.O. 78–257 and 258).
[2] Campbell, August 19 and October 6, 1834 (F.O. 78–246 and 247).
[3] The same, December 21, 1835 (F.O. 78–258).
[4] To Campbell, Nos. 23 and 25, December 8, 1837 (F.O. 78–318).

These words were no idle statement of mere views. Whatever might be the outcome of Chesney's excursion down the Euphrates or the development of the Suez route, the Red Sea and the Persian Gulf formed direct avenues to India which Great Britain was resolved to guard with her own forces.

The events which led to a further and sharper clash of Anglo-Egyptian interests began simply enough in a mutiny of Muhammad 'Ali's troops in Arabia. The Syrian war had severely strained the viceroy's finances. The pay of the troops in Arabia fell into arrears, and two Albanian officers exhibited great discontent. Early in 1832 the viceroy was writing to the governor of Hijaz that 5000 purses were being sent with which to appease the troops, but that "the two hogs of leaders" were to be persuaded to return to Egypt or else seized and sent thither in irons.[1] Neither measure bore fruit. The troops broke into open mutiny and their leaders defied the governor. One of their "ancient comrades" sent to restore discipline was forced to flee and returned to Cairo in disgrace, while the money sent to buy coffee on the pasha's account was seized and plundered.[2] At Jidda all public property and both the viceroy's and private shipping were captured.[3] Late in 1832 the rebels were firmly established in the Yemen,[4] making Mokha their headquarters, where they seriously interrupted the Surat trade.[5] For the moment nothing effective could be done, but in the middle of 1833 Muhammad 'Ali informed Campbell that he proposed to send an expedition to reduce Mokha[6]—a project with which the East India Company was in hearty

[1] To Hasan Aga, Ramzan 7, 1247 (Abdine Archives).
[2] Barker, July 21, 1832 (F.O. 78–214).
[3] The same, December 10, 1832 (*ibid.*).
[4] Campbell, April 16, 1833 (F.O. 78–227).
[5] The same, October 27, 1833 (F.O. 78–228).
[6] The same, June 11, 1833 (F.O. 78–227).

sympathy.[1] At the close of the year an expedition set out, well provided with funds with which to buy off the rebels' Arab allies.[2] These efforts were at last successful. The Arabs changed sides with their customary readiness, and the surviving rebel leader escaped on to a Company's ship of war, while sixteen of his chief officers were beheaded.[3]

But although the Arab chiefs were willing to take Egyptian money for turning against the rebel troops, they were quite indisposed to allow Muhammad 'Ali to enjoy peaceful possession of country lying behind the southern Red Sea ports of Hodeida and Mokha. A long and troublesome war followed between Muhammad 'Ali's officers and the Assiri chiefs of Yemen, the former gaining small permanent advantage, while the state of war hindered trade. Even so late as 1838 Campbell was still urging on the viceroy the unwisdom of seeking to reduce the Assiri tribes to submission instead of simply occupying the seaports and encouraging the inland peoples to bring down their produce for sale.[4]

These operations in any case were of interest to Great Britain only in so far as they brought the Egyptian troops within striking distance of Aden; and indeed their lack of real success down to 1838 did not suggest any great probability that an effective control would be set up over the southern Red Sea littoral. But in the course of the year Muhammad 'Ali suddenly scored two considerable victories. On April 5 Ahmad Pasha contrived to slay 500 and capture 1000 of the hostile Assiri Arabs.[5] In the following month Kurshid Pasha,

[1] East India Company to Board of Control, August 9, 1833 (F.O. 97–411).
[2] Campbell, December 5, 1833 (F.O. 78–228).
[3] The same, February 22, 1834 (F.O. 78–245).
[4] The same, March 20, 1838 (F.O. 78–342).
[5] The same, June 10, 1838 (F.O. 78–343).

who had been despatched into the Wahabi country, reached Aneiza, about half-way across the peninsula in a direct line between Mecca and Basra. It was a place of some trade, frequented by merchants from Baghdad and Damascus, and likely to form a useful base for the further advance of the army. After some hesitation the local chief and principal people of the place came into Kurshid's camp and made their submission. But an accident forced both sides to arms almost at once. In some personal dispute a Turk soldier shot an Arab inhabitant. In the riot that followed the Turk was cut to pieces, and some dozen killed on either side, while the troops were driven out and the gates shut against them. Kurshid was obliged to bombard the place for forty-eight hours before it surrendered.[1] This was followed up the next year by a further advance, which brought the Egyptian troops on to the shores of the Gulf itself. Early in 1839 our agents in the Gulf reported the submission of Al Hassa and Katif, the territory lying along the western coast, and expected that the tribute "usually paid by the island of Bahrein" would be rigidly exacted by the governor whom Muhammad 'Ali had appointed over Najd.[2] Kurshid had written to our resident in the Gulf to announce his intention of occupying Bahrein, if necessary by force.[3] The officer commanding the Egyptian troops who had advanced into Al Katif spoke (rashly indeed) to the British admiral who was visiting the Gulf of proceeding to reduce Basra and Baghdad, and Kurshid himself was reported only to be awaiting the arrival of more men from Medina to advance in force.[4]

These activities were at once most unwise and ex-

[1] Campbell, July 2, 1838 (F.O. 78–343).
[2] The same, April 6, 1839 (F.O. 78–373).
[3] Enclosures to Campbell, May 18, 1839 (F.O. 78–374).
[4] Maitland to Admiralty, April 7, 1839 (Ad. 1–219).

ceedingly ill-timed. They involved a needless penetra-
tion into an area where a strong British influence
existed. The chief of Bahrein was one of "the pacifi-
cated Arabs of the Persian Gulf" (to borrow the extraordinary language of the Indian Political Department)
who had signed the general treaty of 1820, and the
government of India rightly decided to check this
attack upon our position by ordering a firmer and
more peremptory tone to be adopted towards Kurshid
and his people, to be supported by the despatch of
force and the cordial assistance of all chiefs who should
resist the Egyptian demands.[1] Muhammad 'Ali's explanation of his movements—that he only wanted to
check the Wahabis, protect the Holy Cities, and pro-
cure camels,[2] that he was being maligned by reports
from Constantinople and Baghdad,[3] and that he did not
desire any position on the Gulf[4]—had not even the
merit of verisimilitude.

And the movement was ill-timed, for it fell in with
other unfortunate incidents, which, justly or unjustly,
produced all the effect of design. In 1835 the Shah of
Persia had contemplated the despatch of an envoy to
Cairo.[5] In 1838 a member of the Persian mission at
Constantinople visited the viceroy.[6] In the next year
the Shah was reported to be going to send fifty young
Persians to Cairo to be educated,[7] and early in 1840 a
Persian messenger arrived with valuable gifts.[8] All
these comings and goings may have been completely
innocent. But they coincided with a time of Russian

[1] India to Bombay, secret, August 1, 1839 (Ad. 1–220).
[2] Campbell, April 6, 1839 (F.O. 78–373).
[3] The same, July 11, 1839 (F.O. 78–374).
[4] Hodges, February 12, 1840 (F.O. 78–404).
[5] Ellis to Ponsonby, November 21, 1835 (F.O. 78–265).
[6] Campbell, March 19, 1838 (F.O. 78–342).
[7] The same, April 1, 1839 (F.O. 78–373).
[8] Hodges, February 6, 1840 (F.O. 78–404).

predominance at the Persian court; when all the remonstrances of the British agent had failed to dissuade
the Shah from undertaking the siege of Herat, and
when in 1838 an expedition had been despatched from
Bombay to occupy the Persian island of Karak in the
Gulf.

Other queer stories, too, were in the air. In 1835–6
two men arrived at Alexandria from Constantinople,
known respectively as Mahmud and Husain, whose
antecedents and designs were not a little questionable.
They were said to be mere adventurers, but had
visited Russia in the character of emissaries from the
court of Delhi. Mahmud was seen in Cairo and
Alexandria, but then disappeared. Husain some
months later landed with plague upon him. The
English vice-consul, who redeemed a strong partiality
for liquor by his knowledge of Turkish and Arabic, was
asked to take charge of his baggage, as the sick man
had 500 purses of money with him. Noticing the
Indian accent with which Husain spoke, the vice-
consul said he had met his companion when he passed
through the country; Husain admitted that this was so,
but was too ill to continue the conversation, and the
next day fell into a delirium from which he never
recovered. But his papers were secured from the
lazaretto. They proved to be letters in Persian from the
Grand Vazir to various Indian chiefs, together with a
letter of introduction in Turkish from the Vazir to
Muhammad 'Ali.[1]

The troubled political atmosphere inevitably invested Muhammad 'Ali's advance on to the Gulf with
a most suspicious air. The admiral on the East India
station was therefore desired to visit the Gulf and to use
all his influence to prevent any actual attack on

[1] Ponsonby to Campbell, March 31, 1836, and Campbell,
January 18, 1837 (F.O. 78–319).

Bahrein, though Auckland "would not in the absence of specific instructions from home authorize more decisive measures".[1] The attitude at London was much more decided. Ponsonby at Constantinople was ordered to enquire whether Muhammad 'Ali's conquests had been made in accordance with the wishes of the Porte.[2] Campbell at Alexandria was ordered to tell the viceroy that instructions had been sent to Admiral Maitland to prevent the occupation of Bahrein, if necessary by force,[3] and, a few days before this despatch was written, Campbell, acting on earlier instructions and news received from India, had insisted on positive orders being sent to Kurshid to leave Bahrein alone.[4]

At the same period Muhammad 'Ali's activity in Yemen had led to a very similar position at the entrance to the Red Sea. His victory over the Assiri Arabs in 1838 gave him for the moment an undoubted ascendancy in the region known ironically as Arabia Felix. He was disposed to regard the ruler of Aden as a mere dependent, subordinate to the Imam of San'a, who had been compelled to recognise the viceroy's authority.[5] Alternatively he claimed it as formerly part of the Turkish empire.[6]

It was not possible however to treat such claims seriously. The imam had no doubt attempted from time to time to establish his power over Aden; but nothing like a real, permanent control had ever been exercised by him, and British recognition that he had any suzerain powers would have been a gratuitous absurdity. The Turkish claim was equally imaginary. Aden had once been occupied by the Turks in the days

---

[1] India to Bombay, secret, March 13, 1839 (Ad. 1–220).
[2] To Ponsonby, May 11, 1839 (F.O. 78–352).
[3] To Campbell, June 15, 1839 (F.O. 78–372).
[4] Campbell, June 15, 1839 (F.O. 78–374).
[5] Artin Bey to Boghoz Bey, March 22, 1838 (F.O. 78–342).
[6] Campbell, June 9, 1838 (F.O. 78–343).

of Ottoman greatness in the sixteenth and seventeenth centuries. But, as it did not prosper under their rule, they abandoned it as valueless in 1630, and with their evacuation their rights disappeared. On various occasions in the recent past the British had come into friendly contact with the Sultan of Aden. When, in 1799, the British were anxious to block up the outlet of the Red Sea against the feared advance of Napoleon, they had occupied for a short time the island of Perim, that "stone in the sea belonging to the All-mighty, from which no revenue has or ever will be received"; but finding that hot and barren rock untenable, and having worn out or broken all their boring-rods in the fantastic hope of striking water, they removed for a while to Aden. There they were better off, and indeed it seemed almost a paradise in comparison with the little hell they had been occupying, while the sultan welcomed their presence and offered a constant supply of men for the Company's military service.[1] In 1802 Sir Home Popham actually concluded a treaty with the sultan. Valentia, who visited it in the course of his Red Sea travels, reported on it enthusiastically to Canning in 1808. After dwelling on the friendliness always shown by the sultan to the English, he continued, "It is the Gibraltar of the East, and at a trifling expense might be made impregnable".[2] In 1822, when our resident at Mokha visited the place, he found it on the verge of falling into Muhammad 'Ali's hands, the sultan having offered to admit a garrison and allow a small fort to be built on the eastern bay, provided he were to keep possession of the gates of the place, and exercise all civil and military authority within it.[3] Why

[1] From Murray, October 4, *ap*. Bombay Pol. Cons, December 17, 1799.
[2] Enc. in Valentia to Canning, September 13, 1808 (F.O. 1–1).
[3] Hutchinson to Bombay, March 27, 1822 (I.O., Egypt and Red Sea, 7).

Muhammad 'Ali did not take advantage of this opportunity does not appear; and Salt, our consul-general, expected him to do so.[1] He certainly then missed his chance of obtaining complete control of the Red Sea, just as, a little later in the Greek war, he missed the most favourable chance he ever had of securing recognition of his independence.

There matters remained until the project of the Suez route began to develop, and the need for coaling stations appeared. At first Socotra seems to have been chosen for that purpose, and the island was occupied by an expedition from Bombay in 1834–5. But it proved most unsuitable. The high surf made landing difficult; the island was full of malaria; so the idea was abandoned.[2] Already in 1829 Aden had been tried as a coal depot, on the occasion of the first experimental steam voyages from Bombay to Suez. But the *Hugh Lindsay* found she could not take in more than 30 tons a day on account of lack of labour, a very extraordinary reason in the view of a modern traveller.[3]

Then very early in 1837 a Madras-owned vessel under English colours, the *Darya Daulat*, went ashore near by. She was carrying pilgrims and the large donation that the Nawab of Arcot was in the pious custom of sending annually to Mecca. Such of the pilgrims as were not drowned were plundered by the Arabs, and all that could be got out of the wreck was seized under the direction of the sultan's eldest son and sold in the bazaars principally by the sultan's own agent.[4] On a detailed report of these occurrences, Sir Robert Grant, the Governor of Bombay, came to a prompt decision. "The establishment of a monthly communication by

[1] Salt to Hutchinson, December 7, 1822 (I.O., Egypt and Red Sea, 7).
[2] Low, *Indian Navy*, II, 74.
[3] *Idem*, II, 115.
[4] *Parl. Papers*, 1839, XL, 42.

steam with the Red Sea", he wrote, "and the formation of a flotilla of armed steamers renders it absolutely necessary that we should have a station of our own on the coast of Arabia, as we have in the Persian Gulf; and the insult which has been offered to the British flag by the Sultan of Aden has led me to enquiries which leave no doubt on my mind that we should take possession of the port of Aden."[1] He was probably influenced also by the Egyptian expansion in Yemen. Auckland, however, was less precipitate. He directed that reparation should be first required. If it were accorded, an amicable arrangement could be made about the coal depot; if it were refused, then further measures could be considered.[2]

Captain Haines of the Indian navy was therefore sent to discuss matters with the sultan. Early conversations went smoothly enough. After a long confabulation in which the sultan and his advisers "sat up all night with doors closed", the sultan, who was in great fear that Lahej, the capital of his ancestral territory, might be seized by the troops of Muhammad 'Ali, decided to transfer the decaying port of Aden to the East India Company in return for an unspecified number of dollars. He even attached his seal to a document ceding Aden to the English. But at that point troubles arose. His eldest son was opposed to the change, and Haines did not venture to land to complete the settlement.[3] On this news Grant again urged the pressing need "to secure for the British Government, at the only moment when such a step is likely to be practicable for centuries, a possession which unforeseen circumstances have placed within their reach".[4] But the government of India thought the question

---

[1] *Parl. Papers*, 1839, XL, p. 54.
[2] *Idem*, p. 55.   [3] *Idem*, pp. 56–61.
[4] *Idem*, p. 73.

should be determined by the home authorities.[1] Action was therefore delayed until the arrival in August of despatches from the secret committee,[2] on which Auckland authorised the Bombay government to proceed.[3] Haines was at once sent off, with a draft treaty in his pocket, and an escort of thirty men of the Bombay Europeans, for fear lest Muhammad 'Ali should swoop down upon Aden while a more imposing force was under preparation.[4]

Haines reached Aden on October 24, and, as anyone with a knowledge of the East might have anticipated, the inadequacy of his force encouraged the sultan's son earnestly to press his father not to accede to the English proposals. In this he succeeded. Plundered goods from the *Darya Daulat*, which had been given up and stored, were not allowed to be removed. A little later the Arabs, waxing bold, fired on the English boats. Haines retired to a small island to await reinforcements. They arrived on January 16, and two days later the town was carried by assault.

Sir Charles Malcolm, who as superintendent of the Bombay Marine had originally suggested "getting the cession from the Sultan...instead of getting permission for a coal-depot held at the will of an avaricious and capricious Arab chief", was delighted with the issue of events. "The harbour of Aden", he wrote, "with its capacious bay only open to the southward, surpasses my expectations. We could not have desired anything better to answer all our purposes...."[5]

[1] *Parl. Papers*, 1839, XL, p. 76.
[2] Secret Committee to India, May 30, 1838 (I.O., Board's Drafts No. 9).
[3] India to Bombay, September 3, Bombay Sec. Cons., October 3, 1838, No. 650.
[4] Governor's Minute, Bombay Sec. Cons., September 5, 1838, No. 488.
[5] Malcolm to Locke, January 18, 1839 (Brit. Mus. Add. MSS, 36470, f. 57).

This British occupation of Aden was a sharp disappointment to Muhammad 'Ali—far sharper, probably, than our insistence on his withdrawing from the Persian Gulf. It traversed his commercial as well as his political views. It was expected, for instance, although the expectation was never realised, that the whole trade of Mokha coffee would be removed from Mokha to Aden,[1] which would have meant the loss of a very valuable monopoly. The Egyptian commandant complained that the Mokha customs had already vanished.[2] Foreign nations, especially the French and the Russians, disliked a change which could not but strengthen the British position in the East. "I feel certain", Campbell wrote, "that they have worked, and will continue to work on the mind of Mehemet Ali, in giving him false and erroneous impressions of our views in the possession of Aden."[3] But with whatever inward feelings the viceroy regarded this approach of British authority, he carefully avoided protest and limited himself to a statement of wishes and hopes. On learning that the Indian governments had decided to suspend action till they could receive orders from home, Muhammad 'Ali observed "that he hoped the Indian government would be persuaded that Aden formed part of the Yemen..., and that he trusted the Indian government could not for a moment doubt with what pleasure he would permit the establishment of a coal depot there, as well as in any other part of his governments".[4] His nearest approach to a formal protest was the suggestion that it was not reasonable for us to have approved his

---

[1] Campbell, November 1, 1837 (F.O. 78–321).
[2] General commanding Yemen to Muhammad 'Ali, February 12, 1838 (F.O. 78–342).
[3] Campbell, March 27, 1838, and April 8, 1839 (F.O. 78–342 and 373).
[4] The same, June 9, 1838 (F.O. 78–343).

expedition into Yemen and then to seize one of its dependencies.[1]

But Palmerston was not to be appeased. With angry pencil he heavily underscored Muhammad 'Ali's reference to *his* governments, as though the possessive adjective were in itself treason against the viceroy's august master, Great Britain's trusted ally. As to our having sanctioned the expedition into Yemen, he tartly replied that we had raised no objection to Muhammad 'Ali's reducing his mutinous troops, but the expedition had been despatched long before our assent had been received.[2] When the viceroy suggested that it might be well to avoid frontier incidents by recalling his troops from Yemen, the Foreign Secretary retorted that he had no desire that the Egyptian occupation of Yemen should continue, "but on the contrary would be better pleased by any overt act which should show that the pasha is engaged in improving the administration of the provinces confided to his government instead of employing the energies of his mind and the resources of the country he governs in aggressive expeditions against neighbouring districts".[3] And even before Aden had been actually occupied, he warned the viceroy that "any hostile attempt...against Aden will be an attack upon a British possession and will be dealt with accordingly".[4]

From this time onward, as relations became tenser in consequence of the developments in Syria, Aden continued to contribute occasions of bitterness. Muhammad 'Ali was warned not to interfere with the Arab chiefs in the neighbourhood of the new British possession.[5] A little later it was suggested that the viceroy

---

[1] Campbell, April 17, 1838 and enc. (F.O. 78–342).
[2] To the same, May 12, 1838 (*ibid.*).
[3] To the same, May 24, 1838 (*ibid.*).
[4] To the same, June 8, 1838 (F.O. 78–343).
[5] To the same, May 11, 1839 (F.O. 78–372).

would do well to act on his own suggestion and evacuate Yemen altogether.[1] Then came reports that the Egyptians were stirring up chiefs to attack Aden, and the tactless, stupid consul-general who had replaced Campbell swallowed the whole story as literal and exact fact,[2] and, even when Muhammad 'Ali had wholly withdrawn from the country, reproached him with the conduct of those who had succeeded to his authority.[3]

Altogether the period which we have been considering, falling between the first and second Syrian wars, illustrates alike the strength and weakness of Muhammad 'Ali's policy and the actual inconsistency of its several parts. He saw quite clearly the great importance to him of British friendship. He always seems to have desired it. He was constantly seeking the means by which he could increase the value of his co-operation in English eyes. But there he quite misjudged his own position and the position of Great Britain. English and Egyptian interests were indeed closely interwoven. The development of the Suez route to India, gave us the strongest possible interest in preserving Egypt from any foreign domination (except perhaps our own), in promoting the stability of her government and the prosperity of her people, while British sea power rendered Britain the best possible ally for a country that could hardly be attacked but from the sea. An Anglo-Egyptian alliance was therefore a thoroughly sound conception. But from our own point of view there was a wide difference between Muhammad 'Ali, Pasha of Egypt, promoting order, justice, and education in the valley of the Nile, and Muhammad 'Ali, using up the population of his country in order to conquer Arabia

[1] To Campbell, September 13, 1839 (F.O. 78–372).
[2] Haines to Hodges, February 10, 1840 (F.O. 78–404).
[3] Hodges, February 22 and July 6, 1840 (F.O. 78–404 and 405).

and Syria, to spread his power eastwards to Basra and southwards to Aden, and threatening to convulse Europe by overturning the Turkish empire. Nothing could persuade Palmerston—and indeed in this he was entirely right—that British interests needed the support of a great military power in the Near East, such as Muhammad 'Ali, and especially his son Ibrahim, had it in mind to build up. British interests were to be protected by British arms. So the viceroy's expansion necessarily led to a conflict of interests and an opposition of policies. But equally clearly there was not, what some recent Egyptian writers have suggested, the least hostility to Egyptian greatness. Muhammad 'Ali could be as great as he pleased within the natural geographical limits of Egypt. But he was not to endanger the peace of Europe or undertake duties for Great Britain which Great Britain felt very well able to discharge for herself. Palmerston wisely and rightly preferred to establish his country's power in the Persian Gulf and at the entrance of the Red Sea rather than allow any other, however friendly his protestations, to occupy regions that were clearly destined to a high importance.

Chapter VI

THE SECOND SYRIAN WAR AND THE COL-
LAPSE OF MUHAMMAD 'ALI'S PLANS

The tendencies generated by the questions of the Red
Sea and the Persian Gulf unhappily corresponded in
direction and effect with tendencies generated by developments in the Levant. The settlement reached by
the Peace of Kutahia[1] had been no true settlement at
all, for it had left every party dissatisfied and desirous
of further changes, and in particular was this true of
the two principals in the struggle. At Constantinople
the Sultan, Mahmud, and his sar-'askar, Khusrau,
were bent, the one on recovering Syria, the other on
humiliating his old rival. On the other side Muhammad 'Ali had indeed secured a great accession of
territory, but he held it on the least satisfactory of
terms—on grants annually renewable and so annually
revocable by the Sultan. The pasha was growing old.
He could not look for many more years of life; and
what would become of his pashaliqs and of his family
when he died? His disappearance from the scene
would be the certain signal for a strong endeavour to
bring not only Syria but Egypt as well back under the
Sultan's immediate control. His family would be per-
secuted in revenge for his conduct. The countries in
which he had laboured to improve administration and
to spread knowledge would be given over to pashas of
the old school whose only object would be to shear the
people as closely as possible before they were recalled.
As far as Muhammad 'Ali could judge, neither his
family nor his reforms were likely long to survive their

[1] *Vide* pp. 121–2, *supra.*

founder, his own name would speedily pass away and
be forgotten, and the work to which he had devoted his
life and energy would vanish as though it had never
been. The older he grew, the more deeply was it borne
in upon him that his work was still completely un-
secured against future events.

The relations of the Sultan and the pasha immediately after the war showed how hollow had been their
reconciliation. There was the question of the tribute.
Even when the amount payable had been discussed and
settled, the Sultan still claimed arrears which Muhammad 'Ali absolutely refused to pay. While this matter
was pending, advantage was taken of the marriage of a
princess of the Sultan's family to send a special envoy
to the capital, ostensibly on a mission of congratulation, but in fact with a much more serious object. The
envoy was accompanied by a suite of twelve persons:
he was ordered to display all "the magnificence of a
vizir"; he was to distribute a million piastres in
presents.[1] But he was also to represent to Mahmud
that so long as Khusrau continued in the Divan, he
would always be seeking to misrepresent the pasha's
conduct, and that "if the sultan would only consent to
remove the seraskier[2] from his councils, he (the pasha)
would not only pay the tribute regularly..., but he
would also pay a great part of what the Sultan demanded as arrears". It was expected that various
influential enemies of Khusrau would be gathered together at Constantinople for the marriage, so that the
opportunity appeared promising.[3] However, the mission not only failed completely in its object but became
the occasion of slights directed at its sender. The envoy,
Habib Effendi, was not allowed to wear a flag on his

[1] Campbell, April 27, 1834 (F.O. 78–245).
[2] I.e. the sar-'askar.
[3] Campbell, May 10, 1834 (F.O. 78–245).

boat; he was not allowed an awning to shelter him from the sun; his rowers were not suffered to pull in the manner commonly used when conveying a person of distinction; the chief people at the capital were afraid to pay him any public visits, and would only receive him in private; and the Sultan himself showed displeasure when the crew of the frigate that had conveyed Habib to Constantinople manned the yards and cheered, European fashion, in acknowledgment of a gift of 50,000 piastres.[1]

In the course of the year 1834 the question of the tribute was at last arranged, on the basis of the customary rates without arrears. But that hardly signified any real improvement in the difficult and anomalous relations between Mahmud and Muhammad 'Ali. The former, for instance, took every occasion to stir up trouble in Syria. Ibrahim had introduced conscription into the province along with measures of protection for the Christian inhabitants. Both had excited great discontent; a revolt broke out in the country around Jerusalem; and matters became serious enough for the viceroy to visit Syria in person. There was no doubt that the revolt had been encouraged by agents from Constantinople, whose preaching might be reasonably inferred from an incident that occurred at Nablus. There a Turk mounted the minar of the mosque, and cried aloud: "Does the Muslim religion exist no longer? Is it dead? Are we not Turks? Let every man who loves the Prophet take up arms against that man without faith, the Giaour, Ibrahim Pasha! That drunkard who always drinks spirits and wine, who eats pork and every dirt that comes from the sea [alluding to Ibrahim Pasha's eating turtle and other sea-fish forbidden by the Mahometan religion], the same as the Christians do, who lives in the convents with the

---

[1] Campbell's Journal, July 15 and 16, 1834 (F.O. 78–246).

priests and prays with them, but never goes to the mosque".[1] However, vigorous measures were used. Three rebel chiefs brought in to Muhammad 'Ali were beheaded out of hand.[2] The rebellious districts were disarmed. The conscription was enforced. The pasha's power remained unshaken.

But the general position was full of danger. Each party heartily distrusted the other. Each began to prepare for the coming and decisive conflict. "Everything in Syria", wrote the British consul at Aleppo, "is military and every measure is being taken to increase the strength of the army." The defiles of the Taurus were fortified. The pasha's troops were concentrated behind his northern frontier. The position was the same on the other side of the border. Some 9000 men were assembled at Koniah.[3]

What aroused special attention and indeed particular disapproval in England was the conscription by which the pasha's military forces were kept up to strength and enlarged. This was an unwelcome novelty in Syria. The old pashas had never dreamt of such a thing. They had generally maintained Albanian or other foreign mercenaries, despising the military qualities of the native Syrians.[4] Muhammad 'Ali resolved to use them. He had no census to rely on, nor was any census possible. Nothing but Roman discipline could enforce a measure universally considered as unlucky in itself and certain to lead to new taxation. On these points the Syrians still cherished the beliefs they had held in the days of Augustus. The only method by which conscription could be enforced was to order a levy of a

[1] Campbell's Journal, June 30, 1834 (F.O. 78-245). The translation has been modified.
[2] The same, July 17, 1834 (F.O. 78-246).
[3] Werry to Campbell, June 2, 1835 (F.O. 78-257).
[4] Cf. *Memoirs of Lady Hester Stanhope*, II, 113 *sqq.*

specified number of men in a given area, and seize them by force. The Syrians, who much preferred suffering the insults of undisciplined mercenaries to serving in arms themselves, did everything in their power to avoid being caught. In Aleppo, for instance, when a levy of 10,000 men was ordered in 1833, men of military age went into hiding. Some took refuge within consular precincts, and their parents were bastinadoed within sight of the windows in the hope of making the refugees come out. Finally the heads of the quarters of the city were compelled to make up the quota.[1] In 1835 much the same was repeated with the same passive resistance. At Beyrout the mosques were surrounded and the males seized. At Aleppo houses and shops were closed. Trade ceased. For two days neither bread nor meat nor any other kind of provision could be procured. Many fled to the villages at the foot of the Taurus. Others, disguised as women, made their way over the frontier into the Sultan's territories, only to find that Mahmud was following Muhammad 'Ali's example and himself carrying out a conscription with great severity.[2]

These events were reported with much exaggeration, and excited much unfavourable comment. Campbell was directed to suggest confidentially but unofficially to Muhammad 'Ali that if conscription was really needed it should be made on regular lists, on an organised system, instead of men being seized promiscuously by military force "much in the manner in which a given number of wild animals would be caught out of a herd in the desert".[3] These general humanitarian sentiments were reinforced in certain directions by more particular interests. Sometimes this was justi-

[1] Campbell, February 3, 1834 and encl. (F.O. 78–245).
[2] The same, February 18, 1836 (F.O. 78–282).
[3] To the same, December 8, 1837 (F.O. 78–318).

fied, as when in 1835 the troops at Beyrout seized persons in the employment of the consulates; and on this occasion Muhammad 'Ali sent Colonel Sève (Sulaiman Pasha) to make a special enquiry, and invited the consuls-general at Alexandria to depute a person to accompany him.[1] Sometimes, however, Palmerston blazed up over premature and inaccurate reports. In 1835 he heard that Christians had been included as conscripts. "Europe", he wrote, "has a right to hope that the Christian subjects of the Porte who inhabit the countries which the Sultan has placed for the present under the administration of Mehemet 'Ali shall be exempted from that new conscription with which the pasha thinks proper to harass and afflict the Mahometan population whose interests and welfare have been committed to his keeping."[2] But Campbell, ignoring his indignant irony, was able to reply that no Christians had been conscripted. He had recently made a tour in Syria, where he had seen pilgrims with a cross tattooed on their arms, and he had learnt from them it was a common custom, which not only distinguished them from Muslims but also freed them from the fear of compulsory enrolment.[3]

But while humanitarian ideas and Christian sympathy contributed to the disapproval with which the powers, and particularly Great Britain, regarded the Syrian conscription, political considerations made it positively alarming. War between the Sultan and the pasha threatened the reappearance of the Russians and the confirmation of Russian influence at Constantinople under the Treaty of Unkiar Skelessi; and then Great Britain would have either to acquiesce in Russian predominance in the Straits or take up arms to destroy

---

[1] Campbell, September 5, 1835 (F.O. 78–258).
[2] To the same, May 9, 1836 (F.O. 78–281).
[3] Campbell, July 10, 1836 (F.O. 78–282).

it. Neither alternative could be viewed with composure. Muhammad 'Ali must therefore be restrained from attacking the Porte, or, if war could not be prevented, Great Britain must join Russia in supporting the Sultan. Repeated remonstrances were therefore addressed to the viceroy. At the end of 1837 Campbell urged upon him that the powers would not permit him "to keep up large armaments which could have no other effect than to embroil him with the Sultan and prevent the pacification of the east".[1] Palmerston sent loud warnings "of the evil consequences which will infallibly result to himself if he recommences an attack upon any part of the sultan's dominions. You will also represent to the pasha that his extensive conscription, his active military preparations, and his concentration of troops in Syria, are all calculated to excite great distrust as to his intentions with respect to the Porte".[2] But to all remonstrances Muhammad 'Ali had an answer that was difficult to rebut. Mahmud was reorganising his own army; German officers, including the famous von Moltke, were being employed to train and discipline them; fifty-one new regiments, it was reported, were being formed. But the Porte was involved in no foreign war and had no internal rebellion to crush. The preparations must then be directed against Egypt, and the viceroy's measures were dictated by the heartiest desire for peace[3]—a mere eastern version of *Si vis pacem....*

Both Great Britain and France found this rejoinder very irritating. Their consuls-general were instructed to make the strongest representations, and twice in March, 1838, Palmerston wrote on the subject, first demanding a categorical explanation of Muhammad

[1] Campbell, December 12, 1837 (F.O. 78–321).
[2] To the same, February 6, 1838 (F.O. 78–342).
[3] Campbell, February 7, 1838 (*ibid.*).

'Ali's intentions,[1] and later warning him of the dangerous consequences of war. "You will point out to the pasha", he continued in this second despatch, "that he ought to be sensible that his talents and energies, great as all the world know them to be, will find ample scope for their exertion in establishing a good system of administration in the countries already subject to his rule."[2]

But in spite of his fine words and moral indignation Palmerston was not taking, perhaps from his position he could not take, a fair view of the situation. He was demanding of the viceroy what could not possibly be conceded save to force. Campbell had suggested a much juster attitude when at the end of 1837 he had written, "I cannot but feel that if it were possible for Mehemet 'Ali to be secured against any aggression on the part of the Porte, and that he were at the same time obliged to reduce his army and navy to a fixed standard, and prohibited from raising conscriptions in any part whatsoever of his governments, the beneficial change of these measures would be speedily visible in every part of the country".[3] This seems entirely true. Nothing but some such guarantee could free the viceroy from the need of arming unless he was prepared to hand over to the Sultan any of his governments that the Sultan chose to demand. Unfortunately the Russian position made any such guarantee impossible. Palmerston therefore adopted the official theory that Muhammad 'Ali was merely a servant and minister of the Sultan, that the Sultan had every right to require the restoration of his territories at any time, and that the viceroy's warlike preparations were illegal, disloyal, treasonable. So they were in the theory of the Otto-

---

[1] To Campbell, March 16, 1838 (F.O, 78–342).
[2] To the same, March 29, 1838 (*ibid.*).
[3] Campbell, December 21, 1837 (F.O. 78–321).

man empire. But where lies the point at which worn-out fictions such as this cease to bind? In India the government of the East India Company had resolved that it was freed from all obligation to the Moghul Emperor as soon as he quitted their protection and cast in his lot with their possible enemies, the Marathas. Every reasonable person had always held that they were justified. Muhammad 'Ali's position was not wholly unlike that of the Honourable East India Company. The main difference lay rather in political environment than in political principle. Warren Hastings' rejection of the authority of Shah Alam did not imperil the peace of Europe; Muhammad 'Ali's rejection of the authority of Sultan Mahmud would endanger it. While therefore the great pasha deserved sympathy in his endeavours to make permanent the reforms which he had introduced and to save them from the blight of Turkish administration, there still remained, quite apart from the unconvincing arguments on which Palmerston's official case was rested, strong and valid reasons for his policy. In this world major interests must be suffered to prevail, and the consolidation of Muhammad 'Ali's power or even the maintenance of his reforms could not be reckoned to outbalance the evils of a general war. "The great object of the British Government", Palmerston had said in 1833, and it still was true, "is the maintenance of peace...; we are averse to any great changes in the relative distribution of political power because such changes must either be brought about by war or must have a tendency when effected to produce war."[1]

The nature, efficacy and ideas of Muhammad 'Ali's administration must be reserved for treatment in a separate chapter. But, whatever their real value, it was an important element in Palmerston's policy that he

[1] To Campbell, October 2, 1833 (F.O. 78–226).

regarded them with a large measure of distrust. The liberal statesman thought the benevolent, humanitarian, enlightened objects which men said the pasha had set before himself completely inconsistent with the violent seizure of men to serve in the pasha's armies; the whig landlord could not conceive just government compatible with expropriation; while western economists condemned with one voice the trade monopolies which the pasha had set up. These general reasons strongly indisposed him to sympathise with Muhammad 'Ali's claims and views. When Campbell alludes to the viceroy's protection of property, Palmerston comments, "Except that of the people whom he governs", and, when the consul-general refers to the pasha's benevolence, the foreign secretary adds, "I.e. war and conquest and plunder and conscription and monopoly".[1] These expressions, valueless as an estimate of Muhammad 'Ali's work, undoubtedly help to explain Palmerston's conduct in the crisis that was impending.

Nor were these views merely the product of general ideas and the irritation created by the pasha's inconvenient activity. The administration of Syria, as I shall show later, had been less successful than the administration of Egypt, and its defects had been artfully elaborated by sinister interests. The decay of Turkish administration, the neglect of the pashas, the growing inferiority of Turkish military power, and the consequent timidity of the Divan in matters of external policy, had encouraged the growth of extraordinary abuses of the Turkish capitulations. The consuls claimed to be exempt from all but certain fixed dues and to be able to extend this privilege to all whom they employed and to all whom they recognised as their nationals. Layard records that at Salonika most of the

[1] Campbell's Report on Egypt (F.O. 78–408 B).

consuls lived on the sale of passports and protections to the native Christians.[1] In Syria these abuses had been carried on without check. "The consuls and agents", Campbell wrote, "used to protect an unlimited number of rayas of the country, under the denomination of brokers to the merchants, honorary dragomans, etc., and these protections were sold by them to the rayas, some of whom being rich were ready to give large sums for a protection which withdrew them from Turkish jurisdiction."[2] Lady Hester Stanhope, with no better excuse than her own autocratic temperament, gave no less than seventy-seven protections, some to persons of wealth, and nearly all to persons who were not in her service or at all events drew no pay from her. The consuls too were always issuing certificates declaring goods in the Turkish customs houses to be for their personal use (and so exempt from duty or examination) when everyone knew that they were merely covering goods belonging to native merchants.[3] The establishment of Muhammad 'Ali's rule in Syria, involving the introduction of conscription, greatly enhanced the money value of consular protection. Colonel Sève, who had been sent to enquire into the violation of consular buildings,[4] brought back a severe report, confirmed by the consuls-general's agent who had accompanied him. The dragomans were mostly rich native merchants, who, far from being able to interpret for the consuls, knew no language but Arabic; the janissaries kept shops or followed a trade; the clerks were merchants, and some rich. Most of these nominal employees were either above discharging their duties or incapable of doing so,

[1] Layard, *Autobiography*, II, 25. The reader will notice the similarity to the practice of the East India Company's servants in Bengal between 1757 and 1765.
[2] Campbell, June 19, 1834 (F.O. 78–245).
[3] *Ibid.*
[4] *Vide* p.159, *supra.*

but they paid handsomely for their offices, and the more so because consular protection was held to extend not only to their employees, but to their employees' families and servants.[1] Campbell himself furnished specific examples of abuses occurring within his own knowledge. At Beyrout in 1836 he had found the British consul protecting a cargo of wheat which proved to have been shipped by one Greek and consigned to another.[2] When therefore on Muhammad 'Ali's legitimate complaints the consuls-general at Alexandria advised that these profitable protections should be limited[3] at the very moment when they promised to be more profitable than ever, the irony of events bit deep into the consuls' hearts. Far better, they felt, had been the easy days of Turkish misgovernment, when (for a consideration) a raya could easily obtain Russian or French or British status, than the regular system of profitless reforms that were being introduced from Egypt. Their reports inevitably reflected their lacerated feelings and empty hands. Campbell had frequent reason to remark "the extreme eagerness and avidity" with which some of them seized upon every trifle likely to indispose His Majesty's Government against the viceroy. They reported monopolies which had never been established.[4] They demanded that British dragomans, who were Levantines of low birth and small education, should be received with the same distinction as French dragomans, who were educated Europeans, bearing their sovereign's commission, and entitled in due course to promotion to consular rank.[5]

[1] Campbell, November 22, 1835 (F.O. 78–258).
[2] The same, July 19, 1837 (F.O. 78–320).
[3] The regulations are given in Campbell, November 22, 1835 (*ut supra*). They were ratified promptly by Austria, France and Russia. The same, April 4, 1839 (F.O. 78–376).
[4] Campbell, December 3, 1836 (F.O. 78–284).
[5] The same, September 22, 1837 (F.O. 78–320).

And one even got up a bogus petition against the Egyptian authorities, in support of indefensible abuses.[1]

Nor did they lack a convenient channel of communication with the British embassy at Constantinople. The second dragoman there, Richard Wood, was brother-in-law of Consul Moore at Beyrout. His temper may be judged from the following incident. When Campbell was touring in Syria in 1836, he met this man at Beyrout, and listened to a harrowing account of Ibrahim's cruelties in suppressing a recent revolt, and in particular of his having burnt to the ground no less than thirty villages. What were their names? asked Campbell. Wood did not know. Had he seen them? No, but he had been told so. Campbell very properly begged Consul Moore to verify the statement. But although Moore was unable to do so, Wood nevertheless reported the story as a fact to Ponsonby, the ambassador.[2] These consular reports must have fallen in aptly with Palmerston's frame of mind, ruffled by the clashes of policy described in the last chapter, and thoroughly irritated by the threat to the peace of Europe implicit in the relations between Muhammad 'Ali and the Sultan. He was thus strongly predisposed by his view of the European situation and his disbelief in the reality of Muhammad 'Ali's reforms to support the Sultan rather than the pasha.

The attitude of France was somewhat different. The French had never regarded the Ottoman empire as sacrosanct. They had not hesitated to detach Algiers from it. They had on one occasion sent a minister plenipotentiary direct to Alexandria.[3] Louis-Philippe had in private conversation spoken of Muhammad 'Ali's independence as a thing certain to be achieved in

[1] Campbell, October 9, 1837 (F.O. 78–320).
[2] The same, July 31, 1836 (F.O. 78–283).
[3] *Vide* p. 121, *supra*.

time.[1] The French had provided officers for the army, the marine, the dockyard and arsenals, of the pasha. French financiers had offered him a loan.[2] The French consul-general maintained close and friendly relations with him. Like the English, the French wanted peace in Europe; but, unlike the English, they were disposed to seek it by preventing the Sultan from attacking Syria rather than by preventing Muhammad 'Ali from strengthening himself against the Turk. Their first plan was to reconcile the two. "To France belongs the duty of uniting the two halves of the empire", wrote Mimaut, the French consul-general. In the course of 1836 the French ambassador at the Porte was directed to offer French mediation. Apparently the French were willing to guarantee Muhammad 'Ali's position for life provided he reduced his army and marine by half, which would allow the Porte to do the like;[3] and the ambassador, on the eve of returning to Paris to confer with Thiers and the French consul-general with Muhammad 'Ali, declared to the Reis Effendi that the Porte's hostility against the viceroy must be abandoned.[4] As a result of these suggestions and of obscure discussions between the French authorities, the Porte, and agents of Muhammad 'Ali,[5] it was decided to send Sarim Effendi on a special mission to Egypt. But this was only one more example of the Porte's habitual bad faith. At the moment when it appeared to be complying with French wishes, it was writing (with perhaps equal sincerity) to its minister in London that it was seeking to content the French ambassador "without

[1] Campbell, May 30, 1833 (F.O. 78–227).
[2] The same, October 12 and 24, 1833 (F.O. 78–228). Cf. Sabry, *op. cit.* pp. 311 *sqq.*
[3] The same, October 30, 1836 (F.O. 78–284). Cf. Sabry, *op. cit.* p. 319.
[4] Sabry, *op. cit.* p. 320.
[5] Campbell, December 20, 1836 (F.O. 78–284).

opening the door of our mind" and that Great Britain was the only power on whom the Turks could rely.[1] When Sarim reached Alexandria, Muhammad 'Ali found that he was sent merely to flatter him and sound his views. A couple of days after his emergence from the quarantine which fear of plague inflicted on all arrivals from Constantinople, Muhammad 'Ali received Campbell in audience. Their talk chanced to turn on the fits of madness that gossip attributed to the Emperor Nicholas. "I do not believe", said the pasha, "that he is the only sovereign who is so. Mine also does not appear to be right in his head," for he had sent an envoy to arrange for the co-operation of Cairo and Constantinople without empowering him to offer terms.[2] In later discussions Sarim proposed an hereditary tenure of Egypt and Acre, while the pasha insisted that the offer must include all his existing territories.[3] The mission was therefore as complete a failure as the Divan had intended. But the obstacles to a good understanding had been rendered more evident than ever.[4] The bad faith of Constantinople was invincible.

The French share in this abortive overture was well known; and it was generally thought that but for their encouragement and support Muhammad 'Ali would have paid more attention to Palmerston's representations. They certainly were eager to keep the pasha on his guard against what they believed to be a consistent British hostility.[5] And it seems to have been Metternich's policy to promote British suspicion of French plans. All that his agents could discover, steal or invent

[1] Sabry, *op. cit.* pp. 320–1.
[2] Campbell, January 21, 1837 (F.O. 78–319).
[3] *Idem*, and January 27, 1837 (*ibid.*).
[4] The same, April 11, 1837 (*ibid.*).
[5] E.g. instructions to Cochelet as consul-general, September 12, 1837, *ap.* Sabry, *op. cit.* pp. 325 *sqq.*

in this connection was freely placed at the disposal of their British colleagues. De Laurin, the Austrian consul-general, communicated to Campbell not only his despatches to his own furtive Foreign Office, but also documents which he had "conveyed" from the French consulate. He once showed to Campbell, for instance, a letter from Colonel Sève to Mimaut, with marginal comments and signature in Mimaut's own hand.[1] Nor were the French obstructed in the execution of their policy only by dishonest Turks or foreign mischief-makers. With that lack of disciplined subordination which their agents in the East had ever displayed, Roussin at Constantinople or Sebastiani at London might hold language quite inconsistent with the views of the French cabinet.[2]

At last in 1838 Muhammad 'Ali, finding that he had in no wise benefited by the well-meant French endeavours, resolved upon bringing matters to a crisis. This was fancied at the British embassy at Constantinople to be the result of Russian advice. The idea had obsessed the embassy for some years, and there are grounds for thinking that it was promoted by vexed Levantine consuls.[3] Campbell did not believe the story. He pointed out that its truth was hardly consistent with the recall of the late consul-general of Russia before his intrigues had been completed or with the rarity of his successor's visits to the pasha.[4] And in this matter, as in most cases where Egypt was concerned, Campbell's information was better and his conclusions more accurate than those of our impulsive, intemperate ambassador.[5]

[1] Campbell, October 9, 1837, and enc. (F.O. 78–320).
[2] E.g. memo. by Palmerston, July 19, 1838 (F.O. 96–19).
[3] Cf. Wood to Ponsonby, December 31, 1835 (F.O. 195–107).
[4] Campbell, March 21, 1838 (F.O. 78–342).
[5] The correspondence of the Russian consulate, in course of publication, will, I believe, be found to confirm this view.

What external influence moved the pasha to his next step was not the sinister promptings of Russian diplomatists, but the sincere and freely expressed sentiments of merchants, both French and British. I have already mentioned their regret that he was not to be allowed to add Baghdad to the number of his cities.[1] Such feelings might perhaps have been explained away as the ignorant desires of men trading under the burden of corrupt incompetence. But they were held not only by the European merchants of Baghdad but by those of Cairo and Alexandria as well, and by their partners and correspondents at London, Paris and Marseilles. The pasha might pursue a system of monopolies, but under his rule as nowhere else in the Levant strict order and severe justice were established. His was a government with which bargains might safely be made. French and English merchants, however their governments might differ, were emphatically agreed in desiring that his rule should be maintained and perpetuated. Waghorn, for instance, the active transit agent for the Suez route, seems to have assured the pasha that Britain would recognise his independence.[2] British merchants refused to quit Cairo and Alexandria when the British consul-general withdrew and when British forces were attacking Ibrahim in Syria; and when the troubles were all over in 1842, a committee was formed in London to strike a gold medal to commemorate the protection which the pasha had "nobly afforded" to British residents in Egypt,[3] while our consul-general was highly embarrassed at being desired to present to him an address from the Bengal Chamber of Commerce, applauding the dignified and impressive

[1] *Vide* p. 126, *supra*.
[2] Campbell, April 16, 1838, and enc. (F.O. 78–342). Cf. passage marked for omission in confidential to Campbell, June 9, 1838 (F.O. 78–343).
[3] Hoskins, *op. cit.* p. 290.

example which he had set to the nations of Christendom.[1] He must, I think, be excused for mistakenly supposing that the popular view could not remain without influence on a popular government.

On May 25, 1838, Muhammad 'Ali therefore made a formal declaration of his intentions to the French and British consuls-general, and a little later to their Austrian and Russian colleagues. He told them he had resolved to declare his independence of the Sultan. For this he gave two reasons—his family's future, and the maintenance of his reforms. Campbell reports him as saying "that he never can consent that all that which he has been toiling for, and all the useful and costly establishments founded by him at an enormous expense, such as his arsenals, his fleet, his steam vessels, his manufactories with European machines and with workmen either European or natives who have been educated by him at great expense in Europe, the numerous useful schools and literary institutions which he has established entirely on the European system, the mines which he has opened both of coal and iron in Syria, and the roads and canals made there and in Egypt—he cannot, he says, ever permit all those establishments to revert to the Porte and be lost at his death, and that he should have the pang of feeling that all his labours should merely have been for the Porte which would allow them to go to ruin, whilst his own family and children would be exposed to want and perhaps even to be put to death".[2]

This proposal met at once with the strongest discouragement from both France and Great Britain. Cochelet was instructed to say that both states "were resolved if necessary to use coercive measures to contain Mehemet 'Ali in his duty of vassal to his

[1] Barnett, September 30, 1841 (F.O. 78–451).
[2] Campbell, May 25, 1838 (F.O. 78–342).

sovereign".[1] Campbell, with abundance of moral advice, was to express the English cabinet's deep concern mingled with hopes of a more just and prudent decision.[2] But it was still hoped that the crisis might be relieved without any actual explosion. Just at this time it was feared that the Sultan's fleet might appear off the Egyptian coast. Muhammad 'Ali declared that if it did he would attack and destroy it in person.[3] Palmerston at once suggested that the Turkish fleet might cruise in company with the British Mediterranean squadron, and go wherever that might go. This, he thought, would reassure France and the pasha and demonstrate that the Turkish squadron was out for exercise and instruction only, while it would also evince a close union between Turkey and Great Britain.[4]

Meanwhile the pasha received his discouraging answers with considerable calm, merely saying that he could not forgo his design, but that he hoped "the great powers would take a more just and equitable determination in his favour".[5] At this moment his hopes seem to have centred on the possibility of coming to some agreement with the Porte so as to cut away the technical grounds on which the great powers were resisting his proposals. Money was undoubtedly more powerful at Constantinople than at any other European capital. He had already enquired of Medem, the Russian consul-general, and of Campbell what their respective courts would do in case he arranged with the Turks for their recognition of him as an hereditary or independent ruler. He had received little encourage-

---

[1] Campbell, July 17, 1838 (F.O. 78–343).
[2] To the same, July 7, 1838 (ibid.).
[3] The same, July 12, 1838 (ibid.).
[4] To Ponsonby, July 25, 1838 (F.O. 78–329 A).
[5] Campbell, August 11, 1838 (F.O. 78–343).

ment from either.[1] But the French were more favourable. Early in the following year, 1839, they were still
anxious to induce the pasha to abstain from hostilities
by holding out the hope of some "arrangement being
made with the Sultan favourable to the future position
of his descendants".[2] But this proposal Palmerston was
unwilling to accept, at all events unless the pasha
would give up most of Syria.[3]

Much encouraged by the general European attitude,
which promised strong protection in case of defeat,
Sultan Mahmud resolved upon the war which he had
been so long preparing. Russian agents seem to have
played the chief part of provocation, expecting that the
Turks would be well beaten and would then summon
the Russians back to Constantinople.[4] In February
Ponsonby learnt that Mahmud had determined to
make war in the spring.[5] He was reported to have sent
an order to the Grand Council of his ministers, saying
that the sar-'askar, Hafiz Pasha, reported his army
able to beat Muhammad 'Ali's, that the Capitan Pasha
declared the fleet able to destroy the Egyptian fleet,
and that it therefore remained for the Council courage-
ously to do its duty.[6] Hafiz indeed and his German
officers were incessant in their demands to march
against Ibrahim in Syria.[7] In April therefore the Turks
crossed the Euphrates at Bir. For two months nothing
happened. Russia promptly demanded that Ibrahim
should retire towards Damascus, promising in that
event to induce the Sultan to withdraw from the

---

[1] Medem, March 20/April 1, 1838; and Campbell, July 9, 1838
(F.O. 78–343).
[2] Granville, February 15, 1839 (F.O. 27–580).
[3] Cf. to Beauvale, June 28, 1839 (F.O. 7–278).
[4] Ponsonby, January 27, 1839 (F.O. 78–354).
[5] The same, February 12, 1839 (*ibid.*).
[6] The same, March 7, 1839 (*ibid.*).
[7] The same, March 19, 1839 (F.O. 78–355).

Syrian frontier.[1] The pasha's reply was a declaration
that Ibrahim should retire as soon as the Turks had re-
passed the Euphrates, and that if the four great powers
would guarantee him from attack and support his
desire of an hereditary succession, he would withdraw
some of his men from Syria altogether and be prepared
to accept a definite agreement.[2] The French addressed
an urgent demand to Mahmud, calling on him to avoid
hostilities, and declaring that unless Hafiz recrossed the
Euphrates he would be deemed the aggressor.[3] At the
same time they called upon Muhammad 'Ali to withdraw as well.[4] By the middle of June the pasha, tired
of waiting for some acceptable proposal, while the
Turkish commander sought to raise a rebellion in
Ibrahim's rear, announced that he must at last give his
son liberty to act.[5] On June 24, therefore, two hours
after daybreak Ibrahim attacked Hafiz's camp at
Nazib. The German officers abounded with reasons
why the Turks should have won.[6] But the action was
more of a rout than a battle. Ibrahim captured all the
Turks' cannon and baggage, and their army vanished.

This brilliant success was immediately followed by
two other pieces of good fortune. On July 1 was
announced the death of Sultan Mahmud.[7] Disappointment and anxiety had told heavily upon him. Some
months earlier the master of his wardrobe had without
his knowledge caused his dresses to be taken in so as
not to hang too loosely on his shrunken form,[8] and he

---

[1] Campbell, May 7, 1839 (F.O. 78–373).   [2] *Ibid.*
[3] Ponsonby, June 16, 1839 (F.O. 78–356).
[4] Campbell, June 16, 1839 (F.O. 78–374).
[5] The same, June 14, 1839 (*ibid.*).
[6] Ponsonby, July 8, 1839 (F.O. 78–356).
[7] Beauvale, July 11, 1839 (F.O. 7–281), says the death had
occurred on the 29th and had been concealed for thirty-six hours.
[8] MacCarthy and Caratheodory, *Maladie...de...Mahmoud II*,
p. 20.

had followed the preparations for his attack upon Muhammad 'Ali with incessant anxiety, which, it was said, he sought to relieve with forbidden liquors. His obstinate hatred had made him a dangerous enemy, and the pasha had good cause to rejoice at his death. He was succeeded by his eldest son, Abdul Majid, a boy of sixteen, brought up in the harim, with a dwarf and two black eunuchs for his favourite companions.[1] Although Mahmud's obstinacy had been enlightened by but few sparks of intelligence, the counsels of the empire would evidently be enfeebled by his death unless some external guidance could be found.

And while Ibrahim's victory and Mahmud's death were still in all men's mouths, the Turkish fleet appeared off Alexandria, not to bombard the city, but to join the pasha. It has commonly been supposed that this result had been brought about by bribery. But other reasons suffice by themselves to explain the conduct of the commander, the Capitan Pasha. Ahmad Mushir, who held that office, had been ordered to sail for the Syrian coast in order to co-operate with the efforts of Hafiz to raise revolts against Muhammad 'Ali, and for this purpose he had some 6000 troops aboard his fleet.[2] But when he had passed the Dardanelles, he received new orders to proceed to Rhodes. This aroused his suspicions, and he then learnt from the captain who had brought the orders that at Rhodes he was to be dispossessed of his command and the fleet returned to Constantinople. He assembled his officers, told them he was convinced Khusrau meant to give the fleet up to the Russians, and that it would be better to join Muhammad 'Ali, with which they all agreed.[3] He

---

[1] Beauvale, July 10, 1839 (F.O. 7–281).
[2] Campbell, July 11, 1839 (F.O. 78–374).
[3] The same, July 17, 1839 (F.O. 78–375). Cf. Ponsonby, July 8, 1839 (F.O. 78–356).

had always been an enemy of Khusrau. Mahmud's death threatened to invest Khusrau with greater authority than ever. It was natural for Ahmad therefore to proceed to Alexandria and propose to join Muhammad 'Ali in overthrowing the common enemy of both. What would have been an act of treason in a European state was in Turkish politics a mere act of prudent foresight. "I have never known a Turk", wrote Campbell, ". . . who was not in all his acts guided by his own interest, or by ambition of power and the desire to overthrow his personal opponent."[1]

This defection seemed to place the game in Muhammad 'Ali's hands. There was no force to hinder Ibrahim from marching upon the Bosphorus by land, while the united fleets appeared before Constantinople. Ponsonby was sure that the forts at the Dardanelles would show no vigour in opposing them, and that a new Divan might be formed in which Muhammad 'Ali's friends would have a decided control.[2] But the pasha, in accordance with his general principles of moderation, does not seem to have wished to go so far. As soon as he had heard of Mahmud's death, he ordered Ibrahim to suspend hostilities. The day after Ahmad had dropped anchor in the harbour of Alexandria, a messenger arrived with a letter from Khusrau, formally announcing Abdul Majid's accession. It was gracious in tone. The Sultan pardoned the pasha's conduct towards his deceased father, promised new honours and the hereditary government of Egypt and its dependencies, and engaged the pasha to promote the prosperity of the empire.[3] These were not terms with which Muhammad 'Ali was prepared to be content. But he

[1] Campbell to Ponsonby, July 16, 1839 (F.O. 78–375).
[2] Ponsonby, July 21, 1839 (F.O. 78–357).
[3] Campbell, July 11, 1839 (F.O. 78–374). Cf. Ponsonby, July 2 and 3, 1839 (F.O. 78–356).

COLLAPSE OF MUHAMMAD 'ALI'S PLANS 177

was confident he could now obtain what he really wanted, the hereditary government of his existing possessions, and spoke publicly of proceeding to pay his personal homage to the young Sultan.

But "Ottoman ministers are an abject, miserable sort of men".[1] Khusrau, essentially false, and incapable of honest dealing, had sent other letters to Egypt as well as his gracious one to the pasha. He wrote to four of the chief officers of the fleet exhorting them to seize the Capitan Pasha and bring him back to Constantinople. Muhammad 'Ali at once took up the challenge. He wrote to Khusrau calling upon him to resign his office since he could be trusted by neither the chief men nor the "nation" in general,[2] and he sent out a circular to the pashas of the empire demanding their aid in removing this unworthy Grand Vazir, whose conduct had never benefited either the throne or the "nation", and who had been the cause of all the evils that for years had afflicted the state.[3] And at Constantinople men's hearts failed them for fear. The only plan that Khusrau could devise to save him from the impending danger was to comply with the demands that the pasha had made, for the hereditary government of all his territories. But just as this decision had been taken, the Internuncio received instructions from Metternich that transformed the situation. To the Austrian minister, as to Soult at Paris and Palmerston at London, the situation threatened the possibility of Russian intervention under the Treaty of Unkiar Skelessi. The Internuncio was therefore ordered to engage the representatives of France, Prussia, Russia and Great Britain to join with him in presenting a note to the Porte declaring that an agreement between the five powers was

[1] Ponsonby, July 8, 1839 (F.O. 78–356).
[2] Enc. in Ponsonby, August 6, 1839 (F.O. 78–357).
[3] Enc. in Campbell, July 28, 1839 (F.O. 78–375).

assured and that the Porte would do well to take no action without their concurrence. The note was signed the very day the instructions were received and it was delivered to Khusrau early next morning.[1] It gave the Vazir courage enough to reverse the decision which he had taken. By order of the ambassadors their note was communicated to Muhammad 'Ali on August 6. He was deeply preoccupied and his expression betrayed the uneasiness which this new and unexpected change caused him.[2]

Ponsonby was delighted at this development. He suffered from a highly virulent form of Russophobia, and smelt Russian intrigue in everything that transpired. He was particularly convinced that the pasha was sold to Russian interests, and had inoculated Palmerston with his ideas. So early as 1836, a question of trading dues which Muhammad 'Ali had reduced for Russian goods but had been unwilling to lower for British commodities, had been deemed to confirm reports "that there is a closer understanding between the Pasha and the Russian Government than either of the two parties have hitherto acknowledged".[3] Now everything that the pasha did was ascribed to Russian influence. There was an understanding between him, Russia, and Persia.[4] Russia was visibly favouring his cause.[5] A new party had been formed to overthrow Khusrau with Russian aid.[6] In vain did Campbell use every argument he could think of to dispel this illusion. Our sharp-nosed ambassador could not even detect anything queer in the Russian ambassador's readily signing the joint note when his great aim was supposed to

[1] Ponsonby, July 29, 1839 (F.O. 78–357).
[2] Campbell, August 7, 1839, and enc. (F.O. 78–375).
[3] To the same, November 22, 1836 (F.O. 78–281).
[4] Ponsonby to Campbell, July 5, 1839 (F.O. 78–375).
[5] Ponsonby, August 19, 1839 (F.O. 78–358).
[6] The same, August 21, 1839 (ibid.).

be the maintenance of the old precarious situation in order to secure the accomplishment of Russian aims.[1]

The first thing to be done was to prevent the pasha from acting while Europe heavily deliberated. In this both France and England were agreed. The French consul-general warned Muhammad 'Ali that the French and British squadrons might be used for coercive measures. Palmerston wrote, "The pasha must be well aware that he is not in a position which, either geographically or politically or with reference either to military or naval considerations, can enable him with impunity to set at defiance the governments of Europe and more especially the maritime powers".[2]

It was significant that at this time the Foreign Office decided to recall Colonel Campbell. He had then been serving in Egypt since 1833. He had watched closely the progress of the pasha's policy, both internal and external. He had travelled extensively in Egypt, in Syria and Crete. He was no blind admirer of the pasha, whose conduct on occasion he could criticise with due severity; but his conciliating manners, his persuasive address, his commanding presence, his sound, just judgment, had given him great influence with Muhammad 'Ali, who regarded him as a personal friend. But he had forgotten his own interest. When the tide of diplomatic opinion had begun to run against the pasha, Campbell had sought to stem it. He had tried to disabuse Ponsonby of his Russian fantasy. He had pointed out with untimely truth that the Jews and Christians of Syria would suffer acutely if they were restored to the direct rule of the Sultan.[3] He had dared to suggest that the Turkish empire might be restored to progress and prosperity if Khusrau were removed from office and

[1] Ponsonby, August 20, 1839 (F.O. 78–358).
[2] To Campbell, September 13, 1839 (F.O. 78–372).
[3] Campbell, August 7, 1839 (F.O. 78–375).

Muhammad 'Ali invited to co-operate in its reform.[1] It was unbearable that a man who merely knew the people and conditions of Egypt and Syria, and who had only seen with his own eyes the good that had been done, should even hint his disagreement with the official view that Muhammad 'Ali's reforms were sham; and it was monstrous that, on learning of Muhammad 'Ali's demand that Khusrau should be removed from his office, he had not expressed the shocked surprise he would have felt on hearing that Lord Auckland in a fit of madness had demanded that Lord Palmerston should cease to be Secretary of State.[2] In September he was curtly informed that Palmerston intended to advise his recall[3]—a measure which the minister had been contemplating for a year.[4] By an ironical chance the news of Keane's occupation of Kabul could only be forwarded without delay to Malta by a steamer which the pasha placed at Colonel Campbell's disposal.[5]

Colonel Hodges, Campbell's successor, reached Alexandria in December, 1839.[6] He proved to be hot-tempered, blustering and quarrelsome. He began by quarrelling with the packet agent at Alexandria for charging him postage in accordance with instructions from the Postmaster-General.[7] He went on to confide in a most intemperate vice-consul who carried tales well calculated to inflame both the consul-general and

[1] Campbell to Ponsonby, August 6, 1839 (F.O. 78–375).
[2] Cf. despatch to Campbell, August 13, 1839 (F.O. 78–372). Palmerston does not, of course, draw the parallel I suggest, but it seems to represent his feelings.
[3] To Campbell, September 11, 1839 (*ibid.*).
[4] Palmerston's note, October 26, 1838 (F.O. 78–344).
[5] Campbell, October 12, 1839 (F.O. 78–375).
[6] The same, December 18, 1839 (*ibid.*).
[7] Hodges (consular), January 23, and to Hodges, July 3, 1840 (F.O. 78–407).

the Foreign Minister.[1] His own conduct won him the cordial dislike of the whole consular body, and before the consulate-general was reopened in 1841, he was very wisely sent off to cool his temper in the less trying climate of Hamburg.[2] His services in the crisis of 1840 seem to have been more than amply recognised by permission to accept the insignia of a Turkish general of division.[3]

Two other incidents, slight in themselves, may be here mentioned as illustrating the hasty and inconsiderate temper with which matters were being driven on. Hodges mentioned that the Swedish consul-general had defended Muhammad 'Ali's detention of the surrendered Turkish fleet. Without waiting for more, Palmerston at once requested his recall. The Swedish government desired reasons. Palmerston demanded of Hodges a few good damning circumstances; but none were to be had.[4]

The second incident occurred a little later in 1840. On May 5 a despatch was addressed to Hodges relating to the trial of certain Jews at Damascus. He was to represent the disgrace reflected by these "barbarous enormities" on a ruler who prided himself on promoting civilisation.[5] A further despatch dwells upon "the deep and general feeling of indignation" which had arisen throughout the country.[6] Here again is a prompt, unhesitating readiness to believe the worst. The case was one of those in which the Jews were

[1] Barnett to Bidwell, September 20 and December 17, 1841 (F.O. 78–451).
[2] To Hodges, June 25, 1841 (*ibid.*).
[3] To the same, February 18, 1841 (*ibid.*).
[4] Hodges, January 24, 1840 (F.O. 78–404). To Hodges, February 25 and March 25, 1840 (F.O. 78–403). Hodges, March 21, 1840 (F.O. 78–404).
[5] To Hodges, May 5, 1840 (F.O. 78–403).
[6] To the same, May 30, 1840 (*ibid.*).

accused of murdering a Christian in order to mingle his blood with the unleavened bread of the Passover. Belief in the existence of such practices was still as universal in the Levant as it had been in medieval Europe. The accused men had been seized, tried by the ordinary processes, and condemned. Most unhappily, there was but too much reason for thinking that Sharif Pasha, Muhammad 'Ali's governor at Damascus, had acted with propriety. He had followed the advice of the French consular agent. Worse than that, the English consul, Werry, not only considered the guilt of the accused proved by the proceedings on their trial, but testified that the prompt and suitable measures taken by Sharif Pasha had saved the Jews of Damascus from general pillage and massacre.[1]

The nervous irritability which Palmerston displayed in these incidents resulted from the difficulties which he found in bringing the general question at issue to a satisfactory conclusion. Matters had gone very contrary to his expectations. The anticipated difficulty had been to induce Russia to co-operate with the other powers and to prevent her from consolidating her position by separate action. But this proved to have been greatly exaggerated. The Emperor Nicholas was not eager to act under the Treaty of Unkiar Skelessi. The reappearance of Russians at Constantinople would have meant war with England and probably with France as well, and in the Near East the consolidation of Muhammad 'Ali's power—an object remote from the emperor's wishes. Moreover a divergence of views had already appeared between Palmerston and Soult, the French Foreign Minister. The first wished to restore Syria to the Sultan, the second to leave it in the pasha's possession. If therefore the emperor supported Palmerston's policy, instead of attempting to act alone, he would

[1] Hodges, June 18 and July 20, 1840, and enc. (F.O. 78–405).

have a good prospect of breaking up, instead of cementing, Anglo-French co-operation.[1] He therefore sent Baron Brunnow on a special mission to London in 1839.

This cleared away one difficulty, only to raise another. Palmerston was eager to carry with him France as well as Russia, if he could. But French foreign policy was now, as it had been ten years earlier, beset by many difficulties. The July Monarchy, like its predecessor, was never strong enough to ignore currents of popular opinion; and French sympathies were strongly in favour of Muhammad 'Ali. And, as always, policy was liable to distraction by diverse and sometimes con-flicting continental and colonial interests. Fear of the press made it difficult for Soult to withdraw from the position he had taken up. His ministry fell, on a purely domestic issue, at the end of February, 1840, and he was succeeded by Thiers.

The new Foreign Minister pursued Soult's policy but with rising bitterness against England. His first plan was to revive separate negotiations between the Porte and the pasha through Pontois, the French ambassador at Constantinople, in order to confront Great Britain and Russia with a settlement which they could find no pretext to reverse.[2] Probably as a result of these en-deavours, Khusrau was removed; and Muhammad 'Ali promptly decided to send his secretary, Sami Bey, on a mission to Constantinople. His pretext was the offering of congratulations on the birth of the Sultan's daughter, and the concession which was to be offered was the restoration of the Turkish fleet.[3] The immediate answer to this was the signature by Great Britain, Russia, Austria and Prussia of a treaty by which

[1] Cf. Mowat, *ap. Camb. Hist. of Br. For. Policy*, II, 172–173.
[2] Medem to Nesselrode, May 1/13, and May 22/June 4, 1840.
[3] Hodges, Nos. 50 and 53, June 17, 1840 (F.O. 78–405).

Muhammad 'Ali was to receive the pashaliq of Egypt on a hereditary tenure and southern Syria for life, provided he accepted the offer within ten days; if he delayed acceptance beyond ten days but accepted within twenty days, he was to receive Egypt alone; if he refused, the four powers would blockade him; if he advanced on Constantinople, the powers would co-operate at the Sultan's request in its defence; and article 4 re-established "the ancient rule of the Ottoman Empire", that the Dardanelles should be closed to all foreign ships of war whenever the empire was in a state of peace. The treaty was signed on July 15, 1840. Palmerston had succeeded in his great desire to merge the Treaty of Unkiar Skelessi in some more general agreement, although he had failed in securing the co-operation of the French.

The news provoked an outburst of indignation at Paris. The French press, the ministers, the king, talked as though war were imminent. But they knew, and Palmerston knew, that it was not. "France will not help him [the pasha]", Palmerston wrote, "...nor has she the means of doing so." She had indeed fifteen sail in the Mediterranean, but it was almost the whole of her navy. She had an army of 60,000 men in Algiers who needed large reserves to be maintained to fill up the gaps caused by "fever and the Moors". "How in this state of things could France wantonly engage in war with the great military powers of the continent?..."[1]

Thiers' next hope was that matters could be so spun out as to leave the issue undecided when winter would disperse the blockading squadrons and prevent the movement of troops, when he could hope to break the concert that had been formed and reassert the influence of France. With this object in view, he advised the

[1] To Hodges, July 18, 1840 (F.O. 78–403).

pasha to reinforce his position, to remain on the defensive, to hold out.[1] It was the worst advice that could have been tendered. A sudden advance on Constantinople would perhaps have produced such an upheaval as would have enabled the pasha to get better terms. But to refuse the allies' offers and attempt a mere passive resistance was inviting defeat. This also was foreseen by Palmerston. France, he said, "will wait, will lie by, and if Mehemet Ali should be able to resist the allies for any length of time, she will then offer herself as a mediator. But it will be the business of the four powers so to press Mehemet Ali as not to give France such an opportunity".[2]

In the face of the formidable combination that had been slowly forming against him, the old pasha had continued to hold his head high. He probably found it impossible to believe that the great powers would really agree upon a common course of action in a matter over which they had always been sharply divided. He had reckoned on either France or Russia neutralising the action of Great Britain—if Great Britain did attempt to act. When Hodges was ordered to urge upon the Turkish naval officers their duty of rallying "round their sultan and caliph",[3] the pasha leapt up from his divan vowing he would shoot the first deserter, and Hodges decided that he had better not carry his orders into effect.[4] New regiments were raised; troops were recalled from Arabia; a camp of 36,000 men was formed at Damanhur, a judicious choice from its central position; and all with a method and good order that Hodges had not expected.[5] Indeed even Hodges

[1] Instructions to Cochelet, July 29, 1840. Sabry, *op. cit.* p. 501.
[2] To Hodges, *ut supra.* Cf. Palmerston to Hobhouse, July 27, 1843 (Brit. Mus. Add. MSS, 36471, ff. 211 *sqq.*).
[3] To the same, February 25, 1840 (F.O. 78–403).
[4] Hodges, March 31, 1840 (F.O. 78–404).
[5] The same, February 21, 1840 (*ibid.*).

began to be impressed with this old man's life, vigour and intelligence, and to fear lest in despair he should cause some general conflagration "whence might spring new interests, new combinations, new chances in his favour".[1] But by the middle of the year the strain of unceasing anxiety had begun to tell. He was shaken by "feverish and restless starts".[2] In August the Russian consul-general found him asleep on the divan. He said he had been unable to sleep for several nights. "His Highness's state of health, the torments to which he was evidently a prey, the efforts he made to control the irritation caused by his present position, and the conflicting feelings that possess this old man of 70 and combine to wear out the energy which distinguishes him, made our conversation painful indeed."[3]

But he lost neither his grasp of affairs nor his skill in counting chances. Like Thiers, he reckoned the allies would be slow to act, and that their blockade, when formed, would accomplish little immediately.[4] He saw he could rely upon the moral, though not upon the material support of the French. He knew that English public sentiment was far more friendly to him than to the Porte. He reckoned therefore that if matters went ill he could at least rely upon the hereditary government of Egypt, while, if the alliance by some lucky chance broke up, he might get all Syria too.[5] When therefore an agent from Constantinople and the consuls-general presented the allied demands, he refused to listen to the pompous eloquence[6] of Colonel

[1] Hodges, July 26, 1840 (F.O. 78–405).
[2] The same, July 5, 1840 (*ibid.*).
[3] Medem to Nesselrode, August 19/31, 1840.
[4] Walewski's report *ap.* Sabry, *op. cit.* p. 508.
[5] *Idem*, p. 509.
[6] He liked to convey Palmerston's views "impressively", e.g. despatch of January 4, 1840 (F.O. 78–404).

Hodges and desired a written statement.[1] The ten days passed without any formal answer. When the twenty days were almost expired, he offered to accept the second alternative but refused to confirm his agreement by the immediate release of the Turkish fleet.[2] The term expired, but still the consuls-general lingered on at Alexandria, although news arrived on September 7 that the Sultan had removed Muhammad 'Ali from all his offices and that the consuls-general had been recalled.[3] They did not actually quit Alexandria until September 23.[4]

One reason of this delay seems to have been their desire to watch the conduct of the French consul-general. Another was the fact that their own mutual confidence was slender. For instance on September 7 a steamer put into Alexandria harbour from Beyrout, and sent off about £5000 in Turkish money under the English flag to be put on board an English man-of-war lying in the harbour. The boat and money were seized by the harbour-master, because according to the Turkish regulations the currency of the country might not be exported. Hodges in great anger threatened to haul down his flag at once. To the Russian and Austrian representatives this seemed dangerously likely to provoke a direct quarrel between the pasha and Great Britain, which would have given the latter an opportunity of acting separately on her own account. They therefore intervened to smother the business.[5]

This incident, provoking as it must have been, was not, however, the greatest humiliation that Hodges suffered during his last few days at Alexandria. There

---

[1] Hodges, August 20, 1840 (F.O. 78–406).
[2] The same, August 30, 1840 (*ibid.*).
[3] The same, September 15, 1840 (*ibid.*).
[4] Medem to Nesselrode, September 13/25, 1840.
[5] Same to same, September 2/14, 1840.

was the question of the Indian mails. Months earlier
Hodges had been ordered to ascertain the pasha's intentions in this matter should coercive measures be
adopted against him.[1] On September 19 a packet
arrived. Hodges, not knowing what to do, visited the
Divan, and expressed a hope that the mails would not
be molested. The pasha merely nodded. The consul-
general asked assurances. The other replied that he
would give none. Hodges said he was much surprised.
"The powers calling themselves civilised", retorted the
pasha sharply, "have adopted measures which may
perhaps force me to imitate their example"; and when
asked to explain himself added "their declarations are
not to be depended upon". Hodges could not accept
this remark if it applied to Great Britain. With a
sardonic laugh Muhammad 'Ali answered, "You may
take it or leave it; but my remark is in the mouth of
everybody". Finally he said the mails might pass for
this time only. So, very hot and angry, Hodges went
back to his consulate to inform Lord Palmerston and
the Bombay Government that the mails could not pass
in future.[2] The same evening, in conversation with Her
Majesty's Postmaster, Hodges was told that "*some
person* [the italics are his own] had raised *false* and
unnecessary alarm" about the mails.[3] Next day he
heard from the Russian consul-general that Muhammad 'Ali had assured the East India Company's agent
that so long as he ruled Egypt the mails should pass in
perfect safety.[4] On this the consul-general's wrath
boiled over. He sent home an indignant complaint
against the Postmaster and the Company's agent. "The
question comes to be whether Mehemet 'Ali is to make

[1] To Hodges, April 14, 1840 (F.O. 78–403).
[2] Hodges, September 20, 1840 (F.O. 78–406).
[3] The same, private, September 22, 1840 (*ibid.*).
[4] The same, September 22, 1840 (*ibid.*).

a disaffected functionary a stalking-horse in order to deride Her Majesty's Agent, to depreciate his consideration, to erect an anomalous English authority in his stead, and in a word to reduce that agent to a political nullity." He had expected, he says, nothing but hostility from other Englishmen there, but hoped that persons in public employment "would have sympathised with me".[1] Palmerston at least sympathised so far as to complain to the President of the Board of Control against the Company's agent, only to learn that "if the complaint is communicated to the chairman, it will be made known to the court and consequently become public".[2]

Muhammad 'Ali was as good as his word. In spite of the withdrawal of the consul-general, the hostilities that took place in Syria, and the disorders that threatened to break out in Egypt, he not only suffered the mails to pass, but took special measures to protect travellers using the Suez route.[3] His war, he said, was with Lord Palmerston, not with the English.

But although he certainly had the best of the joke, he could not but get the worst of the match. The forces against him were too strong, their direction too prompt and vigorous. On September 11 a force of British marines and Turkish troops were landed on the Syrian coast near Beyrout. For months a general unrest and Ottoman emissaries had been stirring up the Syrians to revolt. Ibrahim's army was scattered, weak, lacking stores and supplies. In October the Druses rose. On October 10 at Bait-hannis, Commodore Napier met and defeated Ibrahim in person at the head of a small body of troops, and captured his standard. Beyrout was taken. On November 4 Acre, which had resisted

---

[1] Hodges, private, *ut supra.*
[2] Hobhouse to Palmerston, October 9, 1840 (F.O. 78–451).
[3] Parbury, *Handbook to the Overland Route,* p. 257.

Ibrahim for six months, surrendered after a single day's bombardment. The Egyptian power in Syria had collapsed. At Paris, the Thiers ministry which had dragged France disagreeably near to war, had fallen a few days earlier, on October 29. On November 15 Commodore Napier appeared off Alexandria with a strong squadron. On the 27th, though invested with no diplomatic authority, he signed a convention with the pasha, who agreed to evacuate Syria, and to restore the Ottoman fleet, on the condition that he should be recognised as hereditary governor of Egypt. Orders recalling Ibrahim from Syria were issued on the 29th.[1]

This news took the diplomats of Constantinople completely by surprise. "Old Napier", wrote Hodges dropping for the nonce his consular dignity, "has kicked up a devil of a row among the *corps diplomatique* here."[2] He had indeed behaved with nautical irregularity in communicating to the pasha the decision which Palmerston and the English cabinet had taken on October 10, in deference to French feeling. This was to recommend Muhammad 'Ali as hereditary pasha in Egypt provided he speedily withdrew his troops from the other Turkish provinces and gave up the Turkish fleet.[3] When Napier's agreement reached London, it was promptly approved. Ponsonby's prejudices still invented obstacles in the way of a full settlement. He induced the Porte to issue a farman—the hatti sharif of February 13, 1841—containing a number of unwelcome restrictions.[4] This, on Napier's advice, Muhammad 'Ali rejected. Both Palmerston and Metternich urged the modification of the grant. This was done by a farman of June 1. It recognised a hereditary

---

1 Letter of Shawal 3, 1256 (Abdine Archives).
2 Hodges to Bidwell, January 21, 1841 (F.O. 78-451).
3 To Ponsonby, October 15, 1840 (F.O. 78-390).
4 Sabry, *op. cit.* pp. 532-533.

right by seniority,[1] in the direct male descendants of the pasha. It fixed the tribute at 80,000 purses of piastres. It limited the pasha's army to 18,000 men save in time of war or by express permission. It forbade the building of new ships. The ruler of Egypt was thus never to be able to threaten again the peace of Europe. Muhammad 'Ali had failed to found his empire. But he had secured much. Egypt was virtually independent of the Porte's control. Its administration was separate. This privilege was guaranteed by the assent of the great powers, and though the pasha had failed in his larger scheme, he had in fact laid the foundations of a new state.

[1] According to the Turkish rule of succession.

Chapter VII

MUHAMMAD 'ALI'S GOVERNMENT IN EGYPT

I have already observed that among the causes leading
Palmerston to oppose the extension of Muhammad
'Ali's power must be reckoned his misunderstanding of
the pasha's administration. It was indeed the object
among contemporaries of immoderate praise and un-
measured blame. Some, like the enthusiastic Waghorn,
would only see the good that had been done and would
not confess that many of the pasha's achievements were
"showy rather than substantial"; while others, like
Dr Holroyd, Palmerston's correspondent, viewed
matters with English eyes and commiserated the
fellahin because they did not live in brick cottages and
eat beef.[1] But in order fairly to judge the pasha's
reforms and administrative ideas, a number of points
must be borne constantly in mind. One is that he was
working in an oriental country, where the functions of
government were poles asunder from the customs prevalent in the West. It was very hard for the zealots of
laissez-faire to appreciate a system which directed the
subject on every point. The parallels of Indian Government were of little use; for in those times few in England
outside the India House and the Oriental Club had any
sound understanding of what their own countrymen were
doing in India, so it is small wonder that the work of
Muhammad 'Ali was misunderstood. Indeed little sym-
pathetic intelligent criticism was to be got except from
men such as Salt or Campbell, who knew the country
well, or from Anglo-Indians who were familiar with
similar problems and an apathetic eastern population.

[1] Campbell, December 1, 1837 (F.O. 78–322).

Then, too, the pasha had taken over a derelict government. It would be difficult to exaggerate the wretched condition of the Turkish provinces at the beginning of the nineteenth century. An honest governor, as Burckhardt said with perfect truth, could not hope long to hold his office. "The Porte demands supplies and nothing but supplies; and the pasha to satisfy her must press upon the industry of his subjects. He who is the well-wisher of his people, who contents himself with the ordinary revenue, and who lets justice preside in his councils will undoubtedly incur his sovereign's displeasure, not because he is just, but because his justice prevents him from plundering and transmitting a portion of the acquired plunder to the divan. To save his existence he had nothing left but silently to resign his unhappy subjects to the rod of a succeeding despot or to declare himself a rebel, and to contend with his rival until the Porte, convinced of the difficulty of deposing him, patiently waits for a more favourable opportunity."[1] These words were written in 1810, but they are curiously prophetic of Muhammad 'Ali's career. Failure to understand this was to lead Palmerston to misjudge the pasha's work completely.

Egypt was probably in the worst condition of all the Turkish provinces, with the possible exception of 'Iraq. The Mamelukes had done nothing but oppress it. They protected the fellah neither from the arms of the Bedouin, nor from the extortions of the tax-gatherers, nor even from the ruin of his lands by the silting up of the canals. The delta, the most fertile land in the world, had lost a third of its cultivable extent. Fayum was dispeopled by Bedouin raids. Nobody knew what was exacted from the peasant or how much of the public revenue was pilfered on its way to the treasury. The revenue farmers—*roznamji* was their local name—were

[1] Burckhardt, *Nubia*, p. xxxviii.

proverbial for their pride and wealth.[1] Justice was a matter of bribes, property a matter of favour, life a matter of luck.

This was the kind of government which Muhammad 'Ali inherited, to which he was accustomed, under which in Albania he had grown up. The establishment of his authority made him an absolute despot. None can wonder that he accepted his inheritance and on occasion acted much as his predecessors would have done. Jabarti, the historian, returning from the Shubra Palace to Cairo one June night in 1822, was strangled and his body tied to the feet of his ass. Men said that the pasha had been annoyed at the freedom of his comments.[2] The bringer of a secret letter is reported to have been thrown into the Nile to make sure he kept the secret if he had it.[3] The pasha beat a Copt until he consented to deliver over half his savings.[4] Even at the end of his days the autocrat ran strong within him. The wealthier people of Alexandria disliked sending their sons to Paris to be educated, and substituted the sons of porters and other mean persons for the children whom Muhammad 'Ali demanded of them. "If these fellows", he said on learning of their conduct, "will neither understand the advantages of education nor of commerce, they are only fit to carry loads on their backs like porters or donkeys." Accordingly an order was made that *all* classes were to work in person on removing the mounds of rubbish which surrounded the city. Shopkeepers, merchants, scribes and theologians, were to be seen on the appointed days with baskets of earth on their backs and wholly unaccustomed sweat running down their faces.[5]

[1] Paton, *Revolutions in Egypt*, i, 79.   [2] Jabarti, *op. cit.* i, p. ix.
[3] Senior, *Conversations in Egypt*, ii, 116.
[4] Burckhardt, *Arabia*, i, 442 n.
[5] Murray, July 8, 1847 (F.O. 78–708).

And he was an Eastern despot not only by inheritance—he was one by environment as well. Apart from
the small, weak European element—consisting of the
consuls-general, a few French and English merchants,
and the few Frenchmen in his service—he lived among
people who expected and desired nothing else. The
despot is always a lonely person. But Muhammad 'Ali
was separated from his fellows not only by his unlimited
power but also by his policy and intentions. "Do not
judge me by the standards of your knowledge. Compare me with the ignorance that is around me", he
once said to Dr Bowring, who had been sent to report
on the trade of Egypt and Syria. ". . . You have numbers
of intelligent persons. . . ; I can find very few to understand me and do my bidding. I am often deceived, and
I know that I am deceived. I have been almost alone
for the greater part of my life."[1] The good in the pasha's
rule was his own; the bad was generally the work of
those whom he was obliged to use for want of better
men—unscrupulous officials eager for money.[2] "When
I came to Egypt", he said again, "it was really barbarous, utterly barbarous. Barbarous it remains to this
day. Still I hope that my labours have rendered its
condition somewhat better than it was. You must not
however be shocked if you do not find in these countries
the civilization which prevails in Europe."[3]

It is certain that thirty years of his rule produced an
extraordinary change. Yet a generation is too short a
time to produce permanent results. The fact that the
pasha found few or none to adopt his views and purposes
with a sincere enthusiasm, and his consciousness of the
gulf between his own policy and other men's, in itself
led to elements of weakness and instability in his work.

[1] Bowring, *Report* (*Parl. Papers*, 1840, XXI, 146).
[2] Campbell to Bidwell, December 1, 1837 (F.O. 78–322).
[3] Hodges, June 18, 1840 (F.O. 78–405).

He felt—and justly—that every improvement depended on himself alone, and that what he left undone would perhaps never be accomplished. Hence arose in some of his undertakings a lack of due consideration at the outset, and a strong impatience to see immediate results. While he should have been busied with laying deep foundations, he was hurriedly raising the walls of the palace of his dreams. "I am old", he would say, "...and what I would have done must be done quickly."

Many influences thus conspired to impair his reforms, to rob them of a permanent driving-force, or to misdirect his activities. Yet it is hard to call to mind an oriental ruler who, under no spur of external necessity but solely from his love for order and justice and well-being, and in spite of the obstinate though passive resistance of almost all around him, succeeded in establishing a greater number of improvements.

In the form of government he made small change. It continued along the lines which an age-long experience had shown to be most appropriate, and which we ourselves hardly ventured to begin to alter in India until a generation ago. The village was the unit of administration, with its head-man, the *shaikh-al-belad*, representing the ruler in every capacity. The villages were grouped in subdivisions under the *hakim-al-khot*. These subdivisions were formed into sixty-one districts, each under a *mamur*, corresponding with the Indian collector. The districts were grouped in seven provinces each under a *mudir*, or governor, the area of whose jurisdiction was formed by an amalgamation of the twenty-four provinces into which the country had been divided in the time of the Mamelukes. In the larger cities some more elaborate organisation was necessary. There were special police and judges to maintain public order and to prevent or punish crime. And there too the population was divided according to trades and

occupations into guilds, each under its special shaikh
or head-man. In Cairo, for instance, there were 164
of these bodies, the shaikhs being responsible for the
conduct of the members of their respective guilds.[1]
This again was the traditional mode of organisation,
prevalent throughout the East.

In order to keep it working with a moderate degree
of honesty and justice, a close, active and perpetual
supervision was needed, the more so because popular
opinion accepted official dishonesty as a thing of course.
The ideal of the system was to maintain one tyrant to
prevent the appearance of many. Left to themselves,
the village shaikhs seized every occasion of oppressing
their fellow-peasants.[2] Mamur and mudir oppressed
all within their reach. Nor was dishonesty their only
vice. They were ignorant as well. The studious might
be deeply read in the philosophy of Islam and the poets
of Arabia and Persia, but their schools bred scholars
only, not men of affairs. Experience was the adminis-
trator's only guide, and that too often only showed the
way to robbing with decency and prudence.[3] The need,
too, of checking dishonest combinations among the
officials demanded their frequent change of office, so
that men were perpetually in control of matters of
which they knew little or nothing. "Little attention is
paid", Bowring observes, "to the fitness of an individual for exercising the functions with which he is
invested."[4] Unfortunately this was inevitable. Campbell, no unfavourable witness, bears strong testimony
to the point. "The vexations to our merchants", he
says, "arise in most cases from a want of system and
from ignorance of business on the part of the local and

---

[1] Bowring, *Report (Parl. Papers,* 1840, XXI, 117).
[2] Cf. Burckhardt, *Arabia,* I, 145.
[3] Puckler-Muskau, *op. cit.* I, 24.
[4] Report *(Parl. Papers,* 1840, XXI, 49).

minor authorities, rather than from any fault of
Mehemet Ali or Ibrahim Pasha, and this arises chiefly
from the absolute want of people as yet capable of conducting affairs in the numerous branches of administration and in the many posts and places where European
commerce extends, and there are also so many in-
herent vices and venality in everything Turkish that it
must be the work of time to prevent many evils which
are at present unavoidable, but which daily diminish."[1]
Indeed no permanent improvement was possible until
a new generation had arisen, better taught and more
reliable.

By exhortation, punishment and inspection the pasha
strove hard to make good the defects of training,
education and character. His exhortations, conveyed
in the form of circular letters, make queer but instructive reading, and range from the ludicrous to the
pathetic. Sometimes they contained awful threats.
One, issued in 1826, complaining that his officials
were not taking pains enough in promoting cultivation,
declares that he is about to make a personal inspection,
and in whatsoever district he finds any trace of negligence he will dig a pit and bury alive all the officials.[2]
But such warnings cannot have been meant seriously,
for a little over a year afterwards, treating of the same
kind of trouble, he merely says that his further advice
will be delivered with the cudgel or the sword.[3] In
others, which the consul-general Barker spitefully sent
home to amuse Palmerston, he runs riot in abuse.
Neglect to pay in the taxes affords the occasion of one.
"From this it clearly appears that you are a negligent
blockhead and affords another proof that you are an
ass." If the money is not immediately paid in, "be

[1] Campbell, December 12, 1838 (F.O. 78–343).
[2] Circular, Jumadi-us-sani 13, 1241 (Abdine Archives).
[3] Circular, Jumadi-al-awal, 1243 (*ibid.*).

assured I will tear thee in pieces".[1] On a failure to
provide the requisite number of conscripts, he writes:
"And thou—ass that thou art!—what art thou doing?
...For want of better men I have placed thee in
office and made thee a governor, and thou! dost thou
neglect thy duty in this way and delay it so long?...
In the instant thou receivest this order, put thy brains
in thy head and send the rest of the men....If thou
dost not, I will make an example of thee to the rest of
the governors of the districts...."[2] In milder vein is an
exhortation addressed to the Governor of the Sudan
who had sent up a bag of rebels' ears as proof of his
activity. "Those in power and authority should know
that the conquest of the country is to be secured by
peaceful persuasion and the awakening of the natives'
confidence by means of justice." The governor should
follow the example which the French had set in Egypt,
and imitate the behaviour of the English after them.[3] But
a circular of 1843 exhibits the nearest approach to anything like an administrative testament. The old pasha,
as he had then become, calls upon the zealous help of
his servants, since his difficulties were far too great to be
overcome by any single man. He reminds them of the
fertility and situation of Egypt. "To possess a land like
ours which has no equal is our great happiness, and to
spare any effort by which her prosperity may be increased would be an act of grievous ingratitude which
my heart cannot accept and in which I will never
acquiesce. I must then ever and severely be summon-
ing you to do your duty so that we may reach the end
we have set before us....Beware of idleness and negligence.... The wise man boasts not of his own conduct,

[1] Enc. in Barker, February 19, 1833 (F.O. 78–231).
[2] The same, January 23, 1833 (*ibid.*).
[3] To the Commandant in the Sudan, Rabi-al-awal 9, 1236
(Abdine Archives).

but of the success of the affairs entrusted to him. Know that I will pursue the well-being of this land even at the cost of my life and the lives of my kindred. All about me well know that I love not to harm any man. For forty years I have held my hand from sharp punishment, but if I am compelled to do otherwise, the fault will lie not at my door.... Of old I did not hope to reach the state to which to-day we have arrived; and now that my ambitions are higher, I will readily sacrifice to the prosperity of my country, which is my great desire, even one of my own kin set over three million men."[1] Three months later he made all his chief officials swear to serve him honestly and to report any abuse of authority that came within their knowledge.[2]

There is no doubt that the circular just noticed marks the real wishes of the pasha's heart. It was addressed exclusively to his officials. It was never communicated to the consuls-general. It was not designed to impress European opinion. It agrees with the language which Muhammad 'Ali used when speaking in confidence with European friends. But he was well aware that punishment was necessary as well as exhortation. It was true that he did not love to injure anyone, and in general withheld his hand from chastisement. But it was no more than a general disposition from which at times he could not help departing. For instance, in 1822 the revenue collector at Ghiza falsely represented that he could get in neither the tithe nor the tax on houses. This was a most serious matter in the pasha's eyes. He believed (it is now impossible to say whether justly or not) that the man was lying, probably from motives of corruption. He therefore instructed Ibrahim Pasha, at that moment acting as mudir of the province,

[1] Circular, Jumadi-us-sani 4, 1259 (Abdine Archives).
[2] Barnett, October 16, 1843 (F.O. 78–541).

to reason with the man and if possible convince him of his error. If he succeeded, so much the better; if not, the collector was to be beheaded, lest the interests of government should suffer by his misconduct. Ibrahim apparently carried out the sentence with his own hand. A later letter declares that the man had been slain by his own obstinacy, not by either the pasha or his son, and his place was to be filled either by a Frenchman or by the deceased's brother.[1] As time passed, and perhaps as the general standard of conduct improved, the death penalty was used more and more sparingly, and all but great misconduct was punished by labour on the public works. An order of 1830 directed that twenty-five officials of middle Egypt were to undergo six months' hard labour.[2] In 1833 the mamurs were warned that they would be thus punished if they compelled the servants of government to till land within their jurisdiction.[3] In the following year, as the spilling of blood was an act evil in itself, the mudirs and mamurs were forbidden to inflict the death penalty without the special orders of the pasha,[4] and in 1836 a village shaikh was ordered to be executed if he proved to be guilty of beating a man to death without provocation.[5]

But the best security against official misconduct lay neither in sound advice nor in bloody punishment, but in frequent and exact inspection. In this matter the pasha did not spare himself. He frequently went on tour, enquiring with the utmost particularity into the state of the accounts and the general administration; and at such times, travelling virtually without a guard, was accessible to the complaints of the humblest fellah.

[1] To Ibrahim Pasha, Shaban 5 and 15, 1237 (Abdine Archives).
[2] To Kotkhuda Bey, Safar 5, 1246 (*ibid.*).
[3] To the mudirs, Muharram 9, 1249 (*ibid.*).
[4] To the same, Rabi-us-sani 20, 1250 (*ibid.*).
[5] To the mudir, Tanta, Jumadi-us-sani 6, 1252 (*ibid.*).

One result of his tour in the Sudan in 1839 was an order for the replacement of corrupt and ignorant officials.[1]

The number of Europeans employed in general administrative business seems to have been exceedingly small. There were in the country a number of French and English, renegades and others, but, while these men were freely employed in the arsenals, and in the army,[2] I think they were seldom set to administrative work, and the only definite reference to their civil employment I have met with is the one noted above, when Ibrahim was told he might appoint a Frenchman at Ghiza instead of the executed Copt.

Nor were natives of the country employed in any of the superior posts. The superior administration was Turkish, not Arab. "The meanest man who speaks Turkish", observed Bowring, "is *ipso facto* considered as belonging to a caste high above the indigenous inhabitant."[3] An Arab servant could hardly even be sent with a message to a high official. The Turk in Egypt, even under Muhammad 'Ali, enjoyed something of the position of unquestioned superiority that the contemporary servant of the East India Company did in India. Foreigners noted with surprise the universal sentiment of inferiority and subjection prevalent among the natives of the land. "We are but fellahin", they would say. They never dreamt of questioning the right of the foreigner to rule over them. They were completely unarmed, completely submissive, asking for nothing but to be allowed to pour Nile water over their fertile lands in peace.[4]

But the pasha was unwilling to allow this state of affairs to continue. He did not trust the Turks very far.

[1] To Abbas, Muharram 11, 1255 (Abdine Archives).
[2] Campbell, June 12, 1837 (F.O. 78–319).
[3] Report (*Parl. Papers*, 1840, xxi, 7).   [4] *Ibid.*

They were likely to sympathise with Constantinople and to yearn for the old, easy, corrupt and profitable ways of government which he was bent on reforming. He therefore sought as far as possible to replace them by Arabs. This bold idea, as it seemed at the time, was first suggested to him by Drovetti, the French consul-general. So early as 1826 no less than forty-five young men, the sons of Arab shaikhs and others, were sent to France to be educated there and rendered less unfit for public employment.[1] In 1833, in the course of a tour in the Delta, he visited the lower Turkish revenue officials with the bastinado, finding they had small sympathy with the Arab population and extorted money for their private use, and he declared besides that in future the Arab shaikhs should communicate directly with himself.[2] One result of this decision was a gathering of the principal shaikhs at Alexandria a few months later. Information given by Muhammad 'Ali's secretary to the consuls-general suggests that this was done in order to permit the pasha to instruct and exhort them on the due discharge of their duties. Campbell reported an amiable dialogue in which the shaikhs promised the most scrupulous observance of the pasha's orders.[3] But the published information does not seem to have told everything. Muhammad 'Ali had found that he could not prudently go too far in the employ-ment of Arabs. The Turks, as a foreign observer said, "always stole more decently than the Arabs".[4] Besides that, [intriguers, who always flourish under a personal despot, however benevolent, were seeking to exploit the pasha's evident good will. Influential village shaikhs, the pasha learnt, were stirring up their

[1] Salt, April 4, 1826 (F.O. 78–147).
[2] Campbell, June 13, 1833 (F.O. 78–227).
[3] The same, October 26, 1833 (F.O. 78–228).
[4] Puckler-Muskau, *op. cit.* I, 24.

brethren to delay the collection of the taxes in the hope that the blame would fall on the Turkish officials and that the shaikhs would be appointed to fill their places. This was to be brought to an immediate end. No time was to be wasted on tedious and inconclusive enquiries which would elicit nothing but lies. Any important village shaikh accused of acting thus was to be punished without more ado.[1] It seems unlikely that this business was forgotten in the shaikhs' assembly at Alexandria, although the report given to Campbell says nothing of it. Further development of Arab employment had to await the slow development of the pasha's educational schemes.

At headquarters the work was divided among seven departments—war, the navy, cultivation, finance, commerce (and external relations) education, and police; but though the ministers in charge of them were reckoned of higher rank than the mudirs of the provinces, they seem to have had no separate authority of their own over the latter, for the pasha was careful to hold all the strings of government in his own hands. Nor did he suffer these central departments to follow their universally instinctive course and swell into vast establishments whose main purpose is to justify their employment by the complication of public procedure. He suppressed 200 posts in the Treasury, and, not content with that, reminded the director that the chief merchants of Alexandria could control with only four clerks a business turnover amounting to nearly a third of the Treasury receipts. Had he forgotten the chief accountant's mania for filling the public offices with Copts? If he could not manage better, the directorship would be given to someone else.[2]

[1] To Abbas Pasha, Jumadi-al-awal 28, 1249 (Abdine Archives).
[2] To Sharif Pasha, Rabi-us-sani 26, 1260 (*ibid.*).

The most interesting aspect of Muhammad 'Ali's
rule is certainly the pains he took to develop and enlarge the practice of discussing public business before
proceeding to any action. In 1819 he set up a council
or divan of seven persons to manage and discuss
transactions between the Treasury and European
merchants,[1] and this system of official deliberation was
applied to all departments of the central government.
Every matter was to be maturely discussed before being
remitted for the pasha's orders. Then in 1829 the
principle was more widely extended. Ibrahim Pasha
presided over a gathering of 400 persons specially
convened, comprising the chief civil and military
officers, the mudirs, and even a number of village
shaikhs, to discuss the best way of correcting abuses and
improving the condition of the peasants. It sat every
night for some time, and the members were sworn to
secrecy.[2] In 1832 a similar plan was tried in Syria.
A small body of Grand Notables, twenty-two in
number, was convoked to deliberate on the affairs of
the people.[3] In 1834 the shaikh of the Al Azhar mosque
and the shaikh of the merchants' guild were directed to
nominate suitable ulema and merchants to sit in the
Superior Council, and at the same time the mudirs
were ordered to convene in each *mudirliq* an assembly
including cultivators, the village shaikhs, and others, to
choose two village shaikhs to represent the cultivators
of the mudirliq in the council.[4] These things were
generally misconceived and misrepresented by the
tourists whose information gave the tone to European
opinion. On the one side was the young Disraeli representing the pasha as saying he would have as many

[1] To Kotkhuda Bey, Shaban 12, 1235 (Abdine Archives).
[2] Barker to Gordon, September 22, 1829 (F.O. 78-184).
[3] Ibrahim's proclamation, Safar 15, 1248 (Abdine Archives).
[4] To Habib Effendi, Rabi-al-awal 25, 1250, and a circular to
the mudirs of the same date (*ibid.*).

parliaments as William IV but would take care to choose them himself. On the other were Philosophic Radicals and Saint-Simoniens who claimed Muhammad 'Ali as a convert to western democracy. The one suggests that the pasha's experiments were mere tricks designed to impress European opinion; the other that they meant the establishment of representative government.[1] Of course they were neither one nor the other. Ordinary public business in the East had always been decided by a group of officials—a divan or durbar—presided over by the pasha in person, or some superior official, and sitting virtually in public, with a constant succession of petitioners and spectators. As Bartle Frere once said, important as is a knowledge of public opinion in a western country, its importance is even greater in the East. The oriental ruler needed urgently to know what men were saying in the bazaars and caravan-sarais. In part he could depend upon his spies—the most permanent of all instruments of government in Asia. But another side perhaps could be revealed by the assemblies which Muhammad 'Ali from time to time convoked. He was much too shrewd to dream of borrowing wholesale from western practice. But he was also much too shrewd not to see that a discreet borrowing of western ideas, adapted in such a way as not to disturb accustomed forms, might prove very beneficial to his government. He must have been influenced too by another motive. A man with so strong and clear a sense of the value of knowledge can hardly have been unaware that his tentative assemblies were instruments not only of government but also of political education. Had chance but provided Egypt with an heir to Muhammad 'Ali's talents as well as to his dominions,

[1] Monypenny and Buckle, *Disraeli*, I, 176–7. St John, *Egypt and Mohamed Ali*, II, 472 *sqq.* Cf. Bentham's memorandum (Brit. Mus. Add. MSS 25663, ff. 139 *sqq.*).

the country would have afforded to western nations an example of political reform as remarkable as that of Japan. But a single life, largely spent in building up a political dominion, cannot conceivably do more than plan the outline of institutional development.

His financial management was extraordinarily successful. Onlookers were always anticipating his financial ruin and declaring that his wars and internal projects would ruin him and the country alike. In 1827, for instance, when he was burdened with the cost of the war in the Morea at the moment that his resources were straitened by two successive failures of the Nile to attain its usual height, he still went on building factories and constructing a mole and dockyard at Alexandria.[1] Four years later he was contemplating projects ten times as great.[2] He kept out of the hands of European moneylenders.[3] In 1837 it was thought that the fall in the price of cotton (of which he exercised a monopoly) would hit him hard: and yet he managed to pay off the arrears due to his troops.[4] Barker thought he really must have found Aladdin's lamp.

But his magic lay merely in prudence and attention. The public accounts, when he obtained the government, were kept by Copts, who made them a perfect model of intricacy. This had two advantages—it made their services indispensable and it hid their defalcations. The public accounts were not centralised. Various taxes would be assigned to various services according to the approved Turkish mode.[5] There was no budget nor any possibility of one. Here as elsewhere the pasha was willing to learn and borrow from the

[1] Barker, *Syria and Egypt*, II, 60–1.
[2] *Idem*, p. 158.
[3] Cf. Campbell, October 12, 1833 (F.O. 78–228).
[4] The same, May 25 and July 13, 1837 (F.O. 78–319 and 320).
[5] E.g. the assignment of the Damascus *Miri* for the *haj*. See p. 42 *supra*.

European. He directed Boghoz Bey, the Armenian, the most trusted and the most trustworthy of all his servants, to obtain a scheme of accounts as used in public offices in Europe;[1] and the Frenchman Jomard was employed to frame a new system.[2] But that still left untouched the vicious method of apportioning "different districts...to different ministers to provide for their expenses instead of sending their revenue to a common treasury. The present state of things leads to great abuses, as every minister has a treasury of his own, and seven doors are opened (those are the different ministries) to fraud and abuse, when one in a country like this is already but too many".[3] When Bowring visited Egypt in 1838 the pasha sought his advice in the matter of accountancy. All the public accounts were produced for inspection, and Bowring made a number of recommendations for their improvement. First came the introduction of a budget of receipts and expenditure at the beginning of each year; then the payment of all revenues into the central treasury; the complete separation of the power to receive and issue public money; the establishment of the power in the Finance Minister to sanction or reject proposed expenditure; and finally provision for the prompt payment, balancing and audit of all public accounts.[4]

The fragmentary evidence as yet available does not permit of any full or exact narrative of the pasha's financial history. But he seems usually to have succeeded in keeping his expenditure well below his revenue. For instance in 1820–1 (the Coptic year used in the Egyptian accounts ended on September 28)[5] the

[1] To Boghoz Bey, Rabi-al-awal 22, 1249 (Abdine Archives).
[2] Jomard, Coup d'Œil, p. 23.
[3] Campbell, February 26, 1838 (F.O. 78–342).
[4] Bowring, Report (Parl. Papers, 1840, xxi, 62).
[5] Murray, March 17, 1848 (F.O. 78–757).

revenues amounted to 240,000 purses against an expenditure of under 190,000. In 1832–3 they were a little over 500,000 against an expenditure of 415,000. In 1846–7 they were over 600,000 against an expenditure of 460,000. It is obvious that there must have been years of heavy expenditure when the accumulated surplus was much reduced; but surpluses seem to have been more frequent than deficits. Land revenue—*miri* —was naturally much the largest item among the receipts, but it scarcely amounted to more than 50 per cent., while on the expenditure side the army and marine seem to have absorbed about the same proportion of the total.[1]

Egyptian land tenures at the beginning of the nineteenth century were in much the same confused condition as when the East India Company undertook the administration of its Indian provinces. All the four orthodox schools of Muslim law recognised it as conquered territory with all its lands vesting in the Caliph. In token of this the leader of the Friday prayers at every mosque throughout the country mounted the pulpit holding in his hands a real or imitation sword. But, as everywhere else, the ruler had always been alienating his demesnes by grants, sometimes revocable at will, sometimes purporting to be irrevocable. The actual form probably made small difference, and Muslim lawyers held the convenient doctrine that even the most binding grant could be recalled in the interest of the state—a matter of which the ruler himself would be sole judge.

However, the confusion of the seventeenth and eighteenth centuries bred a host of proprietors, the most important of whom were the Mameluke chiefs and the tax-farmers called *multazim*. The lands held by

[1] Bowring, *ut supra*, p. 44. Murray, *ut supra*. St John, *op. cit.* II, 469 *sqq.*

the former of course paid no revenue, while those in the possession of the latter included ever-growing areas held tax-free—*ussieh* lands—in consideration of the labour and expense of collecting the revenue on the remainder. One of the pasha's earliest actions, as I have already stated,[1] was to appropriate the Mamelukes' lands, and to hold an enquiry into the tenures by which the other lands were held. Between 1808 and 1814 he appropriated the whole, giving the multazim pensions instead of the ussieh lands held by them.[2] In this the pasha does not seem to have exceeded the theoretical limit of his legal rights, although it must be remembered that "legal rights" did not carry the same connotation as in Europe. The measure was extreme, and Muhammad 'Ali himself would perhaps only have justified it by his extreme financial need at this period. He could not establish a stable government unless he resumed that large proportion of the land, amounting to nearly three-quarters, which had fallen into private hands by the corrupt negligence of his predecessors. The doctrine of necessity may be called in to justify anything. But the measure did not affect the fellah at all, but only a small class of proprietors, and the pasha's English critics might with propriety have remembered that Lord Cornwallis had expropriated not a small class of landlords but a large class of peasants in Bengal. No unjust act can be defended. But the guilt of injustice to the few seems less than the guilt of injustice to the many, for it inflicts a lower amount of avoidable suffering. Both the governor-general and the pasha undoubtedly believed their respective policies to be in the interest of the country at large.

[1] *Vide* p. 32, *supra*.
[2] Artin Bey, *Propriété foncière en Égypte*, pp. 84–6. St John, *op. cit.* II, 456 *sqq.* Jomard, *Coup d'Œil*, p. 11. Missett, March 22, 1814 (F.O. 24–5). Cf. Young, *Corps de droit Ottoman*, VI, 45 *sqq.*

This general resumption of the land was followed up by a cadastral survey of the country. To this the pasha paid a close attention. The mudirliq registers are said almost everywhere to bear the seal of his inspection.[1] But in this matter his work was impaired by the quality of his servants. His surveyors were unskilled, the supervisors dishonest.[2] In fact he had to encounter all the difficulties which in Bengal prevented the East India Company from ever undertaking a revenue survey, and in the other Indian provinces produced a multitude of early errors. The pasha found, for instance, that rich occupiers bribed the surveyors to show their lands as uncultivated and not irrigated, while the reductions thus made in the demand were recovered by over-assessing the lands tilled by poorer cultivators.[3] But though defective in detail and needing much revision, which was only applied gradually as the defects came to notice, the survey revealed much cultivated land which had till then escaped assessment by deliberate fraud.[4]

Another most important measure was the promotion of irrigation. The pasha claimed to have introduced no less than 38,000 sakias—water-wheels—or more than half of those in operation in 1844.[5] He cleared the old irrigation canals and dug new ones, and in Upper Egypt especially brought a great amount of land under tillage. Campbell mentions a new canal designed to irrigate a million acres.[6] Bowring found that 100,000 feddans had in fact been brought into bearing.[7] The

[1] Artin Bey, op. cit. p. 88.
[2] Campbell, February 26, 1838 (F.O. 78–342).
[3] To the Mudir of Ghiza, Safar 8, 1250 (Abdine Archives).
[4] Jomard, loc. cit.
[5] Bowring, Report (Parl. Papers, 1840, XXI, 12). Barnett, December 12, 1844 (F.O. 78–583).
[6] Campbell, January 1, 1834 (F.O. 97–411).
[7] Bowring, loc. cit.

man who was of most service to the pasha in these matters was the French engineer Linant, who also projected a great work which was to have controlled and extended the irrigation of the Delta. This was the famous Nile barrage, to be built near the fork of the Delta below Cairo. This, it was hoped, would permit the complete irrigation of the Delta in even the worst of Niles, and bring into cultivation between two and three hundred thousand acres above the barrage.[1] The difficulty was mainly technical. Linant had had no previous experience of such works. The project was long discussed, and at last a plan was prepared for submission to the French Board of Civil Engineering.[2] Most people doubted the possibility of carrying through so great a work, which was expected to take five years and cost at least a million and a half sterling.[3] It was not till 1847 that the foundation stone was actually laid, and then when accomplished the work failed to do what was expected of it. The great river found its way under the inefficient foundations. The pessimists proved for the moment to have been right. Modern engineers distribute the blame between Muhammad 'Ali's impatience and Linant's inexperience. Indeed the whole episode illustrates alike the pasha's strength and weakness—on the one side his vision and zeal for betterment, on the other his uninstructed haste and the imperfect instruments at his command.

Despite this failure, the cultivated area was considerably enlarged under the pasha's rule; and grants were freely made in order to promote agriculture. From 1829 onwards waste lands were ceded to individuals on condition of cultivation. At first the grants gave only a heritable usufruct; but in 1842 they were

[1] Campbell, November 1, 1834 (F.O. 78–247).
[2] Barnett, October 20, 1842 (F.O. 78–502).
[3] Bowring, loc. cit.

transformed into grants of absolute property. About the same period the lands rendered cultivable by the pasha's new irrigation works were granted out—under the title of *chifliqs*—on condition of progressive tillage. Much of the new area was bestowed on members of the pasha's own family.[1] So private property in land revived. At the same time it extended imperceptibly again over the rest of the country. The individuals registered in the cadastral survey gradually became in fact proprietors. As in India land came again to have a sale value, and Bowring could hear of no one who had been expropriated in recent times except for failure to pay the land revenue,[2] just as would have been done in similar circumstances in India.

The land revenue was payable either in kind or in money. Certain areas, specially suitable for the growth of crops such as cotton or indigo, in which the pasha had established a monopoly, were required to deliver specified quantities of the appropriate article. Elsewhere the occupier might cultivate what he pleased, subject to the payment of an assessment computed on the quality of the soil and the value of the crop that might best be grown on it. Down to 1834 the assessment was levied on a holding, whether cultivated or not, provided there was water enough even partially to irrigate it. But in that year the pasha adopted the much more equitable plan of levying the revenue only on the land which could be fully irrigated.[3] Another important reform was the abolition of the age-old custom of making good the failure of payment on one holding by levying an extra rate upon the rest. The practice

---

[1] Artin Bey, *op. cit.* pp. 95 *sqq.* Cf. to the Director of Roznamah, Zilhaj 24, 1256 (Abdine Archives); Barnett, January 15 and December 12, 1844 (F.O. 78–582 and 583).
[2] Bowring, Report (*Parl. Papers*, 1840, xxi, 123–4).
[3] Campbell, April 27, 1834 (F.O. 78–245).

seems to have been almost universal in the East. It had been as familiar in India as it had been in Egypt. It was defended on the score that it helped to prevent village shaikhs and other influential persons from thrusting an unfair proportion of the assessment on the smaller holders.[1]

The actual amount and rate of the assessments seem to have been considerably increased. It is even said that the actual money assessment was roughly doubled.[2] But this statement by itself is certainly misleading, for it leaves out of account various extra taxes, some recognised, others concealed, which the officials had collected and which had been not only prohibited but in some part suppressed. Nor can the extreme reluctance of the fellah to pay be taken too seriously into account. Centuries of hard experience had taught him, as it had taught the Indian ryot, that willing payment was inexpedient. It always was interpreted as indicating a superfluity of money, and therefore led to a demand for more. The feeling had been strengthened by the period of loose, weak government which had preceded the pasha's as it had the East India Company's Government. French observers of the time of Napoleon bear witness to the extraordinary difficulty which the Mamelukes had found in getting in the revenue. "The peasants...only pay at the last extremity, and sou by sou; they hide their money; they bury their goods and chattels...When they see a body of troops coming, they flee with their wives, children and cattle, leaving only their empty huts behind. If they think themselves strong enough to resist, they fight, calling in to their aid neighbouring villages and even the Bedouin." The Mamelukes had to maintain troops in each of their

[1] Bowring, Report (*Parl. Papers*, 1840, xxi, 15). Puckler-Muskau, *op. cit.* i, 23–4.
[2] Cf. St John, *op. cit.* ii, 450 *sqq.*

provinces solely engaged in trying to force the villages to pay and often enough not succeeding.[1] Muhammad 'Ali's power was more firmly established than this. Open resistance seems seldom to have been attempted. But passive resistance still continued. It was apparently a point of honour with the fellah to pay nothing till he had received a certain number of stripes, and the one who resisted the longest was the most esteemed.[2]

This was not the only parallel that may be traced between the Egyptian fellah and the Indian ryot. By ancient usage both were regarded by the governments which Providence was pleased to establish over them as existing to fulfil one function in life—the tillage of the soil. The duty of the cultivator was to cultivate. If he neglected that duty, the ruler must punish him with sharp penalties. As a recent writer has well said of Hindu and Muslim India, "the agrarian system was a matter of duties rather than rights".[3] Both Muhammad 'Ali and the East India Company inherited that conception unchanged from the past. As was natural, the pasha clung to it more firmly than did the Company's servants. He was not willing to permit land to lie untilled. When he learnt, for instance, that the lands granted to village shaikhs in return for their services were lying unwatered and covered with weeds, he directed the guilty shaikhs to be beaten at the corner of their fields, as an example to others.[4] He judged a state of tutelage to be necessary for the fellah's own well-being. He was extremely active in enquiring into any grievances, and under him, Salt observed, the peasants "are in general better treated and more

[1] Poussielgue's letter, 1 Vendémiaire, l'an vii, *ap. Intercepted Letters*, pp. 46 *sqq.*
[2] Bowring, Report (*Parl. Papers*, 1840, XXI, 47).
[3] Moreland, *Agrarian System of Moslem India*, p. xi.
[4] To the mudirs of Lower Egypt, Rabi-al-awal 2, 1252 (Abdine Archives).

content than for many years past".[1] Salt's evidence, it may be noted, is of more than usual value, because his frequent journeys in search of antiquities brought him into close and varied contact with the peasants of the country. Other observers agreed with the pasha's theory of the need of control. "From my own experience of the Arab character such as it exists at present", Thurburn wrote, "I must confess that there is some truth in the opinion that the Egyptian peasant, if left to the free exercise of his own will, would confine himself to the wants of the moment and long continue to direct his attention to the cultivation of those articles only which are produced with the least outlay of labour and capital...."[2]

However the condition of the fellahin fell away at a later date. This was probably due less to the weight of the land revenue demand in itself than to the fact that the system of conscription, to which I shall return later, reduced the productive capacity of the villages while the revenue demand was maintained at the former rate. From 1829 begins a series of complaints of peasants abandoning their villages, and the severest orders were issued against both the emigrant peasants and the officials in whose jurisdiction they should be discovered.[3] Muhammad 'Ali himself ascribed this practice to two causes—ill-treatment by the local officials and ignorance. "There are two sovereigns", he said, "the Sultan Mahmud and the fellah,...and the fellah must not be regarded with an evil eye."[4] Peasants, he says again, are not to be imprisoned for neglect of cultivation, for the first duty of government is

[1] Salt, April 28, 1817 (F.O. 78–89).
[2] Thurburn, *ap.* Bowring, Report (*Parl. Papers*, 1840, xxi, 64).
[3] To Zeki Effendi, Shawal 14, 1244; Circulars, Muharram 13, 1259, and Muharram 17, 1260 (Abdine Archives).
[4] To the Inspector-General of Factories, Jumadi-us-sani, 1252 (*ibid.*).

to secure the well-being of the people.[1] Villagers were
to be allowed to appeal to the mudirs if they were ill-
treated, and to petition the pasha himself if they failed
to obtain justice.[2]

With this growing restlessness of the population went
an accumulation of uncollected arrears of revenue. In
1833 the mudirs were warned that they would be held
personally responsible for these balances.[3] In 1835 the
pasha made a tour especially to enquire into this
question,[4] and was led to make considerable remis-
sions.[5] Finally he adopted the dubious device of compelling his principal officers to take over the villages
most heavily in debt with the obligation of paying off
gradually the arrears as well as meeting the current
revenue demand. They were very reluctant to undertake the task, but were told that they had grown rich in
the pasha's service and could not be allowed now to
desert him.[6] In general, the revenue management
suffered from much the same defects as the Company's
early revenue management in India. The demand was
pitched too high to be met in an average year, the
revenue subordinates were careless and corrupt, and
the assessments were unequal, so that some villages
could, whilst others could not, pay the demands
made upon them. In other words, the pasha did not
succeed in ridding the revenue system of its traditional
abuses.

The land revenue system, while of prime and essential
interest to the country as a whole, was not of general
concern to foreign countries. But Muhammad 'Ali's

[1] Circular, Rajab 1, 1252 (Abdine Archives).
[2] To the Divan al Chora, Rabi-al-awal 17, 1260 (*ibid.*).
[3] To the mudirs, Safar 10, 1249 (*ibid.*).
[4] To the mudirs, Zilkaidah 17, 1250 (*ibid.*).
[5] Campbell, September 15, 1835 (F.O. 78–258).
[6] Artin Bey, *op. cit.* pp. 128 *sqq.* Barnett, April 16, 1845 (F.O.
78–623).

trade policy closely affected both and received a great deal of attention. Under Mameluke rule the Turkish Capitulations had scarcely been reckoned as applying to Egypt. Life had been too insecure, trade too irregular, the beys too rebellious, and the European trade with Egypt too insignificant for France or England to attempt to stand upon their theoretical rights. This attitude had continued long after the pasha had established himself at Cairo, and for years no one thought of protesting formally, however much he might complain in private, of the regulations introduced in trading matters. It was not till the 'thirties of the century that difficulties began to arise. Then Campbell criticises the apathy and neglect of the earlier consuls, "many of whom, being in trade and in debt to the pasha, were afraid to assert the just rights of their countrymen";[1] while Molé, writing to de Lesseps two years later, lamented the early tolerance of the European representatives which had complicated matters and rendered complaint difficult.[2] In its origin and early stages the pasha's trade policy had been inspired by his need of finding money and by those evident advantages of monopoly which have always appealed to eastern rulers no less than to western merchants. Salt in 1820 and again in 1826 sent home sharp complaints of the mercantile evils flowing from Muhammad 'Ali's position as the chief merchant of the country which he ruled.[3] He not only compelled the fellah to cultivate, but in some areas he determined what crops should be grown, and required the produce to be delivered into the government warehouses at a fixed rate.[4]

[1] Campbell, July 15, 1835 (F.O. 78–258).
[2] Molé to de Lesseps, March 3, 1837 (F.O. 78–319).
[3] Salt, June 30, 1820 and April 4, 1826 (F.O. 78–96 and 147).
[4] The student of colonial history will be reminded of the Dutch system of "cultures" in Java.

The evils of such a practice are too evident to require statement. But there was another aspect of the matter. The resources of the country were being developed as they had not been for ages. "It is also to be remembered", says Salt, "that the pasha had in some sort created all these fine articles of produce which now form the most valuable commodities for export, as cotton, indigo, sugar, by the judicious application of large capital to these several branches of industry, which the peasants would neither have had the means nor spirit to have improved."[1] Later on the poppy culture was introduced on a large scale in Upper Egypt. Plantations of mulberry trees were made. Factories were set up for the manufacture of sugar and distillation of rum. A tannery was established at Rosetta to supply belts, boots and saddles for the army.[2] Mills were built for the manufacture of cotton cloth. At one time the pasha had almost realised at all events one aspect of the socialist ideal.

Many of these activities were based on false notions. The more elaborate factories were a failure. The machinery was neglected, the running parts left unoiled, the management ignorant and careless. Oxen provided the driving power, whereas of course the Nile itself should have been harnessed to the work. The fellahin detested the unaccustomed regularity of toil and had to be gathered as the army conscripts were, by force. The pasha, Bowring observed with complete truth, "takes hands from the fields, where they would be creating wealth, to employ them in...fabrics[3] where they are wasting it".[4] He was said to have sunk twelve million sterling in these factories and the machinery

---

[1] Salt, May 20, 1825 (F.O. 78–135).
[2] Barker, *Syria and Egypt*, II, 157–8.
[3] I presume "fabriques".
[4] Bowring to Campbell, December 17, 1837 (F.O. 78–342).

with which they were equipped,[1] and all to no purpose. But wasted as much of this endeavour was, it is worth noting with respect because it marks a modification of the pasha's conceptions of his duty. He began by seeking only to raise money. He ended by seeking, however mistakenly, to develop and civilise the country. In this matter he was carried away into an excessive and unwise imitation of the West; but he had come to be something far nobler than the greedy adventurer seeking nothing but his own power and wealth. Even his monopolies had their good side. He may have squeezed the fellah, but he squeezed him less closely than the foreign merchants would have done had they been left free to buy and sell as they pleased, and the burden of mercantile advances would have been yet heavier than the arrears of the pasha's revenue. Of this Muhammad 'Ali was convinced.[2]

This policy however could not but provoke the irritation of the British government. Since Egypt was part of the Ottoman Empire it must be bound by the Turkish Capitulations, and these, as read by British merchants, signified the right of free and unrestricted trade. "They may bring", ran the 53rd article, "and may in like manner buy and export all sorts of merchandise without anyone presuming to prohibit or molest them." But in the first place this apparent right to liberty of trade was limited by an ominously obscure phrase elsewhere excluding "prohibited articles" from its operation. Salt argued correctly that "it leaves almost everything to the caprice of governors and commandants, who may take advantage thereof to introduce any articles they may choose on that list"—a view which Stratford Canning, in an appended note,

[1] Bowring, Report (*Parl. Papers*, 1840, xxi, 31 *sqq.*). Campbell to Bowring, January 18, 1838 (F.O. 78–342).
[2] Campbell, March 24, 1839 (F.O. 78–373).

described as "well-grounded and judicious".[1] Hence
the negotiations which Palmerston undertook through
Ponsonby for a revision of British trading regulations
in the Turkish empire, leading up to the commercial
convention which was signed in 1838. It contained
clear stipulations for the abolition of monopolies, which
Palmerston was resolved should be duly enforced in
Egypt, and which he argued would benefit that
country as much as those who traded with it. "It must
be evident", he wrote, "to every person who is at all
conversant with the principles which regulate the
wealth of nations that [the pasha's] system...tends to
keep Egypt and Syria in a state of abject poverty."[2] As
soon as the convention had been concluded, Ponsonby
called on the Syrian consuls for an account of the monopolies established by the pasha's government. The
consuls at Aleppo and Damascus reported there were
none. The consul at Beyrout sent in a long list which
showed on examination that he confused monopolies
with excise duties.[3] In Egypt the position was clearer.
The pasha exercised monopolies. But mainly owing to
delays in the transmission of the necessary farmans
from Constantinople, the question was not really
taken up till after the crisis of 1840 had been settled. It
then proved difficult, because the great quantities of
cotton, sugar and other produce controlled by the
pasha were delivered to him either as the owner of
chifliqs[4] or as part of the land revenue of the country.
Palmerston drafted angry and threatening despatches.[5]
But commercial opinion at Alexandria and Cairo had
been too much annoyed by his late policy and perhaps

[1] Salt, May 20, 1825 (F.O. 78–135).
[2] Memorandum, September 13, 1838 (F.O. 96–19).
[3] Campbell, March 30, 1839 (F.O. 78–376).
[4] Cf. p. 213, *supra.*
[5] To Barnett, August 26, 1841 (F.O. 78–451).

was insufficiently informed of "the principles which regulate the wealth of nations", to aid the consul with complaints.[1] There was moreover another reason why they regarded the commercial convention with marked distaste and were unwilling to see it put into operation in Egypt. So far as that country was concerned, it had been prepared, I think, rather to reduce the pasha's revenues by getting rid of his monopolies than in order to benefit British trade. While it was decidedly advantageous at Constantinople, Smyrna, and other ports under the Sultan, in Egypt the British exporter of cotton would be required to pay 12 per cent. instead of 3, and in Syria all produce, when exported by British merchants, would pay 12 per cent. instead of 2. Foreign merchants would of course continue to pay only the old rates, so perhaps there was good ground for the mercantile dislike of Palmerston's policy.[2] Nor was this all. The rates of the convention were specific, not *ad valorem* rates. When they came to be actually introduced in 1841 they proved to be 22 per cent. *ad valorem* on cotton, 20–25 per cent. on wool, well over 12 per cent. on grain, while import dues, which had been meant to amount to 5 per cent., worked out at nearer 9 per cent. The upshot of the matter was that the pasha finally agreed to levy *ad valorem* rates of 12 per cent. on exports and 5 per cent. on imports payable in Egyptian currency,[3] while in regard to the monopolies he promised in future to sell his produce by public auction.[4] It is difficult to reflect on these blundering, disingenuous negotiations with any feeling of national pride.

One essential condition of the maintenance of the

[1] Barnett to Stratford Canning, December 1, 1841 (F.O. 78–451).
[2] Campbell, September 3, 1839 (F.O. 78–376).
[3] Barnett, May 20 and 26, 1842 (F.O. 78–502).
[4] The same, May 15, 1842 (*ibid.*).

pasha's position had been the assemblage of forces capable of opposing those of his sovereign, the Sultan. That he should create as large an army as he could was a thing of course; but that he should seek to create a navy marks the vigour and the limitations of his mind. It was a prime need if he was ever, as he hoped, to dominate the empire. But it had to be built up from the very foundations, in a country with no trace of naval traditions, by a ruler with not an atom of technical knowledge. He began by building abroad— at Bombay, at Leghorn and Marseilles. In 1821 he asked both the English and the French governments to build him frigates.[1] A little later he made a dock at Alexandria and began to build on his own account, employing French shipwrights to control the work. In 1828 he began to build a naval arsenal for the supply and maintenance of his naval force. He set to work at once to replace the fleet that had perished at Navarino, confident now that his vessels would be superior to any that the Sultan could assemble. Instead of building frigates he began to build ships of the line, mounting a hundred guns or more.[2] In 1829 Cérisy, from the royal dockyard at Toulon, was placed in charge of the Alexandria docks. In 1831 was launched the first of his 100-gun ships, named after himself.[3] In 1833 he had six ships of the line, ranging from 84 to 110 guns, besides seven frigates, and in 1837 he had eight of the former besides one more under construction.[4] In the arsenal was a staff of over 3000 hands under the direction of sixty Europeans. Attached to it was the naval school of Ras-al-tin with 1200 cadets.

[1] Salt, November 6, 1821 (F.O. 78–103).
[2] Barker to Gordon, May 26, 1829 (F.O. 78–184).
[3] The same to Sir P. Malcolm, January 15, 1831 (F.O. 78–202).
[4] Campbell, April 24, 1833 and July 14, 1837 (F.O. 78–227 and 320).

This development was pressed on by the pasha with strong enthusiasm and the closest personal attention, driving on his subjects to co-operate however reluctantly with him. He would often amuse himself by cruising off Alexandria, and I have already mentioned his hurrying off to chase the Greeks with a single vessel.[1] He established a code of regulations, based on those in force in the British and French navies, but carefully adapted to Turkish usage.[2] But while his vigour could get ships, and good ones, built, not even he could raise sailors where no mercantile marine had ever existed. "A hot press is on foot", our consul-general writes in 1832, "not of sea-faring men, for none such are to be found, but of every individual without discrimination." Within forty-eight hours some 1000 men were gathered up in Alexandria to complete the complements.[3] With a stiffening of real sailors and under the command of experienced and skilful officers, something might have been made even of such haphazard crews. But, as the same writer says, "they have no experienced and patriotic officers nor even ordinary seamen".[4] In 1831 Muhammad 'Ali hoped to make good these deficiencies by enlisting English officers and men, and employed Colonel Light—a son, I think, of the grantee of Penang—to engage them for him. He wanted two post-captains, two commanders, several lieutenants, and forty or fifty petty officers and able seamen.[5] But nothing for the moment was done. Not until 1834 did the British government decide to permit naval officers on half pay to serve under the pasha,[6]

[1] Cf. p. 74, *supra*.
[2] Barker to Sir P. Malcolm, *ut supra*.
[3] The same to Stratford Canning, February 20, 1832 (F.O. 78–213).
[4] The same to Mandeville, January 2, 1832 (*ibid.*).
[5] The same, August 11, 1831 (F.O. 78–202).
[6] Campbell, October 25, 1834 (F.O. 78–247).

and by then the pasha had already employed a number of French officers. Besson Bey was vice-admiral with a European-educated Turk, Hasan Bey, under him as rear-admiral. By way of showing his personal interest and placing his navy under powerful patronage in the future, the pasha resolved that one of his sons, Said Bey, should be brought up to the sea. He was therefore sent on ship-board, nominally as a midshipman, at the age of thirteen. He was provided with a tutor, and a special French officer was detailed to teach him his professional duties. After five years' service he was given command of a corvette. But he afflicted his father by his inactivity and premature fatness. He was periodically weighed, and whenever an increase was recorded he would receive a letter exhorting him to discern good from evil, to ensue manly qualities, and to rid himself of fleshliness hateful in the eye of all.[1]

The pasha's navy, like his factories, lacked a solid foundation. It could only be maintained by the closest attention of its founder. It appealed in no way to any class of the people. It had no natural recruiting ground. It was more unpopular than the army. It lay in Alexandria during the brief Syrian war; the Capitan Pasha's surrender robbed it of its chance of performing the service for which it had been called into being; and soon after the pasha's death all the serviceable vessels were sold off to the Porte. The experiment had proved a failure.

The pasha's military labours were much more fruitful and important. I have already mentioned how his original mercenary and foreign army had been transformed into one following European discipline, formed on the European mode of organisation, and raised in

[1] Campbell, August 19, 1834; October 7, 1836; and May 14, 1839 (F.O. 78-246, 284, 373). Also the Pasha to Said Bey, Ramzan 9, 1253 (Abdine Archives).

the country by conscription.[1] By 1832 a very considerable disciplined force had been raised. It then consisted of twenty regiments of infantry, ten of cavalry, with a small body of Turkish and a much larger one of Bedouin irregulars, totalling 83,000 men.[2] Three years later the strength had been raised in Syria alone to 69,000—an increase of 50 per cent.[3] The pasha probably had at this time over 100,000 men under arms. At first they were equipped with muskets imported from France and England: but, the quality being poor, the pasha set up his own factory, and was provided with 2000 stand of arms of the best and latest pattern from the Tower as samples.[4] The training of the troops was at first under the superintendence and control of French and other continental officers, such as Colonel Sève. The officers, for whom special schools were established at Ghiza and elsewhere, were drawn almost exclusively from Turkish and other foreign families,[5] many having been the personal slaves of the pasha who had chosen them as showing fitness for military service. The privates however were exclusively Egyptians with a considerable number of Syrians so long as Syria remained in Muhammad 'Ali's possession.

The methods by which they were raised have generally been considered the worst blot upon his administration. A census had been attempted but abandoned, owing to the universal opposition in which even the pasha's officials had taken part.[6] The only possible procedure was to call upon the mudirs to

[1] Vide p. 65, supra.
[2] Barker, July 21, 1832 (F.O. 78–214).
[3] Campbell, December 12, 1835 (F.O. 78–258).
[4] The same, December 19, 1833, and to Campbell, September 16, 1834 (F.O. 78–228, 244).
[5] Barker seems to have been misinformed when he says they were all Arabs. Despatch of June 23, 1829 (F.O. 78–184).
[6] Campbell, Report (F.O. 78–408 B).

supply a fixed quota of men. This quota was divided out among the villages. The shaikhs seized as many as they could, released those who offered the largest bribes, and sent in the remainder chained two and two like felons.[1] When the pasha's power was at its height he was perhaps claiming one man out of every six for military service.

Nothing in the whole government was so feared and hated as the conscription. The stories of travellers who assert that many cut off their right forefinger in order to escape service in the army[2] might be suspected of philanthropic exaggeration. Campbell, relating that they cut off a finger, drew their teeth, and blinded themselves,[3] might have been misinformed. But such statements are borne out beyond the possibility of error by the pasha's own correspondence. Men who put rat's bane in their eyes, he writes, are beasts in human form who must be sent to forced labour for life.[4] If the barber's wife who assisted them is guilty, she is to be executed and her body exposed for three days.[5] Another woman for a like offence is to be thrown into the Nile.[6] Conscripts are to be warned that if they maim themselves, not only will they be sent to forced labour for life but also another member of their family will be seized in their stead.[7] The officials are warned that the practice must be due to their neglect and that if it continues they also will receive the same punishment.[8] Forced labour proving no deterrent, death was

---

[1] Barker to Sir P. Malcolm, July 8, 1829, and Murray, June 1, 1848 (F.O. 78–184, 757).
[2] St John, *op. cit.* II, 175.
[3] Campbell, February 26, 1838 (F.O. 78–342).
[4] To the Kotkhuda Bey, Shaban 17, 1245 (Abdine Archives).
[5] To the Mamur of Fayum, Ramzan 1, 1245 (*ibid.*).
[6] To the Mamur of Tanta, Zilkaidah 13, 1245 (*ibid.*).
[7] Circular, Shawal 21, 1248 (F.O. 78–231).
[8] Circular to mudirs, Zilhaj 14, 1248 (Abdine Archives).

inflicted instead.[1] Here is something real to justify Palmerston's aversion to the pasha's rule and to reinforce political expediency by humane considerations.

Nor in this matter can the blame fairly be laid upon the Sultan's obstinate hostility, for recruitment might have been fairer, less a matter of official greed and oppression. In this matter the pasha was certainly carried away by his political dreams into a policy which reminds one that he was a Turk first and a benevolent despot afterwards. Yet, if the cruelty of his methods can be put aside, the purpose and the result of his military levies were far from wholly evil. Nothing else could have done so much to raise the spirit of men who had been serfs from before the time when the first of the pyramids was built. No one since the Arab conquest had ever thought of asking them to fight. They had been good to till the fields, to carry burdens, to be beaten, to obey commands, to beget children who would bear the same painful inheritance. Their terrors at being seized and dragged away to serve in the pasha's army was great enough to induce them to hack off a finger, to wrench out their teeth, to blind an eye. But their reluctance to play the part of men does not condemn the pasha for compelling them to play it. Nor was this all. Observers agree that the New Model— the Nizam jadid—was incomparably less oppressive to the general population than the undisciplined foreign mercenaries had been. They did not leave a trail of havoc behind them in their march. They did not move through an Egyptian province as if they were in an enemy's country. The pasha's military organisation was not only an act of power executed in complete disregard of the subject's wishes, but also a measure of education and an administrative reform.

[1] To the Minister of Marine, Rabi-al-awal 3, 1251 (Abdine Archives).

Justice, though urgently needing reform, offered
problems which could not be solved by swift violence.
It was too closely intertwined with the sacred law for
the pasha to touch it with anything but great caution.
In all matters of ecclesiastical law, marriage, divorce
and, above all, inheritance, the only competent
authority was the *mufti*, whose annual appointment by
the Porte was one of the very few remaining relics of
Turkish dominion. This official always bought his
office from the Divan, and so could not be expected to
be over-scrupulous in his administration of justice or in
the selection of the subordinate *qazis* who held posts
under him. Muhammad 'Ali had the poorest opinion
of their integrity. To a family quarrelling over the
division of an inheritance he warmly recommended a
friendly agreement, for, if they fell into the qazi's
clutches, not one alone, but all the claimants would get
the smaller portion.[1] But although the pasha could not
interfere directly with their jurisdiction, he did what he
could to limit its effects. At Cairo and Alexandria he
established two new courts, entirely freed from the
trammels of Islamic law, consisting of merchants instead of theologians, and intended to determine commercial disputes, especially those arising between
Muslims and Christians. What was specially noteworthy was that these courts did not include even a
majority of Muslims. At Alexandria, for instance, it
was composed of nine members, of whom only four
were Arabs, the others being a Frenchman, a Jew, two
Levantine Christians and a Greek.[2]

Criminal justice was normally administered by the
executive authorities. From the first establishment of
his power, the pasha had done his utmost to repress all

[1] Puckler-Muskau, *op. cit.* I, 286–7.
[2] St John, *op. cit.* II, 429. Campbell's Report on Syria, enc. in
despatch, August 23, 1836 (F.O. 78–283).

crimes of violence. Missett in 1813 had commented on the remarkable fact that the inhabitants of Cairo for the first time for many years enjoyed complete personal security.[1] This was only accomplished by the exercise of much severity and many executions. The Bab-uz-zuwaila, where public hangings took place, was at one time constantly adorned by the corpses of malefactors. The pasha's sentences were arbitrary, and he would at times give decisions hardly reconcilable with the ideas of Europe. A man convicted of theft from the musket factory, for instance, was to work for life in irons if young, but if old was to be hanged as a salutary example.[2] But there is little to suggest that the administration of criminal justice was more ferocious than it had been in England at all events in theory until Peel's reforms, and as time went on it became noticeably milder. Labour in chains was frequently substituted for the rope, and the executioner at Cairo told Bowring that he had little then to do.[3]

Slavery and the slave trade were far too well-established institutions to be abolished by Muhammad 'Ali, even had he desired to do so. He had been familiar with them from childhood; they represented the immemorial practice of the East; they violated no moral sentiment of oriental minds; until recently they had not seriously disturbed the much more squeamish conscience of the West. Nothing then was done, or was likely to be done, to limit the slave market of Cairo or reduce the power which Muslim law conferred upon the master over his slave. In 1836 the Russian consul-general, Du Hamel, raised the question, and asked the pasha whether he could not take away from masters the power of inflicting death and wanton ill-treatment.

[1] Missett, November 9, 1813 (F.O. 24–4).
[2] To Habib Effendi, Zilhaj 26, 1252 (Abdine Archives).
[3] Bowring, Report (Parl. Papers, 1840, xxi, 123).

Muhammad 'Ali thought that something might perhaps
be done in the case of male slaves, but gave no hopes of
his being able to interfere with the treatment of women
slaves. The harims, he said, were sacred places to which
no stranger could penetrate.[1] There the matter rested.
The conflict of external policy which speedily arose
between him and the European powers must have
strongly indisposed him to touch a thorny question in
which he had no personal sympathy for reform.

The slave trade itself was one of the oldest branches
of traffic in the countries which he ruled. Slave hunts
were periodically conducted in the Sudan and the
country to the southward, and the captives carried up
in caravans of considerable size. Precise information
on this subject was very hard to get, but a French
enquirer at the time of the French occupation gathered
from the Copt writer who had registered the slaves
brought up to Cairo for thirty years that they had
hardly ever exceeded 4000 in a year.[2] On the establishment of Muhammad 'Ali's power in the Sudan, it is
likely that for a time the number considerably increased. The reader may remember that the pasha had
cherished the design of forming a great army of them.[3]
Every autumn raids were carried out, and for a time
the slave trade in that region was made a government
monopoly.[4] Muhammad 'Ali's southern conquests
were not the only cause making for the expansion of
this traffic. The Russian occupation of Georgia and
Circassia greatly reduced the supply of slaves sent from
those regions to Constantinople, and so increased the
demand for such slaves as could be supplied from

[1] Campbell, December 24, 1836 (F.O. 78–284).
[2] Frank, *Commerce des Nègres au Kaire*, pp. 19 *sqq.*
[3] *Vide* p. 63, *supra.*
[4] To the sar'-askar, Kordofan, Rabi-al-awal 15, 1237 (Abdine
Archives).

Egypt. Then too the matter became much better known. The regularity of the new government permitted Europeans to travel through the Sudan with safety. A certain Dr Holroyd, for example, furnished details of the slave hunts and of the treatment of the captured, which perhaps did not exaggerate the horrors of the practice, but which was certainly employed by Palmerston to prejudice the English public against Muhammad 'Ali's government.[1] After the pasha's prolonged tour in the Sudan in 1838, he took measures to limit the slave trade there. The land revenue, which till then had been paid in slaves, was ordered to be collected in future in grain and other produce; but, although this no doubt did some good, the barbarous, time-honoured custom of slave raids long continued to persist.[2]

A strong contrast to the pasha's attitude to slavery and the slave trade is afforded by his policy in matters of sanitation and education. He was not much impressed by the western arguments in favour of universal liberty. But he was quite sure that western physicians knew more than Arab *hakims*, and that his people would greatly benefit from western knowledge. In sanitation and medical organisation he placed great and deserved faith in the French doctor, Clot Bey, under whom was established a medical school at Abuzabel. The general level of education rendered this attempt premature. The chief instructors were Frenchmen who knew no Arabic; the students were Arabs who knew no French. The net result can hardly have exceeded the production of a number of "surgeons" with no adequate knowledge of western medicine. It

[1] Bowring, Report (*Parl. Papers*, 1840, XXI, 83 *sqq.*). Campbell to Bidwell, December 1, 1837 (F.O. 78–322).
[2] Campbell, March 15, 1839, and Barnett, April 19, 1843 (F.O. 78–373, 541).

would have been wiser no doubt to have begun by
sending a limited number of men to be trained abroad.
But the pasha wished to have surgeons and assistant-
surgeons attached to the various units of his army and
insisted on immediate provision for them. He was
however always eager to encourage skilled visitors. In
1836 an oculist, Dr Charles Nayler, visited Alexandria.
He was so successful in treating cases of ophthalmia
that he was besieged by men of all classes, seventy or
eighty daily gathering outside his house in the hopes of
attracting his attention and benefiting by what seemed
to them more than human skill. The pasha, in the hope
of securing his services, offered him a salary of £1200 a
year.[1]

One of the most horrible sights of Cairo had been
"the hospital of the Moristan"—a charity attached to
one of the mosques, where one could visit sick men
stinking with filth and over-run with vermin, or, better
still, peer through square gratings at chained and naked
maniacs. These most pitiable of beings were in charge
of an old Arab who showed them off in the hope that
visitors would make him presents. At Clot Bey's suggestion the pasha agreed to the abolition of this medieval
relic and ordered another hospital to be prepared in
the great square of Usbekiah.[2]

Another illustration of Muhammad 'Ali's readiness
to adopt improvements is afforded by the Board of
Sanitation. In 1831 a very severe epidemic of cholera
broke out. It had been brought by pilgrims from the
Hijaz to Suez, where 150 died in two days, and then a
fortnight later it broke out suddenly at Cairo. In the
hope of preventing the disease from spreading to
Alexandria, the pasha invited the aid of the consuls-

[1] Campbell, October 5, 1836 (F.O. 78–284).
[2] St John, op. cit. II, 309. Bowring, Report (Parl. Papers, 1840,
XXI, 141).

general, placing all his troops in the neighbourhood at
their disposal and giving them complete liberty in the
matter of expenditure. They accepted the call, although
they seem to have despaired of staying the disease. Two
cordons were established between Cairo and Alexandria. But, as might no doubt have been expected, the
cordons themselves speedily were attacked. In less
than a week 800 soldiers were in hospital, the physicians
and apothecaries either died or ran away, all public
services fell into confusion, and protective measures
were abandoned. Before the epidemic ceased, not far
from 9000 persons had perished at Cairo, and over
1500 at Alexandria. At this time the populations of
the two cities were computed at 300,000 and 90,000
respectively.[1]

Cholera was only an occasional scourge on so large a
scale as this, and did not again become epidemic until
1848.[2] But bubonic plague was a constant source of
terror. Readers of *Eothen* will remember how the
Franks were accustomed, when plague was abroad, to
shut themselves up in strict seclusion, while the Muslims
gloomily attempted to ignore the danger that encom-
passed them. But it was not Muslims of all ranks who
in such times were to be met striding defiantly through
the streets. Such confidence in the irrevocable decrees
of Allah was displayed by few save the poorer sort,
whom narrow circumstances made less careful of the
continuance of their earthly penury. Those whom
wealth allowed a foretaste of the delights of heaven
were as cautious as the unbelieving Franks themselves.
The pasha could be visited by none—not even the
consuls-general were allowed to break his quarantine.
The public offices were closed. Business came to a

[1] Barker, August 18 and 23 and September 2; Barker to Gordon,
September 29, 1831 (F.O. 78–202).
[2] Murray, July 26, 1848 (F.O. 78–757).

stand.[1] The worst outbreak was the one that fell upon
Lower Egypt in 1835. It was thought even more
destructive than the Great Plague that had raged forty
years earlier. In three months the casualties were
announced as 31,000 at Cairo alone. But Campbell
believed that they had been much more numerous.
He reckoned that more than this number of Muslims
alone had died. In a single great household 135 deaths
had occurred. Twelve hundred Muslim houses were
shut up because every inhabitant was dead. A quarter
of the Copts perished, adding 20,000 to the roll.[2]

Since quarantine was the only protective measure
that had as yet been adopted against the plague, the
pasha had again invoked the services of the consuls-
general, without whose aid and concurrence it would
be difficult and perhaps dangerous to enforce quarantine on a large number of European ships and sailors.
The consuls had therefore formed a committee which
was known at different times as the Board of Sanitation
and the Committee of Health. A lazaretto had been
built, near the place where Cleopatra's Needle then
stood, on the shore of the New (or eastern) Port at
Alexandria, where all vessels undergoing quarantine
were required to anchor;[3] and the chief of police at
Alexandria was warned to enforce all the rules that the
consuls might adopt. This was no easy matter. The inhabitants were unwilling to follow rules, the object of
which they could not understand, and which they
fancied were contrary to the rules of their faith. The
avoidance of contagion, the pasha declared, is not contrary to the law; he promised to obtain a *fatwa* or
declaration to that effect from the theologians. The

[1] Salt, June 15, 1816 (F.O. 24-6). Campbell, March 29 and
April 15, 1835 (F.O. 78-257).
[2] Campbell, June 25, 1835 (F.O. 78-257).
[3] The same, October 16, 1835 (F.O. 78-260).

citizens, he concluded, "are like beasts, unable to discern good and evil".[1] A little later another committee was formed, with Campbell at its head, to improve the general sanitation of Alexandria. A large number of "filthy Arab huts" were destroyed; the old ruined ditch, full of stagnant water, was filled up; the government tannery standing in the middle of the city was removed; a broad road was cut from the European quarter to the Custom House.[2] In 1837, despite the constant influx of pilgrims from plague-stricken regions, Campbell was able to report that plague had disappeared. He ascribed it, of course, to the system of quarantine, which had been strictly maintained. "The pasha leaves the whole affair", he writes, "in the hands of the consular Board of Health, and not only puts in force...every measure ordered by the Board, but he moreover supplies without ever making any difficulty all the funds required...for the service of the lazzaretto, and which is very costly from the great number of Europeans employed in that service."[3]

The recall of Campbell and the events of 1839–40 broke up this organisation. Campbell's successor, Hodges, was much more interested in obtaining information about the defences of Alexandria than in aiding the administration. A new Board of Health was therefore set up, to which Muhammad 'Ali nominated three of the consuls-general, but over which the consuls-general as such had no control. Disputes followed about the proper composition of the board. Physicians too began to question the efficacy of quarantine and to suspect that plague might be conveyed by other means than personal contact. The old system was therefore relaxed and finally abandoned. But it exhibits another

[1] To the head of the Divan, Shawal 13, 1250 (Abdine Archives).
[2] Campbell, October 16, 1835 (F.O. 78–260).
[3] The same, November 7, 1837 (F.O. 78–321).

undeniable proof of the pasha's willingness to adopt
European ideas and guidance where he believed they
might be of real service.

But his educational measures afford the most remarkable evidence of his policy of reform. Cairo was of
course one of the great centres of Islamic culture. To its
great university housed in the old Al Azhar mosque
came students of all the nations of Islam. But its
organisation and studies were alike medieval. It bred
theologians and ecclesiastical lawyers. It did not breed
men of affairs and administrators. All western knowledge was completely excluded. New schools were
needed to provide the wider outlook which the pasha's
administrative ideas required. While Muhammad 'Ali
continued to protect and maintain the ancient university, he set up beside it a whole series of institutions
designed indirectly to modify and modernise the
popular mind. An English contemporary well summed
up his purpose and attitude. Whereas Sultan Mahmud,
he says, by his sudden, violent reforms had weakened
the allegiance of the Turks, Muhammad 'Ali had
always maintained a high character among Muslims
"by adopting the only wise course to be pursued with a
nation in so low a scale of civilisation. By a system of
gradual ameliorations, without violating religious prejudices, he has laid the foundation of a permanent
reform in the institutions of the nation, trusting to the
progress of knowledge from the general establishment
of public schools throughout his government for the
final establishment of his plans of reform".[1]

This policy seems to date from about 1820 and was in
origin the natural corollary of the reform of the army.
The introduction of European methods of organisation and training clearly demanded officers capable
of studying European military science, engineering,

[1] Memorandum, Thurburn, October 14, 1836 (F.O. 78–295).

mathematics. The first indication that this was recognised seems to be the establishment of an Italian, Costi by name, in the citadel of Cairo, to teach drawing and mathematics. Then come orders for the teaching of Italian—the *lingua franca* of the Levant—and demands for teachers of French and Turkish, and a capable engineer.[1] From this simple beginning arose schools designed to train officers for the five branches of the pasha's service—the artillery, engineers, cavalry, infantry, and marine—under European direction.

In order to broaden the basis of instruction, a considerable number of young Egyptians were sent to France, and a few to England, to be educated at the pasha's expense. The fruits of this were seen in 1833 when a Polytechnic School was established as a training school for the officers' colleges. The teaching staff included two Europeans only, one for chemistry and one for mathematics. Beside them were four Armenians, one of whom had spent ten years at Stoneyhurst, and six Muslims, three of whom had been educated at Paris and three in England.[2] This expansion was followed up by the establishment of several primary schools in each mudirliq, with two large "preparatory" schools, one at Cairo and one at Alexandria, designed to feed the Polytechnic School. Admission to the schools was in effect reception into the pasha's service. The pupils were fed, clothed, and lodged at the public charge, and received besides small monthly allowances, rising in amount as the boys passed from class to class. Their future career, the branch of service into which they were drafted, the technical training which each received, was a matter for the determination of the pasha or his officials. Egypt was the first oriental country in which

[1] Letters of Zilhaj 4 and 8, 1235, and Rabi-al-awal 5, 1236 (Abdine Archives).
[2] Campbell, November 14, 1833 (F.O. 78–228).

anything like a regular system of westernised education was established.[1] Bowring was right in criticising the scheme as founded on too narrow a basis of primary education, and as designed to secure superior education for the few instead of providing a universal system for the many. But the pasha cannot reasonably be condemned for not adopting a system which the most advanced western nations had not yet adopted.

This foundation of schools and colleges was accompanied by the establishment of printing presses and the appearance of a newspaper and a gazette. By the end of 1837 seventy-three oriental works had been printed at the press set up at Bulaq, then the suburb of Cairo abutting on the Nile. These included translations of a good many technical works for the use of the new schools.[2] The pasha projected a newspaper to be printed in French and Arabic.[3] The *European Press* existed at Alexandria in 1824, and in that year printed a descriptive poem by Salt, the consul-general.[4] At the same time the position of the European and the Christian were transformed. Before Muhammad 'Ali's rise to power native Christians had been subject to many disabilities. They were obliged to distinguish themselves by the colour of their dress. They were forbidden to ride horses. They were forbidden during the month of the great Muslim fast to eat, drink, or smoke in the streets by day, so as not to remind the true believer of his compulsory abstinence.[5] The Frank inhabitants of Cairo and Alexandria lived in separate quarters with guarded entrances, and, when they went abroad, wore Turkish dress in order to avoid insult.

[1] Puckler-Muskau, *op. cit.* I, 125 *sqq.* Bowring, Report (*Parl. Papers*, 1840, XXI, 125 *sqq.*).
[2] Medem to Nesselrode, January 12/24, 1838.
[3] St John, *op. cit.* I, 54.
[4] *Egypt: a descriptive poem.*
[5] Politis, *op. cit.* I, 175. Jabarti, *op. cit.* VI, 95.

"As is known to every prudent person", ran the Turkish declaration of war on Russia in 1827, "every Muslim is by nature the mortal enemy of infidels, and every infidel the mortal enemy of Muslims." But under the pasha's rule the spirit of the government was transformed, and that of the people sensibly modified. Two of Muhammad 'Ali's relatives, made prisoners by the Russians in 1827, returned from captivity in 1829 full of the good treatment they and other prisoners of war had experienced.[1] In a year when the Nile threatened not to rise to its accustomed height, joint supplications were offered on its bank not only by the heads of the different Muslim sects, but by Jewish rabbis and Christian priests as well.[2] Wolff, the mad missionary, was suffered readily enough to preach in the streets in an Arabic that no one could understand, but, when he placarded Cairo with too legible inscriptions, then indeed the pasha requested his departure since nothing could be done to protect him from a chance attack.[3] Throughout the crisis of 1839–40 Englishmen continued to dwell in Cairo and Alexandria without insult.

This policy was of course unpopular with the shaikhs of Al Azhar. One popular preacher, Shaikh Ibrahim, was bitter in his denunciations. The Jews, for instance, secured a monopoly of the butcher's trade at Alexandria, and so imperilled the salvation of all true believers there, for they would not use the sacred formula, or turn the animal's head towards Mecca, and the hafts of their knives were fastened with only three nails instead of five.[4] But the shaikh was exiled to Tunis.

In all these matters, in compelling toleration, in promoting health and knowledge, in dispensing strict

[1] Barker to Gordon, May 20, 1829 (F.O. 78–184).
[2] Clot Bey, *Aperçu*, I, 317.
[3] Barker, *Syria and Egypt*, II, 142.
[4] St John, *op. cit.* I, 43.

justice, in reorganising his troops and building up a naval force, in defining taxation, in encouraging new crops, in watching closely over the conduct of his officials, the pasha had to work against the opposition of almost all his own people. Most of his most cherished projects were neglected or abandoned by his immediate successors. Some, such as the formation of a navy, were opposed by obstacles too great to be overcome. Most were weakened and impaired by his lack of confidence in the future and his sense that whatever was done must be done by himself and within the limited duration of his own life. So that his work must be adjudged hasty, premature, unfinished. But in spite of that, in spite of the reaction which followed on his disappearance, it would be quite unfair to regard his work as wasted. The strong impulse which he had given, the contacts which he had established with the West, continued, so that when at a later time Egypt began once more to go forward, she began her new movement far in advance of the point at which the great pasha had found her, thanks above everything to the cultural influences to which he had opened his country so widely and so wisely.

Chapter VIII

MUHAMMAD 'ALI'S GOVERNMENT IN
CRETE AND SYRIA

In the course of the Greek war, both Cyprus and Crete had been placed by the Sultan under the care of Muhammad 'Ali, presumably because he alone could secure them from Greek attacks. In 1830 the government of Crete was formally confided to him. He had made it a condition of accepting the charge that he should be allowed to send away the Turkish troops there and garrison the island solely with his Arab regiments.[1] He first sent as commandant a Turk named Usman Bey, whom he had sent to Italy and France to be educated.[2] The population was mixed, rather more than half being Greek by race. Fifty years earlier Savary had reckoned the total at 380,000 persons; but war, plague and misery had reduced it to less than 100,000 at the time when the pasha undertook its government. The mixture of peoples promised much trouble. Nor was the administration likely to be a gainful affair. The revenues were under four million piastres against an expenditure of over eleven. It seems probable that the offer was accepted because it gave the pasha a naval station well to the northward of Alexandria. He had been twice warned by Great Britain that any violent oppression of the Christian inhabitants might provoke the interference of the great powers.[3]

---

[1] Barker to Sir P. Malcolm, August 31, 1830 (F.O. 78–192).
[2] Same to same, September 17, 1830 (*ibid.*).
[3] To Barker, October 15 and December 31, 1828 (F.O. 78–170).

Such a warning was probably quite needless. The ruler who protected Christian minorities in Egypt and Syria was not likely to persecute a majority in Crete. His first act after the proclamation of his farman of appointment was to issue an address to the Candiotes. He assured them that they had nothing to fear, that he would smite any who smote them, and that he would establish two councils, one at Canea, the other at Candia, composed of both Christian and Muslim members, to hear and determine all but strictly legal questions such as inheritance. He intended to introduce material improvements too, such as a breakwater for the harbour of Canea, the re-afforestation of the hills, and the extension of cultivation.[1] Another project was to develop the port of Suda, both as an entrepôt for the Syrian trade and as a base for the Egyptian fleet.[2]

In 1833 the pasha visited Crete in person. Campbell at his invitation accompanied him and sent to England some interesting notes on the island. Under the Sultan it had been misruled by three pashas, all frequently changed and invariably oppressive. At the time of the Greek war the Turks would certainly have been driven out but for the troops sent by Muhammad 'Ali. Since the island had been transferred to him, he had sent as governor Mustafa Pasha, feared by the Turks but much esteemed by the Greek inhabitants. He had set up the promised mixed councils and two tribunals of first instance—one at Sphakia composed entirely of Greeks, as no Turks were living there. Loans of money and cattle had been made to enable the impoverished peasants to recultivate their farms, and a proclamation was issued that those Greeks who had fled might return and reoccupy their farms on condition of paying out those who had bought them at the same price as the

---

[1] Barker to Gordon, September 8, 1830 and enc. (F.O. 78–192).
[2] Campbell, May 26, 1833 (F.O. 78–227).

latter had paid. Many had done so and settled down as rayas under the pasha's government.[1]

However, in spite of the mildness of the administration, a good deal of discontent appeared. Many refugees refused to return except with Greek passports as Greek subjects, and some landed secretly in the hope of raising new troubles. The Candiote emigrants published a journal of their own called the *Minerva*, the main object of which was to arouse discontent in the island.[2] The pasha wisely refused to allow the refugees to re-enter the island except as rayas, declaring that any other course would greatly discontent the 60,000 Christians who had remained there and not demanded a new status.[3] But while the former irregular exactions were suppressed, regular taxation was increased. The *karach* or capitation-tax, levied on all Christian subjects of the Porte,[4] was collected with greater rigour and fewer exemptions. A duty was laid on wine, whether made for sale or for the private consumption of the maker. The monopoly of selling tobacco, wine and leather in the towns was farmed out. Much excitement arose. Miracles were reported to have occurred at different convents, and the peasants began to assemble in crowds. All this seems to have resulted from the *émigré* propaganda, and, when the time was judged ripe for an explosion, an unfortunate Turkish traveller was set upon and murdered. The assassin, a returned emigrant, was duly hanged. But this was the only execution. The remainder of the returned emigrants were either deported or permitted to resume their raya status on condition of their villages'

[1] Campbell, August 29, 1833 (F.O. 78–228).
[2] The same, August 21, 1833 (*ibid.*).
[3] The same, August 28, 1833 (*ibid.*).
[4] The word is properly *khirāj*, land revenue; but the Turks seem to have dropped this use of the word, and applied it to what was called the *jaziya* elsewhere.

standing surety for their good conduct,[1] and the pasha, having issued orders which were intended to increase the cultivation of the island, returned to Alexandria.

But unluckily his orders provided the occasion for fresh trouble. One of them directed the appointment in each district of two persons acquainted with the laws of Egypt, to visit each village, to consult with the rich as to the best means of assisting the poor, and to concert methods of transferring labour from the more populous villages to those in which men were few and lands uncultivated. Although this measure was accompanied by others undeniably calculated to benefit the people at large, such as the establishment of schools and the payment of allowances to the pupils, the Candiotes felt that the pasha was seeking to introduce the same control of the soil as prevailed in Egypt. They broke out into revolt, despite the fact that "the system of Mehemet Ali in Candia, however mistaken it may perhaps be in some points, breathes a spirit of benevolence, a liberality of principle in religion, a love of justice and an evident desire for the happiness and welfare of the people which reflect great credit to him".[2]

The pasha was indignant at this reception of his plans for the betterment of the island and determined to make an example of those mainly concerned; he ordered a certain number to be hanged if found guilty of rebellion, and he told Campbell that he expected a certain number of Turks would be found concerned in the revolt as well as the Greeks. If so, they too should be hanged.[3] In the end thirty-one persons, including five Turks, were executed. The French consul, who chanced to be an ardent Phil-hellene, said they were

[1] Campbell, August 29, 1833 (F.O. 78–228).
[2] The same, October 10, 1833 (ibid.).
[3] Idem.

put to death without trial.[1] The pasha seems to have
been convinced that the whole affair was the work of a
small number of agitators, and to have determined to
inflict a punishment which all the protests of all the
powers could not revoke, so restricted as to give none
an excuse for intervention, but so extended as to give
the Candiotes a sharp lesson. If so, he reckoned justly,
for he had no further trouble in Crete.

The administration of Crete had been entrusted to
Mustafa Pasha, who continued to exercise it during
practically the whole of Muhammad 'Ali's possession
of the island. The consuls of the English, French and
Russian governments all agree that his management
was mild, popular, and in a high degree successful.
Of course he was not able wholly to quench political
discontent. Crete was still a part of *Grecia Irridenta*.
There were always societies in Greece eager to add the
island to their national kingdom. There were always in
the island a number of persons who dreamt of reunion
with their fellow-countrymen or the establishment of
some sort of independence.[2] But so long as Mustafa
Pasha ruled Crete, it remained quiet and contented.
The Russian consul reports that taxes were paid without resistance, that complete tranquillity reigned, that
the municipal councils were always ready to do as the
governor wished.[3] In 1838 he was ordered to Syria to
take command of troops sent to suppress an insurrec-
tion that had broken out there. The English consul
remarks that his departure occasioned "the most spon-
taneous, disinterested and unequivocal marks of...
affection" from every class of the people. When he left
Canea, he was accompanied to his boat by the whole
population, young and old, lamenting with tears his

[1] Campbell, December 31, 1833 (F.O. 78–228).
[2] Lyons, August 2, 1838 (F.O. 32–78).
[3] Thoron to Medem, January 10, 1838.

departure and entreating him to return to them.[1] He had in fact protected the Greeks and soothed the Muslims.

In accordance however with his custom of believing the worst about Muhammad 'Ali's government and designs, Palmerston could not leave the island alone. The hanging of twenty-six Greeks and five Turks is mentioned by him "if report speaks true" as great severity and numerous executions. He suggested that the pasha might resign the island to the beneficent rule of the Sultan, who might be induced to bestow on it a constitution such as that existing in Samos.[2] Several discussions followed between Campbell on the one hand and the pasha and his chief minister Boghoz on the other, but the latter declined absolutely the proposals made to them. Crete, they said with truth, was not like Samos, populated only by the Greeks. There lived a large body of Muslims who could not reasonably be subjected to Greek rule, while the settlement of Greeks in the island showed conclusively that the pasha's rule was neither severe, intolerant nor unjust.[3] So matters remained till 1840 when the pasha lost Crete as well as Syria. Palmerston at once revived his former project of establishing the Samian constitution there—a plan to which he seems to have been specially attached. Perhaps he thought that when Campbell had discussed the question with Muhammad 'Ali, it could not have been fairly presented; Campbell must have been tactless and perhaps unconvincing; and the pasha had of course been unwilling to make any real reform. But Ponsonby in fact could do no better with the Porte

[1] Campbell, April 24, 1838 (F.O. 78–342).
[2] To Campbell, March 3, 1834 (F.O. 78–244). This island was wholly peopled by Greeks and governed in the Sultan's name by a Greek chief.
[3] Campbell, May 17, 1838 (F.O. 78–342).

than Campbell had done with Muhammad 'Ali. At Constantinople as at Cairo the Samian plan was deemed unsuitable to Crete—and Ponsonby agreed. The Turk inhabitants, he said, could not be subjected to Greek tyranny, nor the forts occupied by Greek garrisons. It would mean constant rebellions, and the island would pass to Greece, or France or Russia. So Crete was given back to the Sultan, without the constitution which Palmerston had at one time judged so important to its well-being.

The administration of Crete by Muhammad 'Ali deserves to be regarded as a success. But the same can scarcely be said of Syria, where the task was heavier, more complicated, and worse controlled. In Crete the Turks formed a minority, and submitted with what grace they could to the reforms which the viceroy ordered and Mustafa Pasha carried into effect. In Syria the population was still more divided by race and creed. It was intensely fanatical. Both main divisions were cloven by the teaching of rival sects. Out of a total of 1,800,000, nearly a million were followers of the Prophet. The 600,000 Christians were divided between the Catholic and the Orthodox Churches; the remainder consisted of minor groups. So that the Muslim majority could lord it over these small and disunited bodies with little fear of possible reprisals. Secular authority was disputed and defied by territorial chiefs who had ruled with little interference from the Turkish authorities. Above all, while Crete was sheltered from external interference by the pasha's fleet, Syria lay open to the active intrigue of the Sultan's agents and the attacks of the Sultan's forces all along a lengthy land frontier.

The Turks had divided the region into four pashaliqs—Acre, Tripoli, Damascus and Aleppo. But Abdullah, the gallant defender of Acre against Ibrahim,

had obtained, besides Acre, Tripoli and the districts of
Nablus and Jerusalem. But within his government
were a number of chiefs who paid no obedience to his
authority. One was the Amir Beshir, the prince of
Lebanon. Another was the Bedouin chief Abu Ghosh,
established between Gaza and Jerusalem. A third was
Mustafa Barbar who had driven the Turkish deputy
out of Tripoli and whom Abdullah had to expel by
force of arms. In the hills of Nablus was a shaikh
whose authority had been recognised by the Porte
itself. Aleppo was torn in pieces by rival Muslim
factions. In Damascus Christians and Jews lived in
perpetual fear for their lives and goods. Not even the
pasha himself was safe. "The Porte on learning that the
citizens of Damascus had cut his pasha's throat, merely
sent them another."[1] The reader of *Eothen* will remember with what delight a raya saw Kinglake
boldly walking along the raised footway which the
true believers had been wont to reserve for themselves.
Indeed, as the French agent Boislecomte most judi-
ciously observed, religion in Syria occupied much the
same position as race in Egypt. In the latter a man
belonged to the ruling or the subject class according as
he was born a Turk or an Arab. In Syria Turk and
Arab stood on a common footing, and a man's degree
depended on his being bred a Christian or a Muslim.[2]
But this solidarity of feeling within the two faiths did
not extend to the desert Arabs on the east and south.
In the days of Wahabi greatness ibn Saud in two days
and a half over-ran at least 120 miles and plundered
thirty villages,[3] while the Bedouin were always raiding
the settled country and driving the inhabitants west-
wards, so that the eastern borderland was full of

[1] Douin, *Mission de Boislecomte*, pp. 220 *sqq.*
[2] *Idem*, p. 199.
[3] Burckhardt, *Nubia*, p. xli.

deserted villages. Nor had the Turkish government
been in any way calculated to reform these evils.
"Everybody knows", wrote Campbell with unhappy
truth, "that the few pachalics of which the Porte could
dispose...were put up to the highest bidder at Constantinople every year, who had no other object in view
but that of making a fortune upon the poor and unfortunate population which thus became a prey to
their rapacity and avarice....Hence their utter negligence in every part of the administration, their total
indifference to the shameful and numerous depredations
of the richer over the poorer classes, and the total
absence of troops and means (for purposes of private
gain) to repel the attacks of the surrounding Arabs."[1]

Stern military rule was the first condition of restoring
peace and order to this unfortunate country, and that,
at all events, was what the inhabitants might rely on
getting from their new ruler. Ibrahim was entrusted
with the government of the territory which he had
conquered. The governor of Damascus, Sharif Bey,
coolly reckoned that the tranquillity of the city would
not cost the citizens more than one head a month.[2]
Every revolt that occurred was made the occasion of
disarming the guilty district. Every inroad of Bedouins
led to swift reprisals. The Syrians too were not merely
to be protected from themselves or their neighbours.
They were to be taught to protect themselves. However averse they might be to military service, military
service would be forced upon them. Under Ibrahim's
drill-sergeants they would at least acquire habits of
discipline to which they had long been strangers. The
Syrian, like the Egyptian, conscription was cruel,
capricious and corrupt.[3] It was conducted, as in

[1] Campbell, Report on Syria (F.O. 78–283).
[2] Douin, op. cit. p. 231.
[3] Cf. p. 226, supra.

Egypt, by a series of haphazard seizures from which the wealthier redeemed themselves by bribing the inferior agents who had seized them. But it must have carried with it fortifying virtues in which the Syrian was peculiarly lacking. It was natural for Palmerston to condemn on moral grounds what he had political reason for disliking. But after the passage of a century the need for moral indignation has vanished, and later experience suggests that the Syrian would have lost little had he enjoyed a longer period of Ibrahim's government.

As in Egypt religious toleration was enforced in a way till then completely unknown. Once the ulemas and theologians of Damascus waited on Ibrahim to complain that Christians were suffered to ride on horseback and that the due distinction between Muslim and infidel was being obliterated. Ibrahim ironically agreed that a distinction should be kept, and proposed that in future the Muslims should ride dromedaries, which would set them high above all Christians.[1] On one tragic occasion, commemorated by Robert Curzon, Ibrahim himself attended the Miracle of the Holy Fire at Jerusalem.[2] These two measures—conscription and toleration—incensed the whole Muslim population against the new government.[3] When Marmont visited Syria in 1834 he found all the Turks very hostile to Ibrahim, although in the Ottoman provinces through which he had just passed the Turks there were quite as bitter against the Sultan.[4] The English consul at Aleppo describes Syrian feelings as those of disgust and even hatred.[5]

[1] Campbell, March 17, 1834 (F.O. 78–245).
[2] Curzon, *Monasteries in the Levant*, chapter XVI.
[3] Cf. p. 156, *supra*.
[4] Campbell, October 9, 1834 (F.O. 78–247).
[5] Picciotto to Campbell, March 3, 1835 (F.O. 78–257).

This feeling was no doubt strengthened by another most disconcerting innovation—the discouragement of bribery in matters of justice. All the English consuls in 1836, who assuredly cannot be cited as witnesses favourable to Ibrahim's administration, are agreed on this point. The least favourable admits that it was diminished. Another believes that it still existed but in a very limited and secret way. A third declares that it was rigorously checked.[1] All agree, though reluctantly, that justice was no longer an ideal applicable to Muslims only. One laments the absence of a code of laws. But even he recognises the establishment in the larger towns of courts, like the new courts established in Egypt, in which Jews and Christians were admitted to sit among the judges. The new system had indeed the merit of a wide elasticity. The plaintiff had the option of laying his grievances before either the old mufti's court or the chief executive official. If he selected the former, the sentence had to be reported to the executive government which could confirm or refuse to execute the decision. If a plaintiff applied to the executive official, the latter could, if the case were simple, hear and decide it himself; if it demanded a knowledge of Islamic law, he could refer it to the mufti's court; if it was a case of complicated accounts or commercial usage, he could refer it to the new courts. The system of justice contained thus a new and most important element. It provided that there should be a much greater probability that a non-Muslim party should receive an impartial consideration of his case. It is perhaps worth noting that under the older system which had been displaced the evidence of a non-Muslim was completely inadmissible against a true believer.[2]

[1] Answer to Query 11. Campbell, July 31, 1836 (F.O. 78–283).
[2] Query 10 (*ibid.*).

One of the Syrian consuls summed up the results of
the establishment of Muhammad 'Ali's government as
including security from arbitrary acts—except in the
case of the conscription—security of property, a new
liberty of religion, of life and of amusements, a fair
distribution of taxes, and in general as near an approach to the liberty enjoyed under a free government as
could be attempted. In many respects he found the
administration to have been improved beyond what
anyone could have expected. But, he adds, the people
"do not appreciate it and are prone from their old
feelings, habits and ideas to turn it solely to their
individual profit".[1] Another observes that "native
capitalists now venture to embark their fortunes in
commercial speculations which formerly they did not
venture to do".[2]

Trade and especially agriculture were much increased.
The rent of land in some areas more than trebled. This
change was occasioned, we are told, by the rise of
competition. Round Aleppo, for instance, the rate of
rent increased because lands were no longer allotted on
a system of favouritism and influence, and that despite
the fact that lands abandoned owing to Bedouin raids
had been brought again under cultivation.[3] Endeavours were made to bring the nomads into more
constant commercial relations with the settled inhabitants, to press eastward the line dividing the desert
from the sown, and to induce the Bedouin themselves
to take to cultivation. "This system, if steadily pursued", Werry writes, "must be productive of great
benefit to the Syrian and Arab populations thus
brought into contact for a peaceable object." In the

[1] Werry, answer to Query 27. Campbell, July 31, 1836 (F.O.
78–283).
[2] Moore, answer to Query 20 (*ibid.*).
[3] Werry, answer to Query 9 (*ibid.*).

rich and extensive plain of Adana, for instance, peopled by a mixture of Anatolians, Turkomans and Kurds, and previously given over to anarchy, the pastoral tribes were induced to spend part of the year in cultivation.[1]

It is impossible to judge with precision how the taxation levied under Ibrahim compared with what had been gathered in under the previous rule. The revenue brought into the public treasuries certainly rose. Collections were more regularly made and more closely controlled. At least one new tax, the *firdeh*, was established. This was a capitation tax which (like the income tax of Great Britain) had originally served to provide extraordinary revenue in time of war. Muhammad 'Ali made it a regular source of income. At first it was based on an estimated payment of 50 piastres a head, but this was soon modified by the establishment of a sliding scale ranging from 30 to 500 piastres, according to the individual's supposed wealth. On this basis an assessment was made on groups of families. The group had to provide the amount appointed, but were free to apportion it among the members as was thought best. Under this arrangement, it is said, the poor were often quite exempt while the rich paid more than the maximum rate.[2]

The infidel poll tax, in Syria as in Crete miscalled the *khiraj*, was collected under special farmans issued by the Porte and remitted to Constantinople for the Caliph's use. This was collected at the rate of 15, 30 and 60 piastres, according to the wealth of the raya. But the officials charged with the collection had always made it a pretext for laying the Christians under private contribution. In 1835 special measures were taken to end this abuse.[3]

[1] The same, answer to Query 27. Campbell, July 31, 1836 (F.O. 78–283).
[2] Werry, answer to Query 8 (*ibid.*).   [3] *Idem.*

As elsewhere, the miri or land revenue formed the main financial resource of the country. But it had been governed by no rule, and was based upon no actual measurement of the land. The nominal unit employed was the extent which in any region a pair of oxen could plough in a day—a system which gave the largest possible opening to evasion and fraud. No attempt had ever been made to fix an assessment on specific land holdings, but the governor of a district was required to find miri to such and such an amount, which was by him distributed among the villages in his jurisdiction, and by the villagers among themselves. The basis of sound administration—a cadastral survey—was completely lacking, though one may reasonably suppose that had Muhammad 'Ali's rule continued, that reform would have been extended from Egypt to Syria.[1]

The land revenue administration does not seem to have provoked complaints or ill-feeling. But military requisitions are frequently mentioned by the consuls as excessively vexatious. Provisions were requisitioned at less than market price in order to supply marching detachments; trees might be cut down for firewood; beasts of burden might be seized to provide transport for a considerable distance; and although some payment was made for them, it never rose to the peasant's demand or compensated the owner for having to follow his beast a long way in order to get him back. Allied to these was the impressment of artisans to work on the fortifications which Ibrahim constructed. The men were paid about half the market rate and might be detained indefinitely.[2]

For many reasons then Ibrahim's administration in Syria ran far less smoothly and successfully than his father's in Egypt. His conscription alienated all the

[1] Campbell, Report on Syria (F.O. 78–283).
[2] *Idem.*

256 MUHAMMAD 'ALI'S GOVERNMENT

Muslim classes, which alone were exposed to it. Toleration enraged every fanatic in the country. His requisitions annoyed the peasant and the artisan. His severity alarmed officials, muftis, qazis, fearful for their time-honoured but iniquitous perquisites. Added to this was the fact that he was regarded as a foreign ruler, bringing with him maxims and principles of government borrowed from Egypt. The Arabs of Syria had always regarded the Arabs of Egypt as immeasurably their inferiors. Ibrahim's conquest enabled the latter to return this scorn with interest. The fellah soldiery was not nearly so forbearing to the Syrians as he was to his own villagers.[1] Ibrahim might establish a system of posts between the chief towns, but men distrusted it and continued to send their letters by messengers hired specially for the purpose.[2]

Another source of difference and difficulty lay in Ibrahim's political ideas. He, far more than his father, cherished the idea of reviving the Arab caliphate. Muhammad 'Ali was not himself strongly possessed of this design, although from time to time he would play with it. He fluctuated between political independence and the reformation of the Turkish empire as his great political aim. To him the Arab always appeared an inferior race, in need of a prolonged and vigorous education. Under him the Arab was never admitted to high office either in administration or in the army. His son, on the contrary, encouraged the Arab. A French observer, Boislecomte, relates that this involved him in difficulties of military administration. He loved to live freely with his men, sometimes even sporting with them, and always praising the race from which they sprang, and contrasting it with the stupid, incorrigible Turk.

[1] Douin, *op. cit.* p. 240.
[2] Werry, answer to Query 12. Campbell, July 31, 1836 (F.O. 78–283).

An Arab soldier once asked him how he, a Turk, could say such things. "I am not a Turk", Ibrahim replied warmly. "I came as a mere child to Egypt, and since then the Egyptian sun has changed my blood and made it wholly Arab." The same conception was voiced by his suite. Mukhtar Bey, for example, declared that he and his like, brought to Egypt in childhood, had nothing in common with the Turks, and claimed to belong, not to a race that would leave only a trail of ruin as its memorial, but to that which had led the way in science and discovery, and covered the earth with noble cities and splendid monuments from farthest Persia to the mountains of Spain.[1] This fantastic pedigree did not carry conviction to Arab soldiers who saw themselves deprived of promotion in order to make room for men who claimed to be descended (spiritually) from the same stock as themselves. The feeling was strengthened by a regulation of Ibrahim's founded on the French code, prohibiting arbitrary punishments. The slightest reprimand led to an immediate demand for a divan (or court of enquiry) and on occasion men threatened their officers with an appeal to Ibrahim himself.[2]

The weakening of military discipline was not the only disadvantage flowing from Ibrahim's pan-Arab views. He would speak openly of reviving Arab nationality, of uniting under one rule all who spoke Arabic, of opening to the Arabs every office of the state and every rank in the army, of sharing with them the enjoyment of the public revenues and the exercise of power.[3] But these notions, popular as they would have been in Egypt, were looked on with different eyes in Syria. There the great division of the people, as I have already said, was not that of Turk and Arab, but that

[1] Douin, *Mission de Boislecomte*, pp. 249–50.
[2] *Idem.* p. 239.   [3] *Idem.* p. 248.

of Muslim and Christian. Ibrahim's theories promised to the Syrians nothing that they did not enjoy already, while at the same time the Syrians were threatened with being placed on the same level as the Egyptian Arab whom they despised. So far from winning for Ibrahim any popularity in Syria, these ideas rendered him and his policy more suspect than ever.

Indeed he had little of his father's talent for governing men. The great pasha always knew just when to cajole, when to threaten, when to strike. His caresses always had something of the terrifying velvet of the tiger's paw. He was never at a loss for an expedient, and could always devise a score of ways of enforcing his will. Ibrahim only had one. He was a vigorous, gifted soldier; force was the only way by which he would overcome obstacles. Left to himself, he would have defied a united Europe, and broken down in an hour what had taken his father thirty years painfully to build. He could never win the Syrians over to his side. He established order, he enforced tolerance, he chastised the raider, he promoted cultivation, did something to purify justice, and augmented trade. But the Syrian Muslims never passed beyond a sullen submission to his rule and were ever on the watch to seize the first reasonable chance of shaking themselves free, of returning once more to their old allegiance, of recovering their traditional superiority over the hated Christian, and of wiping out the humiliating memory of Egyptian domination.

CONCLUSION

The crisis of 1839–40 brought the active career of the great pasha to a close, although he was to rule Egypt for almost another decade. The strain had been too great, the disappointment too severe for this old man of seventy to resist. The responsibility, the effort, the need to take decisions and plan alternatives, had fallen upon him alone. Sleep deserted him. He could not control the starts of his over-wrought nerves. He would break out in sudden bursts of fierce anger. And, even when the crisis had passed and the sharp bitterness of disappointment had been dulled, his mind remained shaken and uncertain, although his bodily health seemed restored.[1] In the middle of 1844 an alarming collapse took place. One night at Alexandria, after a most angry council with the managers of his estates, he was too restless and excited to sleep. Very early next morning he rose and went into the audience hall. It was empty, for none of his ministers was in attendance at such an hour. He cast himself upon his divan and burst into loud convulsive sobs. After a while he called for food, but would not touch it when it was brought. He refused both coffee and his pipe. After about an hour, he called for a carriage and went downstairs. The ministers, hastily summoned, were all in waiting, but had not dared approach their master. On seeing them, he declared that they had all betrayed him, that he would abandon everything and go on pilgrimage to Mecca. He then drove to the country house close to the Mahmudieh Canal from which he usually embarked when going up to Cairo. No boat being ready, he shut himself up there alone, and to a message from the

[1] Barnett, October 18, 1841 (F.O. 78–451).

French consul begging to know what report should be sent to his government would only answer, "What is done is done, what shall be shall be". The following day he embarked, and on reaching Cairo again shut himself up in his riverside palace at Shubra. Clot Bey hastened to attend upon him. He was still so agitated that he could hardly raise a cup of coffee to his lips, and he could not move about without assistance.[1] Yet, when all men expected to hear of his death, or at least that he would never again be able to transact business, rest, joined with Clot Bey's services and his own extraordinary vigour of constitution, enabled him to recover. His melancholia dropped away from him. His mind cleared. He gave up the project of a pilgrimage to Mecca; and inflicted a fine upon the ministers who had incurred his special anger.[2]

Meanwhile the pasha's relations with Great Britain had notably improved. This was mainly brought about by the fall of the Whig ministry in 1841. Peel and Aberdeen were willing to smooth matters over, and not sorry to mark their disapproval of the late policy. In 1843 the government resolved to send the pasha a steamboat as a token of national gratitude.[3] The East India Company presented him with a silver fountain.[4] The Queen sent him her portrait set with brilliants.[5] About the same time the King of the French gave him the Grand Cordon of the Legion of Honour.[6] Ibrahim Pasha visited France and England, where he was well received, and showed he could drink champagne with anybody. Muhammad 'Ali himself spoke of following in his son's footsteps, and in 1847 was assured by his old

[1] Stoddart, August 6, 1844 (F.O. 78–582).
[2] The same, August 7, 1844 (ibid.).
[3] Bowring to Boghoz Bey, June 15, 1843 (Abdine Archives).
[4] Barnett, August 17, 1845 (F.O. 78–623).
[5] To Barnett, September 23, 1845 (ibid.).
[6] Barnett, November 4, 1845 (ibid.).

enemy, Lord Palmerston, once more back at the Foreign Office, that he would be very graciously received by the Queen and might rely on a cordial welcome from Her Majesty's Government.[1]

That visit never took place. But in 1846 the pasha did actually proceed to Constantinople, where he received a warm welcome, and returned (after a short visit to his birthplace of Kavala) in better health and spirits than he had enjoyed since 1840. He was reported to have lavished a quarter of a million sterling on the chief people at Constantinople.[2] But this was his last effort. The administration of the country from 1847 onwards was virtually in Ibrahim's hands, for the pasha himself had at last fallen into real senility. Ibrahim died at the close of 1848, only a few weeks after he had publicly read the *hatti sharif* conferring on him the government of Egypt in consideration of his father's being too afflicted with disease to administer the country.[3] Ibrahim was then succeeded by Abbas I. Ibrahim had in general maintained his father's traditions. But with Abbas came in a new and very different world. The great pasha had been scrupulously moderate in his personal expenditure; Abbas thought little else worth money. "One by one", wrote the British consul-general, "he is abandoning all the works commenced by the old pasha. Schools are abolished, factories done away with, and I expect to hear that the famous Barrage, which has occasioned so much talk in Europe, will shortly be abandoned. It has probably cost 2 million sterling up to this present time and would have required half a million more to finish it....As a set-off against these reductions Abbas is building and

---

[1] To Murray, November 17, 1847 (F.O. 78–706).
[2] Stoddart, nos. 7 and 8, August 29, 1846 (F.O. 78–661 B).
[3] Murray, October 4 (and enc.) and November 15, 1848 (F.O. 78–757).

furnishing palaces, making enormous presents to the
Sultan's family at Constantinople, and talking of
buying steamers as if they were as plenty and cheap as
figs."[1]

Happily Muhammad 'Ali knew nothing of all that
was going forward, or how his most precious schemes
for the development of his country were being abandoned. The knowledge would have been harder to
bear than physical pain or the growing feebleness
of age. At last, when he was eighty years old, he
died about noon on August 2, 1849, at Alexandria. His
body was carried from the palace, by the route which
he had followed in such anguish of mind in 1844, by the
Mahmudieh Canal and up the Nile to Bulaq. There his
body was met by all the surviving members of his
family except Abbas, and borne with scant ceremony
to the place which he had years earlier chosen for his
tomb in the new mosque that he had built up on the
citadel of Cairo, overlooking the great city, and the
river, and the pyramids beyond. "The attachment and
veneration", the British consul-general wrote with un-
wonted eloquence and feeling, "of all classes in Egypt
for the name of Mahomet Ali are prouder obsequies
than any which it was in the power of his successor to
confer. The old inhabitants remember and talk of the
chaos and anarchy from which he rescued this country:
the younger compare his energetic rule with the capricious vacillating government of his successor; and all
classes, whether Turks or Arabs, not only feel but
hesitate not to say openly that, the prosperity of Egypt
has died with Mahomet Ali....

"In truth, my Lord, it cannot be denied that
Mahomet Ali, notwithstanding all his faults, was a
great man....Without any of the advantages of birth or
fortune, he carved his way to power and fame by his

[1] Murray to Palmerston (private), April 6, 1849 (F.O. 78–804).

own indomitable courage, perseverance and sagacity."
Though capable of acts of cruelty, he was not a cruel
man. He loved and sought fame and power, but cared
nothing for money save as a means to great ends. In the
course of his last illness, the consul-general heard more
than one say, "If Allah would permit me, gladly would
I give ten years of my life to add them to that of our old
pasha". When in Aleppo or Damascus or any other
town under the Sultan's immediate government no
Christian could be secure from injury or insult, he had
brought it to pass that the European could walk unarmed in Cairo as safely as in London. "Probably",
the consul-general concludes in needless apology for his
enthusiasm, "I have not been able to resist altogether
the influence which the old pasha's high breeding and
winning manners exercised over all who were in
habitual intercourse with him."[1]

And what is his claim to our remembrance? On my
title-page I have set a phrase of his own, comparing his
work with that of my own countrymen in India. The
comparison is far from being completely true. Yet
there is, I think, more truth in it than many will be
willing at first sight to concede. He had many things in
common with the English administrators who built up
the Company's Indian dominion. Like them, for
instance, he found himself ruling provinces of a derelict
empire under the shadow of a majesty that had ceased
to have any real justification for existence beyond the
memory of vanished glory. Like them, he was impatient of the corrupt stupidity ruling at the imperial
court and refusing to look even a little way beyond
existing circumstance. Like them, he sought independence, in part no doubt from personal ambition
and the strong desire that his name should survive to
coming generations, but in part also because he hated

[1] Murray, August 5, 1849 (F.O. 78–804).

disorder and corruption and misgovernment. Like them, he desired freedom in order that a new and better form of administration might be framed. But in seeking this he had to confront difficulties of an entirely different nature from those which confronted the governors-general. They only had to face the opposition of weaker powers within the Indian frontiers or of European rivals who could never break through the strong guard of naval power set upon the eastern waters. But Muhammad 'Ali's policy ran counter to the desires of great states too jealous one of another to agree upon the destruction of the Turkish empire whether by one of themselves or by another hand, and the only conjuncture which would really have given the pasha his freedom—namely a great war in Europe—never arose. If then Muhammad 'Ali failed to build up a great empire which could compare with that acquired by the East India Company, the cause clearly lay in no lack of skill or perseverance on his side, but because might and luck, which favoured the Company, were against him. He could not escape the overwhelming pressure of the great European states.

In this matter of external policy, however, comparison and contrast are less remarkable than they are in matters of administration. The duty that fell to the pasha in many respects closely resembled the duty that faced the Company. The government of Egypt, like that of Bengal or the Carnatic, had lost even the least pretence of seeking public welfare. The rulers and their agents desired nothing but personal advantages. The subjects, wholly unorganised, offered a sullen, separate and futile opposition to their demands. Justice had become no more than a lucky accident. Protection had vanished. There was none to oversee the conduct of the overseers. To rebuild an administration on a basis so rotten and undermined is one of the hardest of political tasks, and one that never has been accomplished without many blunders by the way.

The types of administrative system which had to be reconstructed in India and Egypt were of much the same pattern. Both were despotisms unlimited save by the moral conceptions of the despot. He was, so far as he chose to be, the universal master, the universal landlord, the universal merchant. The fundamental questions confronting both Muhammad 'Ali and the Company's early servants were at what point would it be right and best to limit these pretensions, and to what extent could the lessons of western experience be applied to these exceedingly different conditions. In some, but not in all respects, the decision of these questions was easier for the pasha than for the Company. Egypt was no larger than a single Indian province. Its population might be called homogeneous when compared with the diversities of India. Its social system was free from the complexities of Indian caste. It was not rent between two rival faiths. But as against these advantages, great as they were, must be set the overwhelming disadvantage of not being able to draw upon an almost unfailing supply of men who could be trusted to carry out their orders. The pasha's administration was differentiated from the Company's by this lack of a covenanted civil service. No really fair comparison can be drawn between Egypt under his rule and India under Bentinck's. The parallel should be sought in an earlier age, before the Company's servants had developed their special virtues—in Bengal, say, under the government of Clive or of Warren Hastings.

This fact, far more than any variation of theory or idea, produced the differences between the pasha's land revenue administration and the Company's. Muhammad 'Ali did not, of course, ever even dream of making a permanent settlement. But, after all, Cornwallis's revenue policy was nothing more than a local aberration, speedily discarded save in the province of its origin. Save that in certain areas he dictated the crops that should be planted, his methods bear a family resemblance to those used in a ryotwari province. High annual settlements, calculated on what could be paid in a good year rather than in an average one; considerable arrears of revenue; the use of stripes to compel the cultivator to pay—all these might have been matched in one or other of the Indian provinces, not only before but also during the earlier years of the English government. Even the doctrine that all land belonged to the state had long before been advocated by the Company's servants.

True, British India had nothing to offer comparable with Muhammad 'Ali's conscription. But conscription was needless and inconceivable in India. It was needless because such large numbers held arms in abhorrence, and it was inconceivable because custom and the social system decreed that arms offered the proper occupation for certain classes only. Perhaps the whole advantage in this matter did not lie on the side of India.

Again the attitude of the pasha was far more frankly despotic than that of the Company's governors. He did not hesitate to enforce his will, if necessary by the sternest measures. He was not separated from his people by the deep differences of religion and culture which separated the Company's servant from the ryot. He would not only compel men to serve in his army, but he would force them to grow cotton, and sugar, and mulberry trees, to send their children to school, to do whatever he thought for the good of the state. Nor is he to blame for this. There was no other way in which the improvements which he sought could be secured.

He was also much more cautious—it is perhaps one of

his greatest merits—in the policy of westernising the administrative system. Material advantages, once achieved, could not but be recognised. But the perception of moral advantages, he knew, could come only gradually. He was therefore in no haste to rule by western methods. He did not, as Cornwallis did in India, try to separate judicial from executive functions or set up a brand-new code which the people could neither read nor understand. He made no attempt to change the basis of administration from executive to judicial. But he did much to purify justice, to control the ancient courts, and to introduce new and better ones. He attempted nothing in the way of legislative institutions, but he did everything in his power to develop the disposal of public business by discussion, and to bring together representatives of various classes, whose views could assist the transaction of public affairs. Above all he sought, both by establishing schools within Egypt and by sending individuals abroad, to bring his people into touch with western ideas, and to breed up a generation imbued with truer ideas and higher conceptions of political duties than that with which he had to work.

In all this he was far more truly inspired than were the Englishmen who were seeking to impose English ideas and culture wholesale upon Indians. His real misfortune was that he was a man, not a system. One generation can lay foundations; but others are needed to carry the edifice above the first course. His early successors betrayed him, abandoned his work, and in many ways frustrated his purposes. The minor variations between Bentinck and Bentinck's successors were nothing compared with the differences of purpose and attitude between Muhammad 'Ali and Abbas I. His work was put to a strain such as that of no governor-general ever had to bear. It is no wonder if much of it was wasted. And yet it is clear that he created modern Egypt, bringing it into new and fruitful touch with the West. That part of his work was not, and could not be, undone. He succeeded, for he had impressed his purpose deeply on the people over whom he ruled, and even now, almost a century after his death, his tradition still lives.

Index